MathFlare

Name: ____________________

Class: __________

Teacher: ____________________

Introduction

As parents and educators, we recognize the pivotal role mathematics plays in shaping a child's academic journey and future success. Yet, the path to mathematical proficiency can often seem daunting, fraught with challenges and complexities. That's where the transformative power of MathFlare Workbooks shine through, illuminating the way forward with clarity, precision, and purpose.

Introducing MathFlare Workbooks – a beacon of guidance, a testament to excellence, and a catalyst for achievement. Crafted with meticulous care and expertise, MathFlare Workbooks stand as paragons of educational excellence, designed to nurture young minds, ignite a passion for learning, and develop a deep-rooted understanding of mathematical concepts.

Picture this: your child eagerly delves into the pages of Mathflare Workbook, greeted by a step-by-step guide illuminated with vivid examples that demystify complex mathematical concepts. With each turn of the page, they embark on a journey of discovery, encountering thoughtfully curated practice questions that reinforce learning and hone problem-solving skills. And when they unveil the answers to those very questions, a sense of accomplishment blossoms within them – a tangible reward for their hard work and dedication.

But MathFlare Workbooks are more than just tools for learning; they are pathways to comprehension, fostering a deep-seated understanding of mathematical concepts through a sequential, logical flow. From fundamental principles to advanced problem-solving strategies, every chapter builds upon the last, ensuring a robust foundation upon which future knowledge can be constructed.

As parents, we yearn for nothing more than to see our children thrive, to witness the spark of inspiration ignited within them as they conquer academic challenges with confidence and poise. MathFlare Workbooks serve as partners in this noble endeavor, offering not just practice questions, but the keys to unlocking a world of opportunity.

And for teachers, MathFlare Workbooks stand as invaluable allies in the quest to cultivate mathematical proficiency in the classroom. With answers readily available, instructors can focus on guiding and nurturing their students, confident in the knowledge that MathFlare Workbooks provide a solid framework upon which to build.

In the pages of MathFlare Workbooks, we find not just the promise of academic excellence, but the seeds of a brighter tomorrow. So let us embrace the power of mathematics, let us champion the journey of learning, and let us pave the way for a generation of young minds poised to shape the world. With MathFlare Workbooks as our guide, the possibilities are infinite, and the future, bright.

Table of Contents

MathFlare
MATH WORKBOOK
Grade 2
Step by Step Guide and Essential Practice with Answers
Addition Subtraction
Multiplication
Place Value and Expanded Notations
Geometry
MathFlare Publishing

MathFlare
MATH WORKBOOK
Grade 2-3
Step by Step Guide and Essential Practice with Answers
Addition Subtraction
Multiplication and Division
Place Value and Expanded Notations
Geometry
MathFlare Publishing

MathFlare
MATH WORKBOOK
Grade 3
Step by Step Guide and Essential Practice with Answers
Multiplication and Division
Decimals
Place Value and Expanded Notations
Fractions and Geometry
MathFlare Publishing

MathFlare
MATH WORKBOOK
Grade 1
Step by Step Guide and Essential Practice with Answers
Counting and Numbers
Addition and Subtraction
Place Value and Expanded Notations
Understanding Time
MathFlare Publishing

MathFlare
MATH WORKBOOK
Grade 1-2
Step by Step Guide and Essential Practice with Answers
Counting and Numbers
Addition and Subtraction
Place Value and Expanded Notations
Understanding Time
MathFlare Publishing

MathFlare
MATH WORKBOOK
Grade 3-4
Step by Step Guide and Essential Practice with Answers
Addition Subtraction
Multiplication Division
Place Value and Expanded Notations
Fractions and Geometry
MathFlare Publishing

MathFlare
MATH WORKBOOK
Grade 4
Step by Step Guide and Essential Practice with Answers
Addition Subtraction
Multiplication Division
Place Value and Expanded Notations
Fractions and Geometry
MathFlare Publishing

MathFlare
MATH WORKBOOK
Grade 4-5
Step by Step Guide and Essential Practice with Answers
Multiplication Division
Place Value and Expanded Notations
Fractions and Geometry
Unit Conversion
MathFlare Publishing

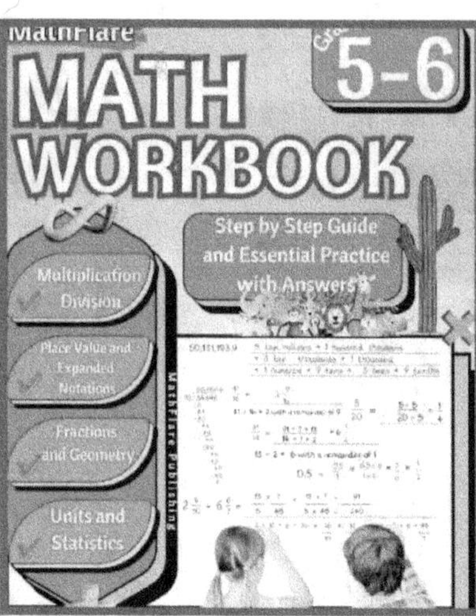

Chapter. 01

Pre-Algebra

Simplifying expressions

It involves combining like terms and performing operations to make the expression easier to understand and work with.

Let's simplify the expression:

$$2x - 2x + 8 + 4$$

- **Combine like terms:** First, we look for terms with the same variable and exponent. In this expression, $2x$ and $-2x$ are like terms, so they can be combined:

$$2x - 2x = 0$$

- **Substitute the simplified terms:** After combining the like terms, the expression becomes:

$$0 + 8 + 4$$

- **Combine the remaining terms:** Now, we add the constants together:

$$8 + 4 = 12$$

Let's solve another problem:

$$-7m - 3 - 3 - 6m$$

combine like terms

$-7m - 6m - 3 - 3$

$13m - 6$

<u>Order of Operations (PEMDAS)</u>

The order of operations, often remembered by the acronym PEMDAS, stands for:

- **Parentheses**: Perform operations inside parentheses first.
- **Exponents**: Evaluate exponents (powers and roots) next.
- **Multiplication and Division**: Perform multiplication and division from left to right.
- **Addition and Subtraction**: Perform addition and subtraction from left to right.

The order of operations helps to clarify which operations should be performed first in a mathematical expression to ensure consistent and accurate results.

- **Parentheses**: Evaluate expressions within parentheses first. If there are nested parentheses, start with the innermost ones and work your way out.

  1. Example: $2 \times (3 + 4) = 2 \times 7 = 14$

- **Exponents**: Evaluate expressions with exponents (powers and roots) next.

  1. Example: $2^3 + 4 = 8 + 4 = 12$

- **Multiplication and Division**: Perform multiplication and division from left to right.

  1. Example: $2 \times 3 + 4 = 6 + 4 = 10$

  2. Example: $6 \div 2 \times 3 = 3 \times 3 = 9$

- **Addition and Subtraction**: Perform addition and subtraction from left to right.

  1. Example: $2 + 3 \times 4 = 2 + 12 = 14$

  2. Example: $10 - 4 \div 2 = 10 - 2 = 8$

<u>Simplify Equations</u>

Evaluating expressions involves substituting given values for variables in an expression and then performing the indicated operations to find the result.

For example: Let's evaluate 4x – 10, when x = 3:

Step 1: Substitute the given value for the variable:

Replace every occurrence of x in the expression 4x – 10 with the given value, which is

3:

$$= 4(3) - 10$$

Step 2: Perform the operations:

Perform the indicated operations according to the order of operations (PEMDAS - Parentheses, Exponents, Multiplication and Division, Addition and Subtraction):

$$= 4 \times 3 - 10$$

Step 3: Simplify:

Calculate the result:

$$12 - 10 = 2$$

Solving Inequalities

Inequalities are mathematical expressions that compare the relative sizes of two values. They are used to express relationships where one quantity is:

- "<" (less than),
- ">" (greater than),
- "<=" (less than or equal to),
- ">=" (greater than or equal to),
- and "≠" (not equal to) another quantity.

For example:

$$y + -10 \leq -8$$

To isolate y, we need to get rid of the constant term -10. Since -10 is being subtracted from y, we can undo this operation by adding 10 to both sides of the inequality:

$$y - 10 + 10 \leq -8 + 10$$

$$y \leq 2$$

To check the solution:

$$2 - 10 \leq -8$$

$$-8 = -8$$

The inequality is true when $y = 2$

Verbal Algebra Expressions

Verbal algebra involves translating word problems or verbal statements into algebraic expressions or equations.

For example: The product of the two numbers is 91. One number is six less than the other. What are the numbers?

We're given a verbal description of a problem, and we need to represent it using algebraic symbols and equations.

Let's break down the given problem into algebraic expressions:

- Given that the product of the two numbers is 91, we can write the equation: $xy = 91$
- Also, given that one number is six less than the other, we can write another equation: $x = y - 6$

Now, we can use algebraic techniques to solve the system of equations to find the values of x and y, which represent the two numbers.

$$x(x - 6) = 91$$

1. Solve the equation:

- Expand the equation:

$$x^2 - 6x = 91$$

- Rearrange the equation into standard quadratic form:

$$x^2 - 6x - 91 = 0$$

- Factor the quadratic equation:

$$(x - 13)(x + 7) = 0$$

2. Find the solutions for x:

- From the factored form, we have two possible values for x:

$$x = 13 \text{ or } x = -7$$

3. Check the validity of the solutions:

- Since one number is six less than the other, we discard the negative solution.

- Therefore, the solution is $x = 13$.

4. Find the other number:

- Substitute $x = 13$ into the expression for the other number:

Other number $= x - 6 = 13 - 6 = 7$

So, the two numbers are 13 and 7.

Solving Equations (One Step)

Solving one-step equations involves performing a single operation to isolate the variable and find its value.

Let's solve an equation step by step: $16 + x = 31$

1. **Identify the Goal:**

    The goal is to isolate the variable x on one side of the equation.

2. **Simplify the Equation:** Combine like terms on both sides of the equation, if necessary.

    The equation is already simplified.

3. **Undo Addition or Subtraction:** If there's addition or subtraction involving the variable, undo it by performing the opposite operation on both sides of the equation.

    Since x is being added to 16, we'll undo this operation by subtracting 16 from both sides of the equation:

    $$16 + x - 16 = 31 - 16$$

4. **Isolate the Variable:** Ensure that the variable is alone on one side of the equation.

    $$X = 15$$

5. **Check Your Solution:** Substitute the value of x back into the original equation to verify that it satisfies the equation.

    $$16 + 15 = 31$$

    $$31 = 31$$

    The equation is balanced, so the solution.

<u>Equations (Two Sides)</u>

A two-sided equation is an equation where both sides have expressions with variables and constants. The goal when solving a two-sided equation is to find the value of the variable that makes both sides equal.

For example: Let's solve an equation:

$$9 + 8x + 8 = 64 + x + 2$$

- **Combine Like Terms:** Simplify each side of the equation by combining like terms (terms with the same variable or constants).

$$9 + 8x + 8 = 64 + x + 2$$
$$17 + 8x = 66 + x$$

- **Isolate the Variable:** Use inverse operations to isolate the variable on one side of the equation.

subtract x from both sides:

$$17 + 8x - x = 66 + x - x$$

$$17 + 7x = 66$$

subtracting 17 from both sides:

$$17 - 17 + 7x = 66 - 17$$

$$7x = 49$$

divide both sides by 7:

$$\frac{7x}{7} = \frac{49}{7} = x = 7$$

- **Check Solution:** Once you find the solution, substitute it back into the original equation to ensure it makes the equation true.

Substitute $x = 7$ back into the original equation:

$$9 + 8(7) + 8 = 64 + 7 + 2$$

$$9 + 56 + 8 = 64 + 7 + 2$$

$$73 = 73$$

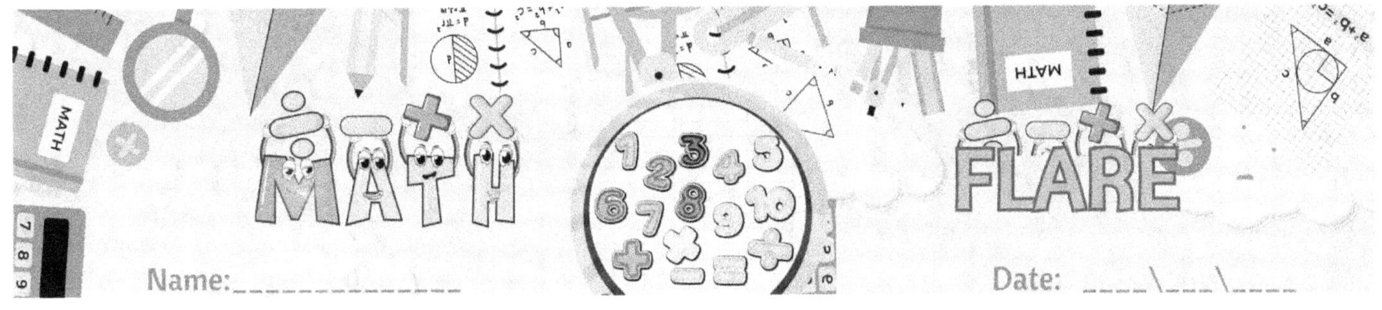

Simplify Expressions

①   -7m – 3 – 3 – 6m

     combine like terms

     -7m-6m-3-3

     13m – 6

②   3z + z

③   8x – 6 + 5x – 9 + 3x + 1

④   9 – 6(9m – 8)

⑤   -4z + 8 + 8z

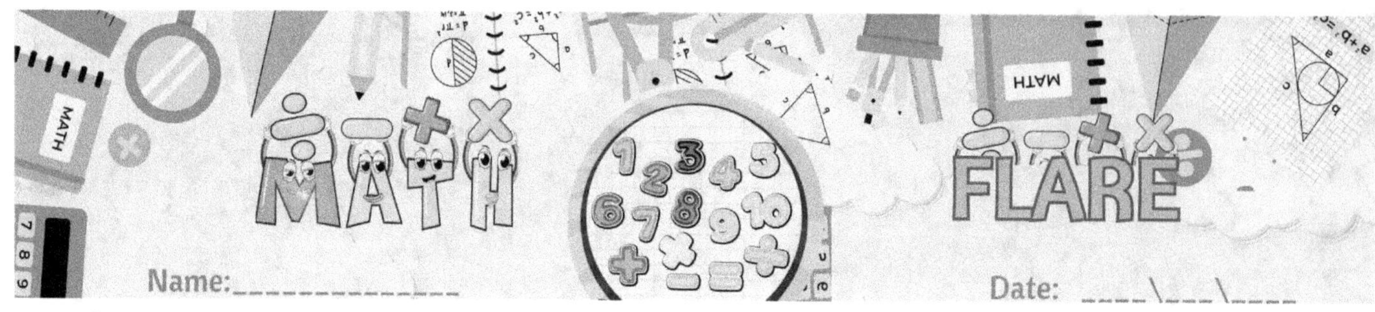

⑥ $2m + 5m$

⑦ $2x + 6 + 8x$

⑧ $z + 2 - 7 - 3z + 9z$

⑨ $-6m + 7m$

⑩ $9x + 4 - 4x - 3 + 5x - 3$

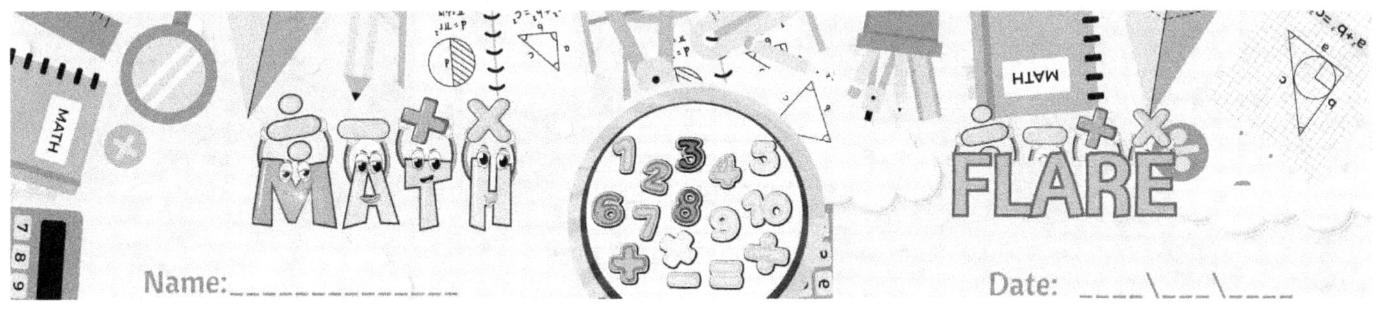

⑪ -6 + m + 6 - 5m

⑫ k + 7 + 5k

⑬ 3z - 8z

⑭ -z + 1 + z + 8 + 3z - 3

⑮ -5m - 7m

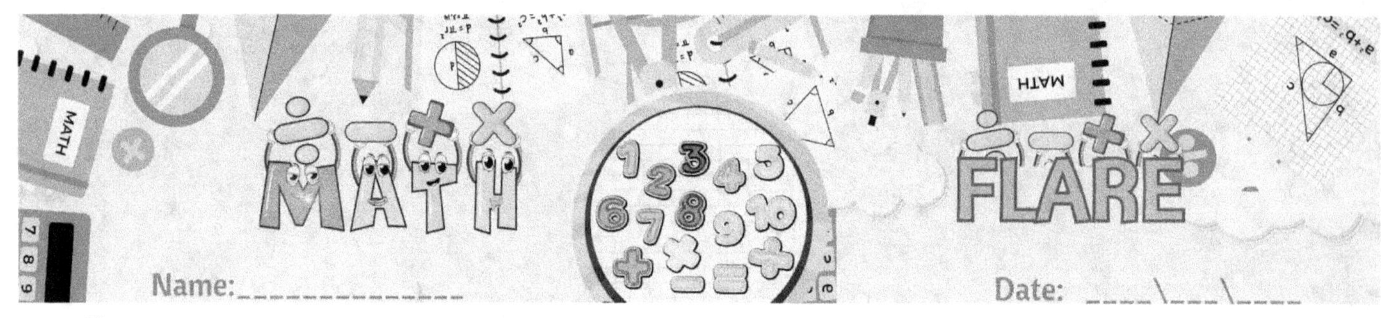

⑯ $-6 + 7x - x - 1 - 8x$

⑰ $9x + 6 + 5x$

⑱ $-5z + 3z$

⑲ $9 - 2x + 1 - 3x + 1 - 9x$

⑳ $-6y + y$

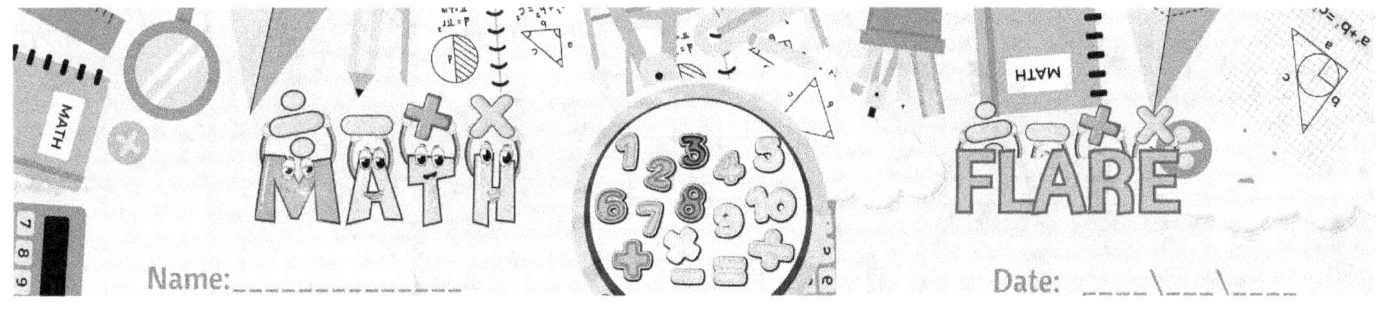

㉑ -4 – 2x + 2x – 6 + 8x

㉒ 8k + 1 – 7k + 6 + 6k + 1

㉓ 3m – m

㉔ -5y + 2 – 8y

㉕ -8z – z

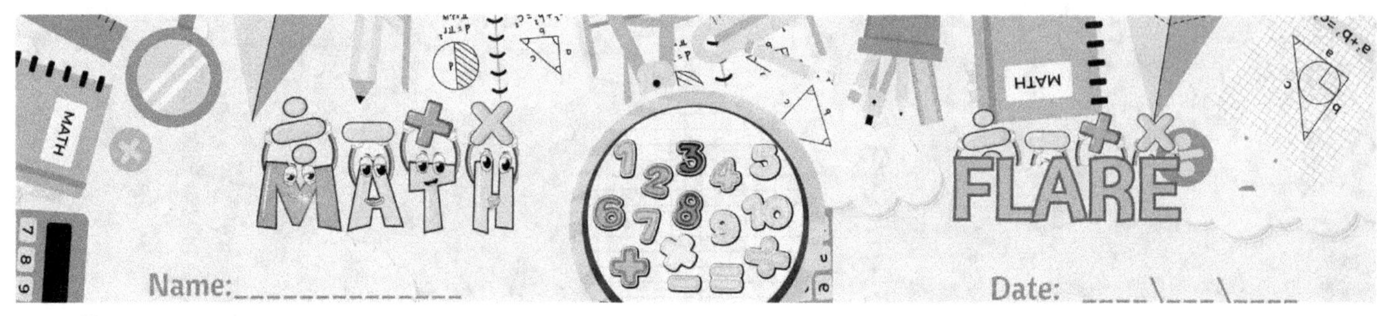

26) $4 + 3(4k + 2)$

27) $y + 5 + 3y$

28) $9 + 5m + 1 + 2m$

29) $4 + 8 + 6z - 3z + 2 - 8z$

30) $5k + k$

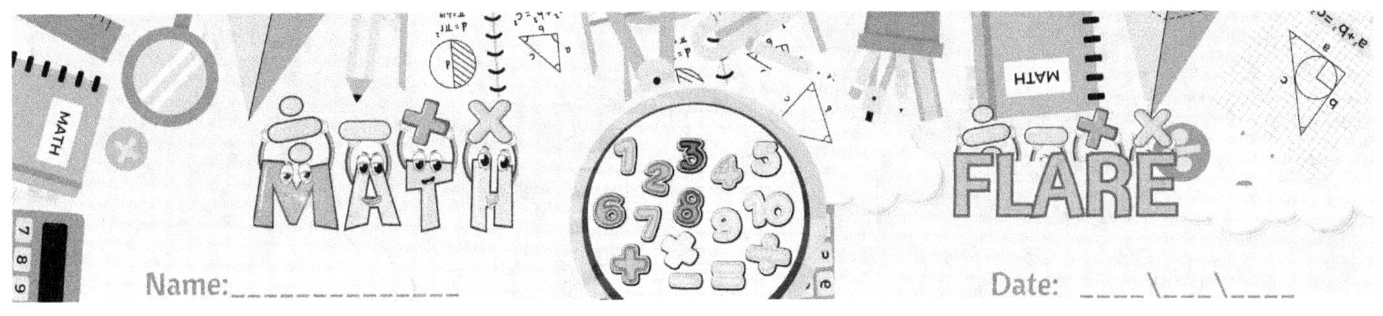

31. $x + 1 + 7x$

32. $8 - 8z + 5 - 9z + 8 - 2z$

33. $m - 7m$

34. $9 + 8x - 7 + 4x - 8 + 4x$

35. $x + 1 + 2x$

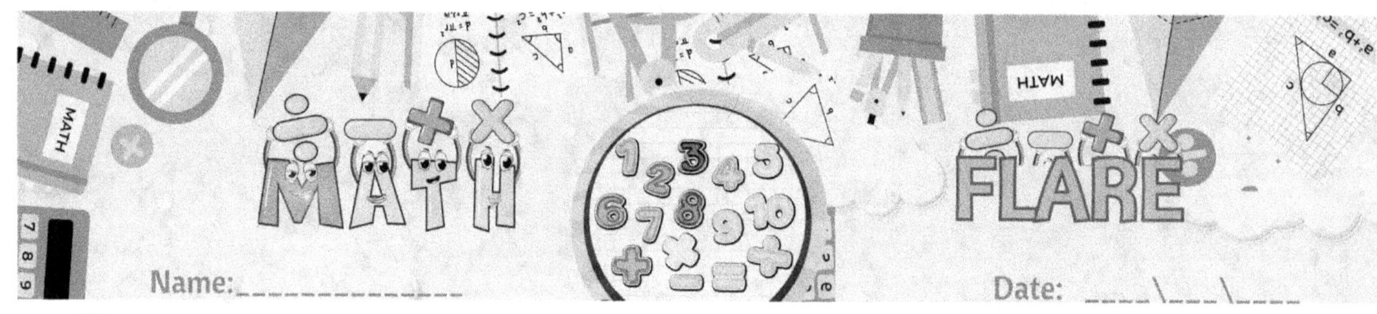

(36) $-6 + 5k + 9 - 2k$

(37) $9x - 9x + 6 + 1$

(38) $-2 - 9m + 4m - 7 + 4m$

(39) $1 + 9(8k - 7)$

(40) $8m - 5m$

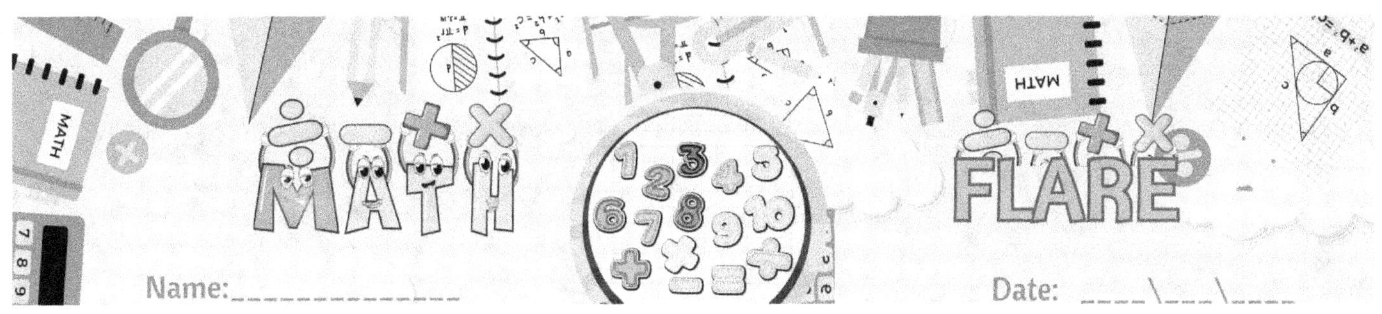

Name:____________   Date: ____________

Order of Operations (PEMDAS)
Evaluate Expressions.

① $6 + 3^2 + 5 + 7^2 =$

6+9+5+49

= 69

② $(10 + 5)(9 + 6) =$

③ $5 + 3 - 9 + 5 =$

④ $(7 \times 1) - (7 + 5) =$

⑤ $1 + (5 + (1 - 3))^2 =$

⑥ $3 \times 7 \times 10 =$

⑦ $(2 + 1)(10 + 1) =$

⑧ $(8^2) \times (4^2) + 3 =$

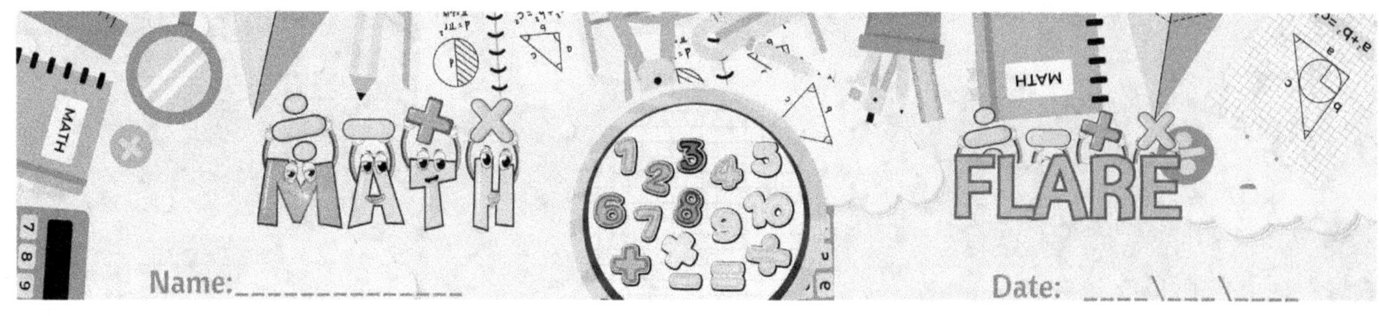

⑨ $10 + 4^2 =$

⑩ $[2 - (2 + 9)] + 2 =$

⑪ $8 \times 6 =$

⑫ $(2 + 4) \div 3 =$

⑬ $8 + 8 + 2 + 7 =$

⑭ $[4 + (7 - 7)] \times 1 =$

⑮ $3 \times 7 =$

⑯ $(9^2) \times (8^2) + 3 =$

⑰ $(6 + 9) \div 3 =$

⑱ $(3 + 6) \div 1 =$

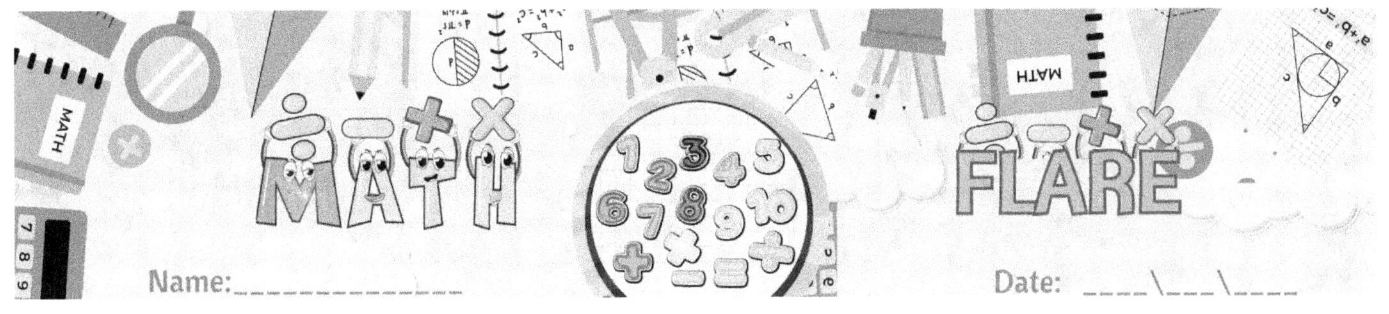

(19) $(4 + 1) \div 2 =$

(20) $[3 - (4 + 6)] \div 4 =$

(21) $6 + (2 + (5 \times 8)) =$

(22) $5 + 4^2 + 7 + 10^2 =$

(23) $6 \times 10 =$

(24) $9 \times 6 \times 8 =$

(25) $3 + 5^2 =$

(26) $8 + 1^2 + 6 + 1^2 =$

(27) $6 + 9^2 =$

(28) $6 + 10^2 + 9 + 5^2 =$

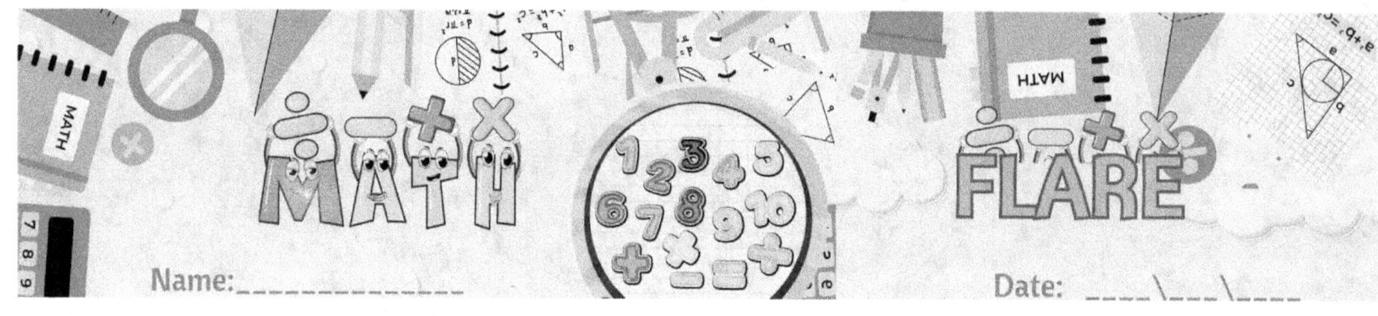

(29) $10 + 2^2 + 1 + 2^2 =$

(30) $[6 - (6 + 8)] \div 1 =$

(31) $(10 + 2)^2 + (5 + 6)^2 =$

(32) $6 \times 2 =$

(33) $6 + 1 - 3 + 10 =$

(34) $10 + 5 - 8 + 8 =$

(35) $[9 - (10 + 4)] + 2 =$

(36) $[7 - (3 + 10)] - 5 =$

(37) $(10 \times 3) - (6 + 3) =$

(38) $[6 - (2 + 7)] + 8 =$

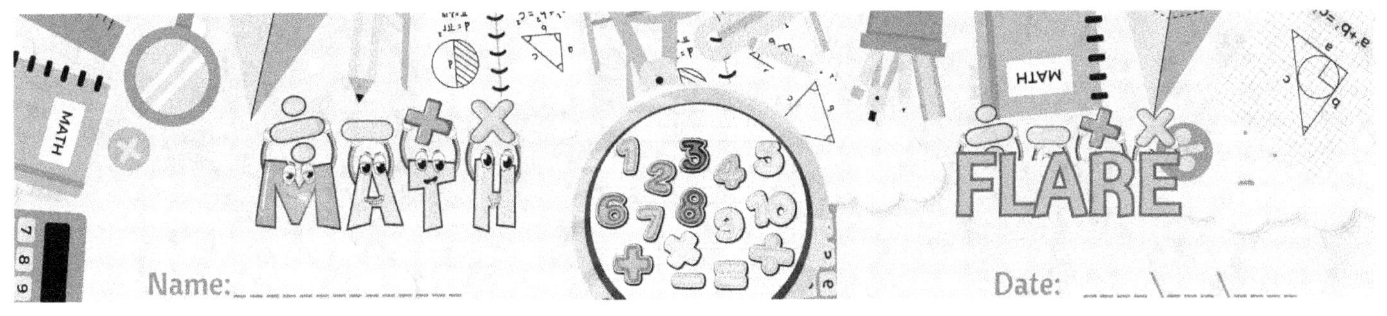

(39) $[1 - (4 - 1)] \times 5 =$

(40) $8 + 1 + 10 =$

(41) $2 \times 5 =$

(42) $[4 - (6 + 6)] + 7 =$

(43) $7 + (1 - (5 - 7)) =$

(44) $[2 - (4 + 2)] - 9 =$

(45) $5 \times 9 + 6 =$

(46) $2 + (6 - (2 + 3)) =$

(47) $[10 - (4 + 7)] \div 4 =$

(48) $(5 \times 5) - (10 + 6) =$

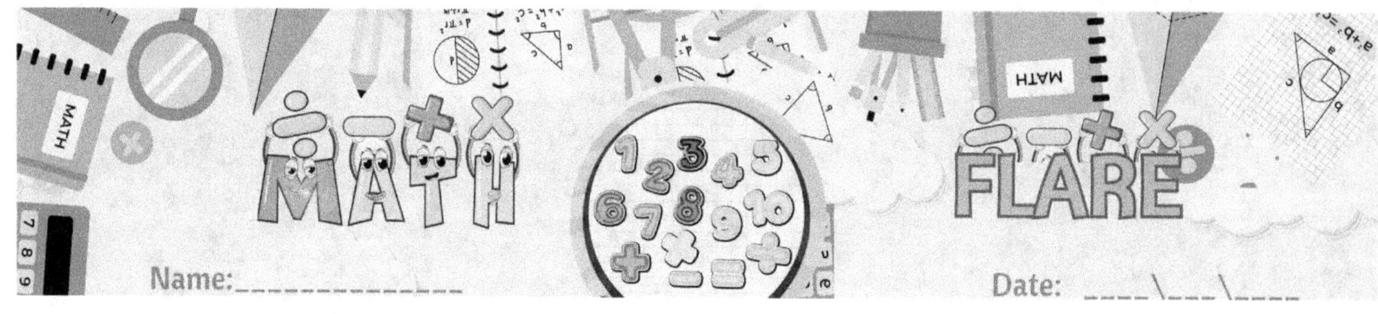

Simplifying Equations

Simplify the following equations when the value of $z = 3$

① $-3(7z) =$

$= -3(7 \times 3)$

$= -3(21)$

$= -63$

② $-3z + -6 =$

③ $-7z - 2 =$

④ $\dfrac{-4 + 15}{z + 8} =$

⑤ $1(9z) =$

⑥ $2z^2 + z^1 =$

⑦ $1 \div z + -4 =$

⑧ $z + -6 + 9z =$

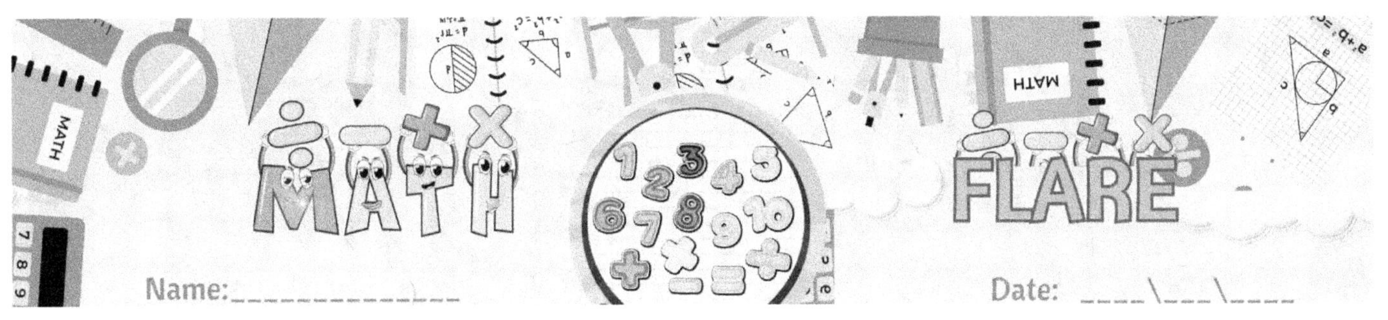

Simplifying Equations

Simplify the following equations when the value of $z = -3$

① $-10 - z =$

② $z \div -2 =$

③ $(z^2 + -7) - 2(-7 + z) =$

④ $5 + \dfrac{5 + z}{-1z} - 6 =$

⑤ $(z^1 + 6) - 5(6 + z) =$

⑥ $z^1 + z - -10 =$

⑦ $7(5z) =$

⑧ $(z^3 + -4) - 0(8 + z) =$

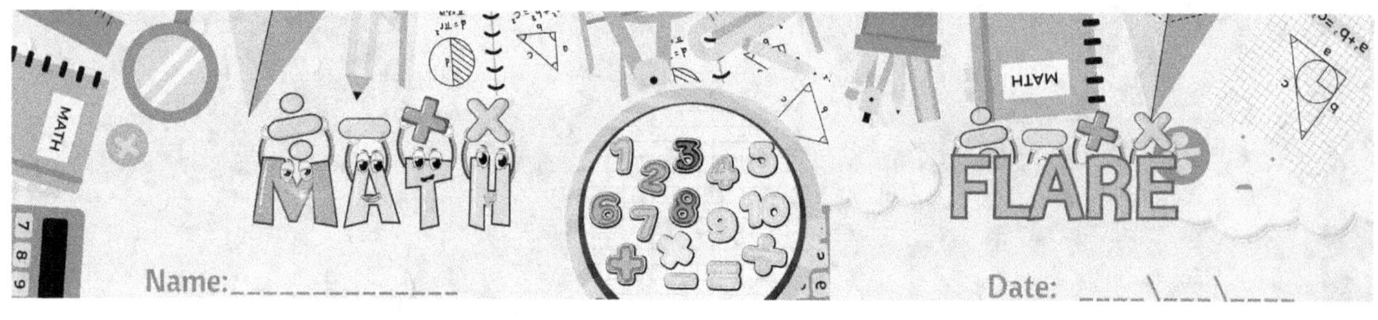

Simplifying Equations

Simplify the following equations when the value of $z = 7$

① $z - 2 =$

② $2z - -5 + 3z =$

③ $z + 4 =$

④ $(6 + -7z) + (-7z - -7) - (-5 + -3z) =$

⑤ $\dfrac{42}{z} =$

⑥ $z + -6 + 8z =$

⑦ $-10z - 5 =$

⑧ $(z^2 + 0) - -1(-8 + z) =$

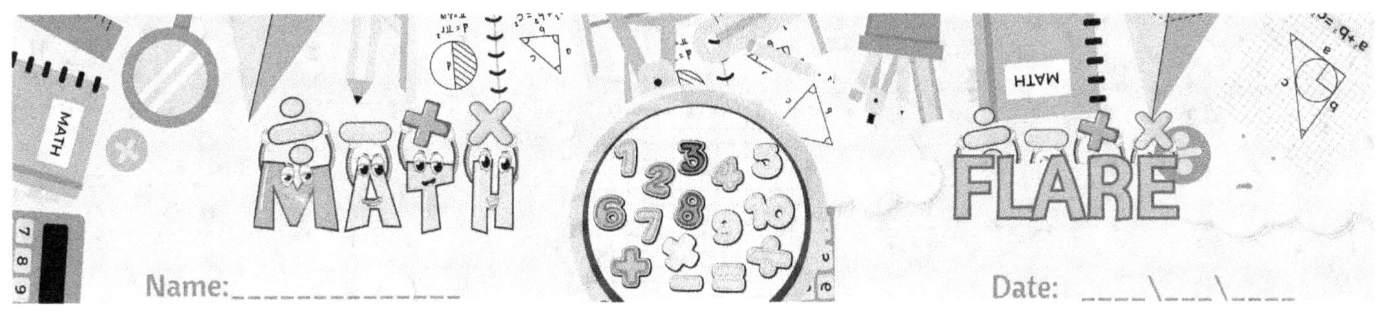

Simplifying Equations

Simplify the following equations when the value of $k = -3$

① $-8 + k =$

② $(-1k + -3) + (7k + -10) =$

③ $6 \div k =$

④ $(k^3 + -6) - 9(-6 + k) =$

⑤ $k^1 + k - 1 =$

⑥ $-8k - -9 =$

⑦ $k^1 + k - -6 =$

⑧ $3k + 1 =$

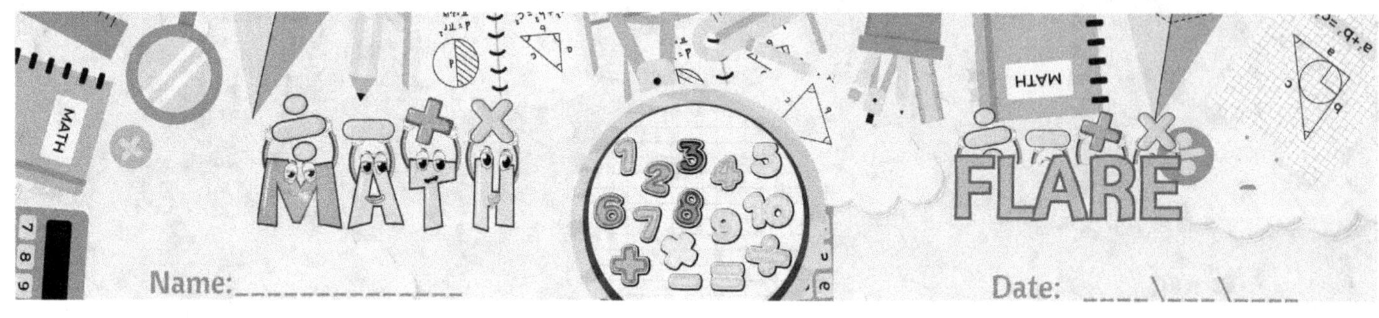

Simplifying Equations

Simplify the following equations when the value of $x = -4$

① $3x + -2 =$

② $2 + \dfrac{x}{-4} =$

③ $x - -9 =$

④ $-7x + 8 =$

⑤ $(x + 10) \div -10 =$

⑥ $\dfrac{-2 + x}{x + -3} =$

⑦ $(-10x + 5) + (7x + -1) =$

⑧ $\dfrac{-28}{x} =$

MathFlare - Math Workbook 8th and 9th Grade

18

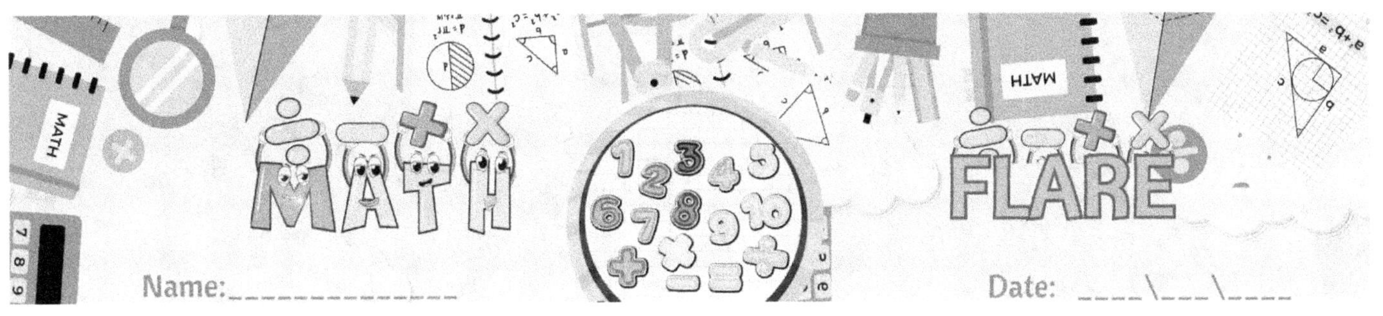

Simplifying Equations

Simplify the following equations when the value of y = -1

① $y + 4 + 8y =$

② $y \div -5 =$

③ $-2 \div y =$

④ $(6y + -4) + (7y + 0) =$

⑤ $-10y + 9 =$

⑥ $10 \div (y + -7) =$

⑦ $(3y + -7) + (-8y + 5) =$

⑧ $-5(2 + y) =$

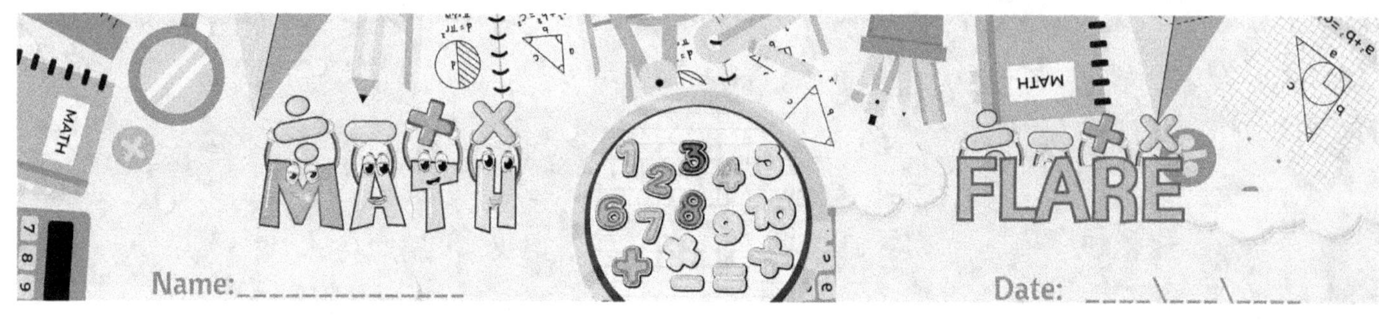

Simplifying Equations

Simplify the following equations when the value of n = 5

① $6n - 7 + n =$

② $(n)^2 =$

③ $n^1 + n - 10 =$

④ $(2 + 7n) + (8n - -6) - (9 + n) =$

⑤ $-7n + 4 - n =$

⑥ $7n + -10n - 6 =$

⑦ $7n + -5 =$

⑧ $4 \div n =$

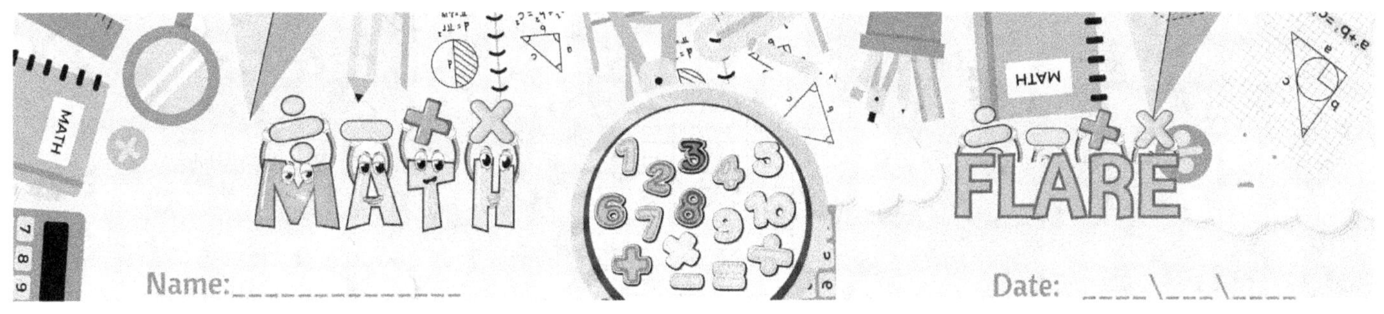

Solving Inequalities

① $\dfrac{k}{-2} > -4$

$\dfrac{-2}{k}$ x−2>−4x−2

  k < 8

$k > 8$

② $x - 2 \le 3$

③ $-2 < k + 1$

④ $2k > -6$

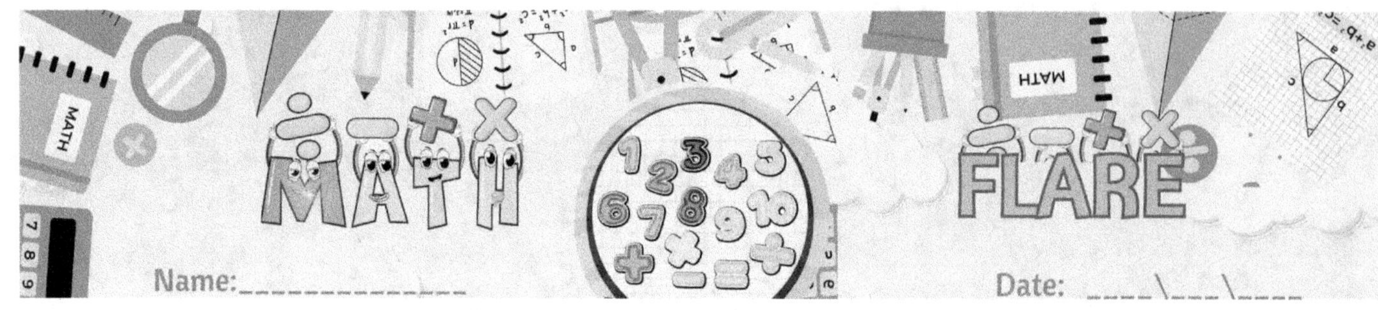

⑤

$$5 \geq 8 + y$$

⑥

$$-2 \geq 6x$$

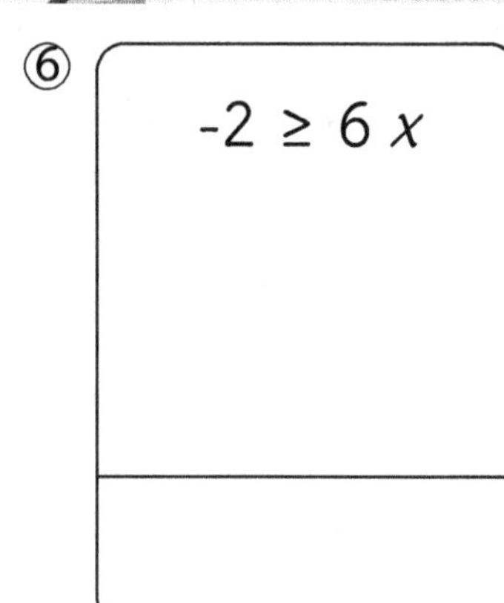

⑦

$$2 - z \leq 6$$

⑧

$$-5 > \frac{y}{-1}$$

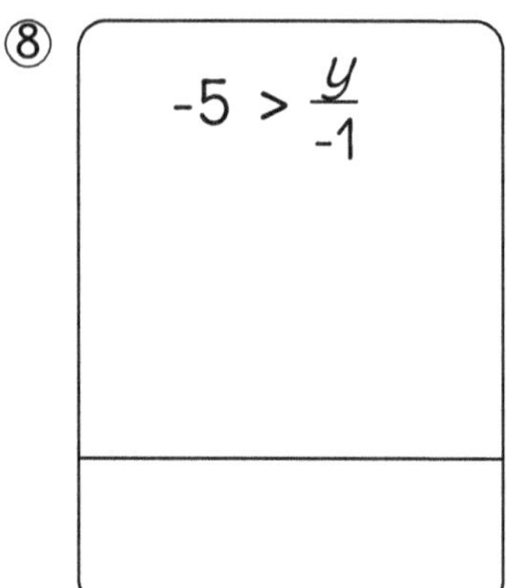

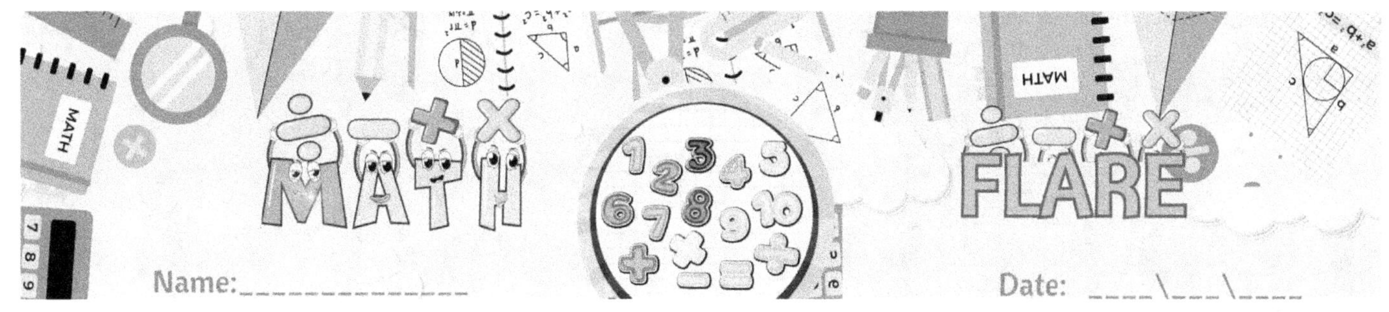

Name:_________________   Date: _______________

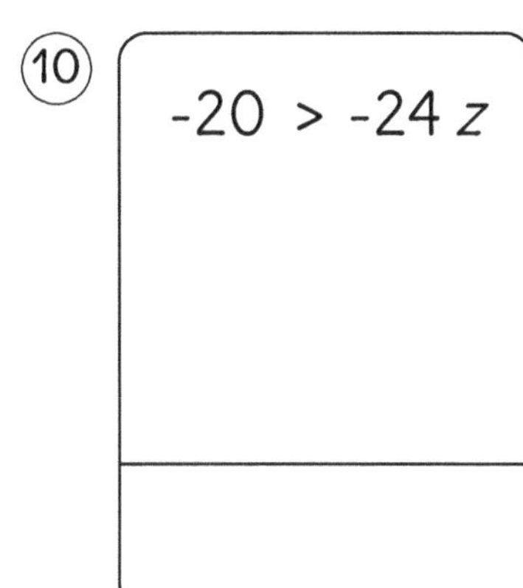

⑨
$$\frac{k}{-6} > -6$$

⑩
$$-20 > -24z$$

⑪
$$m + 1 < -4$$

⑫
$$9 \leq 8 - m$$

13) $9 < 15z$

14) $-2 + m \geq -10$

15) $-3 \leq m - -6$

16) $\dfrac{k}{-3} \leq 1$

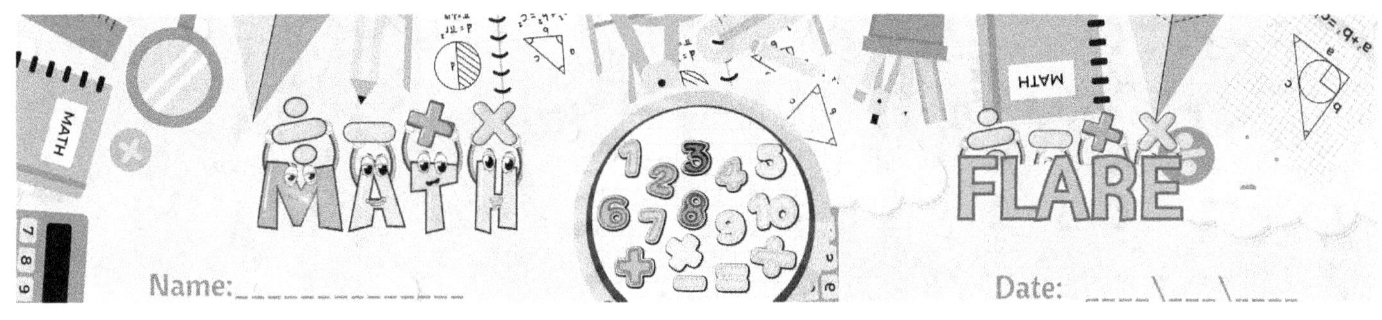

17. $6 \le 5 + z$

18. $-14\,k > 10$

19. $2 \le \dfrac{m}{2}$

20. $7 < -5 - k$

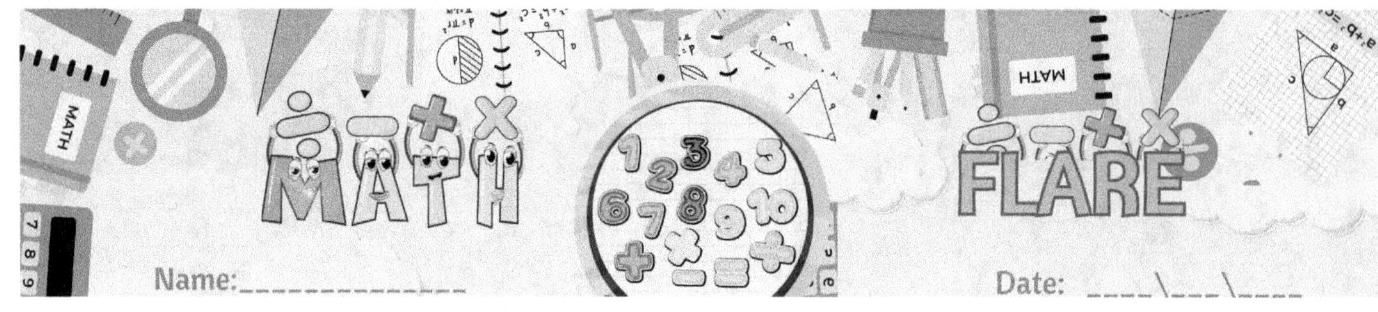

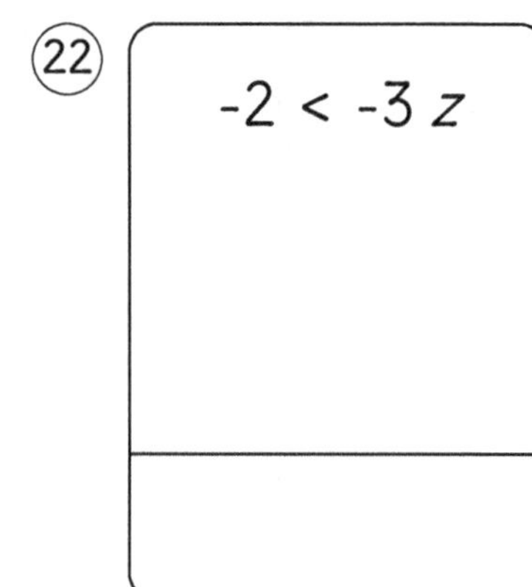

㉑ $1 \geq -7 + m$

㉒ $-2 < -3z$

㉓ $\dfrac{m}{1} < -4$

㉔ $m - 6 \geq 9$

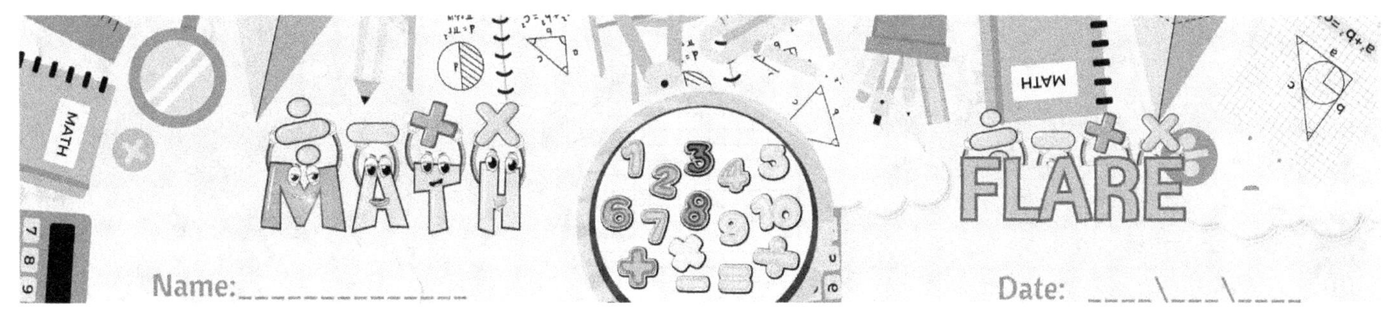

Name:_________________   Date: ______________

(25) $7 < m - 5$

(26) $\dfrac{k}{-7} \geq -2$

(27) $k + 2 \leq -10$

(28) $-15\,z \leq 12$

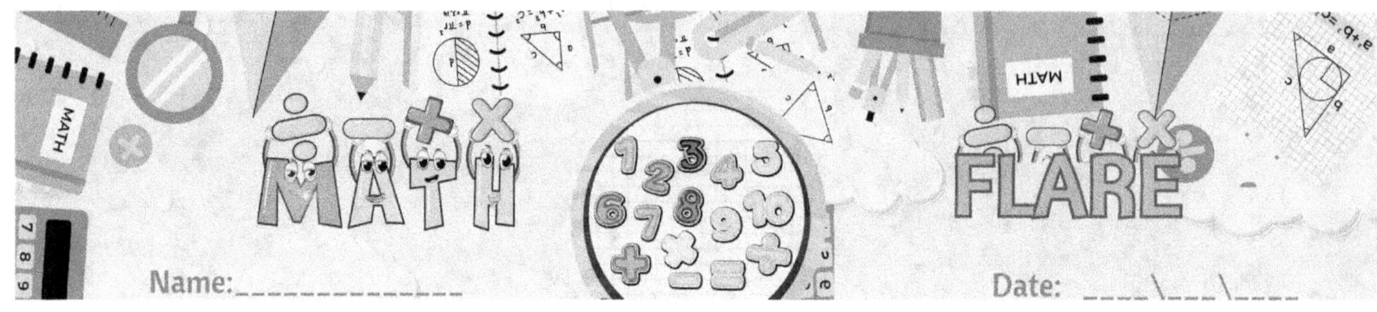

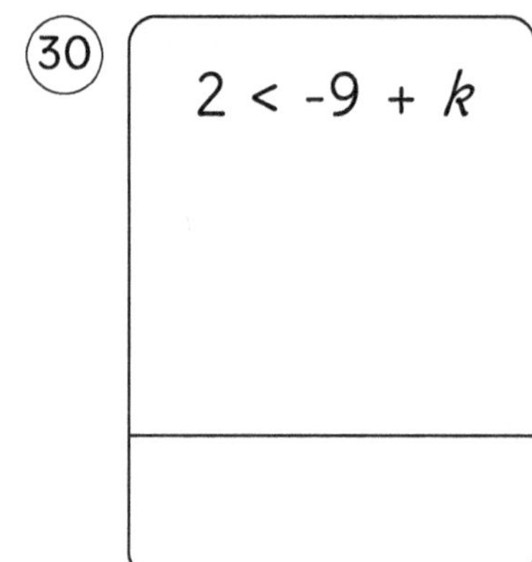

(29)

$$-6z \geq -4$$

(30)

$$2 < -9 + k$$

(31)

$$z - 8 > 9$$

(32)

$$\frac{y}{-1} < 5$$

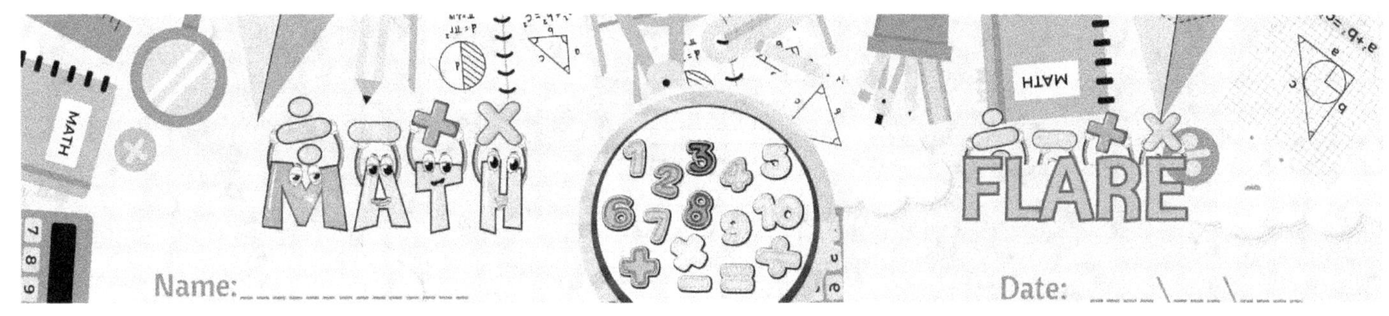

Name:_________________ Date: ______________

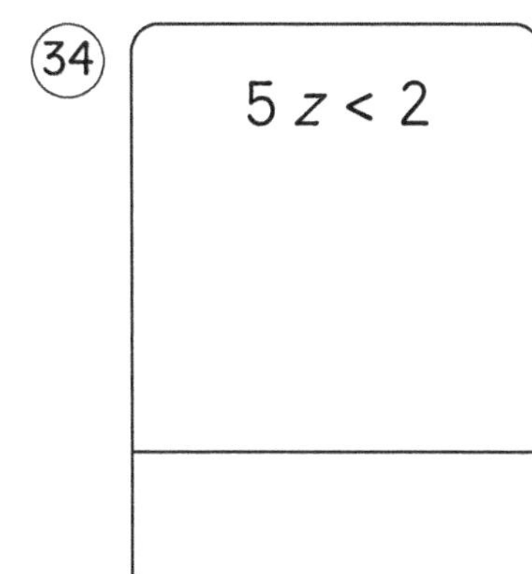

33 $6 \leq 5 - m$

34 $5z < 2$

35 $-3 \geq y + -5$

36 $7 > \dfrac{m}{6}$

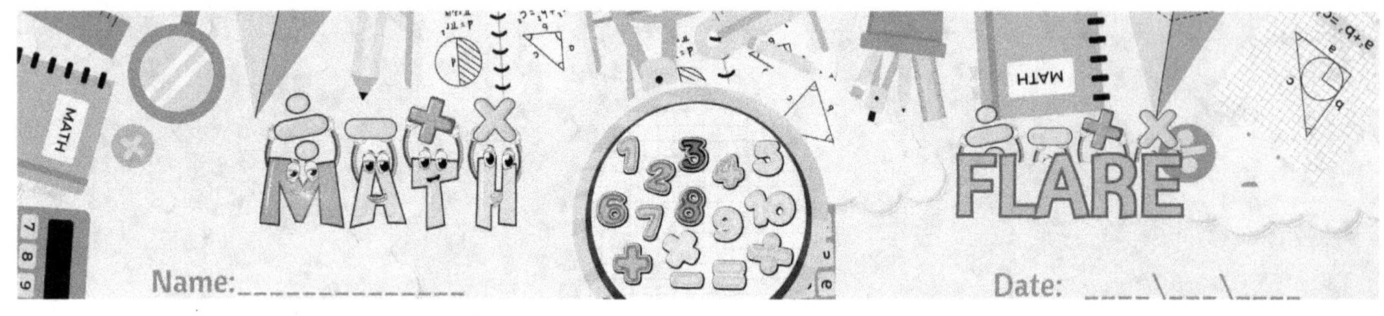

37) $8 \leq m - 3$

38) $5 > \dfrac{z}{8}$

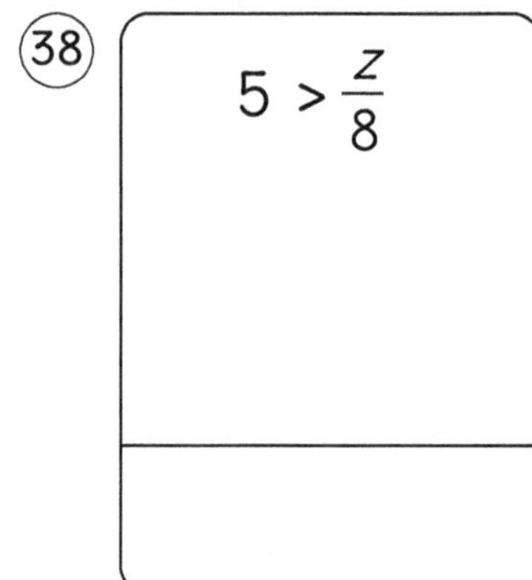

39) $8 \leq k + -5$

40) $-2 k \leq 2$

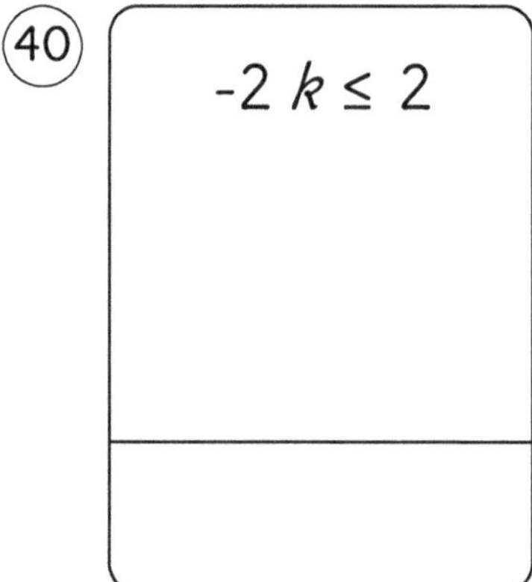

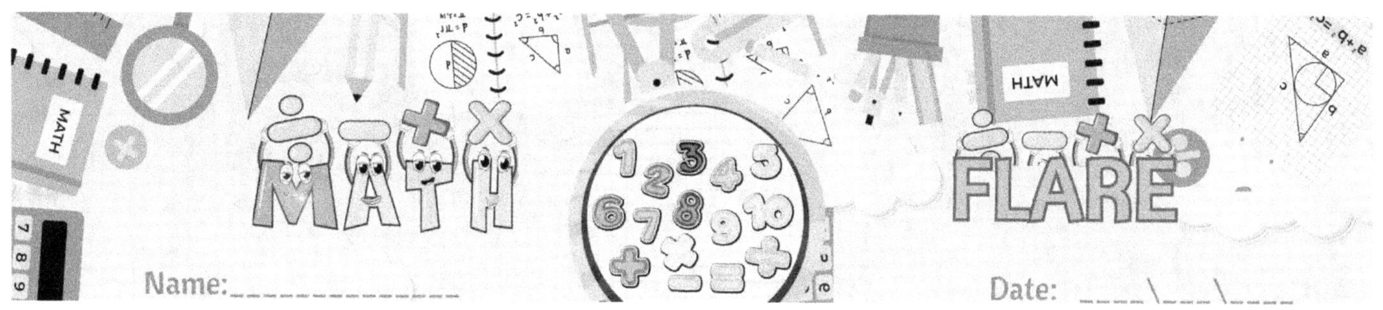

Name:_______________ Date: ______________

Verbal Algebra Expressions

①   11   The difference of a number and seven is equal to 4. What is the number?

$$x - 7 = 4$$
add 7 to both sides
$$x - 7 + 7 = 4 + 7$$
$$x = 11$$

②   The sum of two numbers is 15. The larger number is four times the smaller number. What are the numbers?

③   The difference of two numbers is 76. The larger number is 4 more than ten times the smaller number. What are the numbers?

④   The difference of two numbers is 29. The larger number is 8 more than four times the smaller number. What are the numbers?

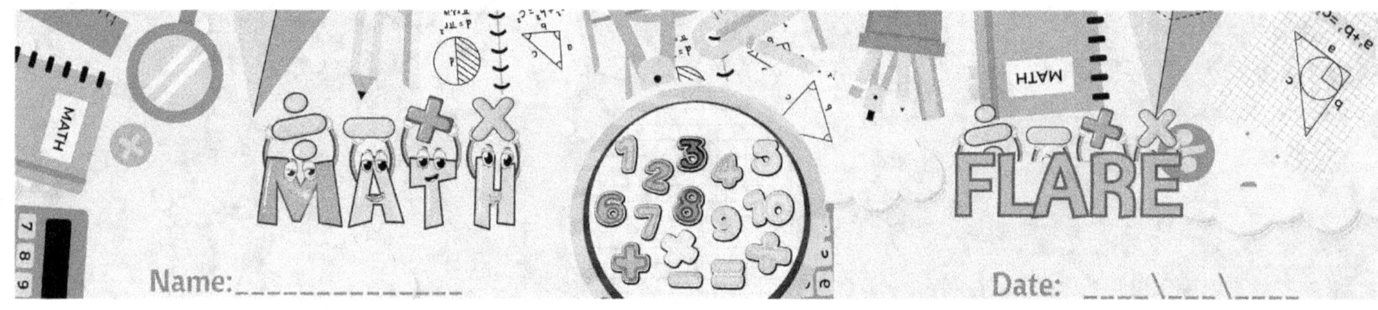

⑤   One-third of a number decreased by 2 is 0. Find the number.

⑥   One of two numbers is three more than the other. The sum of the numbers is 5. Find the numbers.

⑦   Seven times a number increased by 2 is 79. Find the number.

⑧   Three more than six times a number is 45. What is the number?

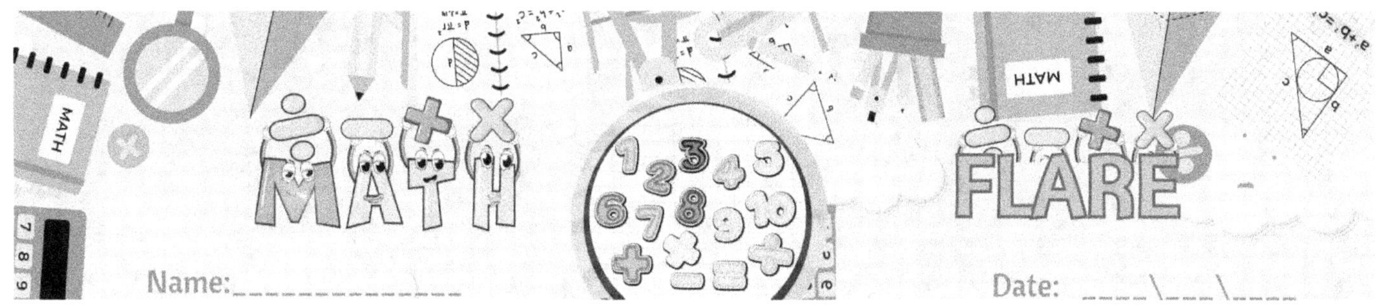

⑨ Find two consecutive even integers such that twice the smaller decreased by the larger is 0.

⑩ The greater of two numbers is 2 less than four times the smaller number. Their sum is 28. Find the numbers.

⑪ Three times a number is 0. What is the number?

⑫ The greater of two numbers is 2 less than three times the smaller number. Their sum is 30. Find the numbers.

⑬ Two more than nine times a number is 74. What is the number?

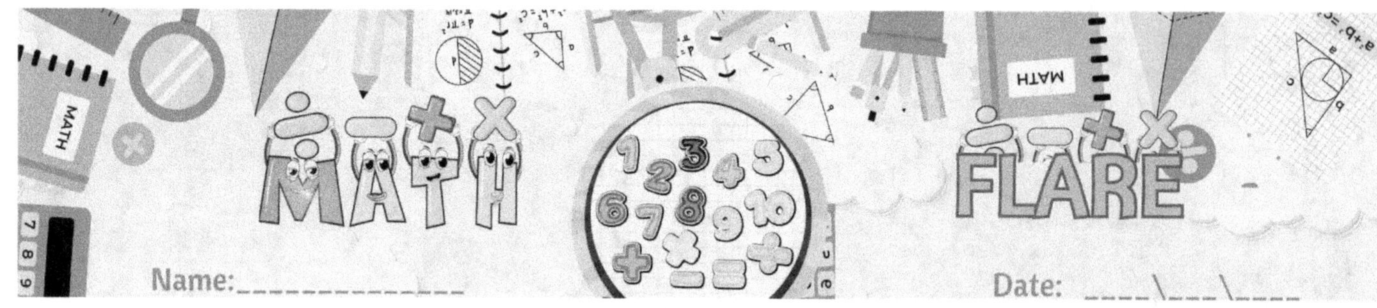

(14) One number is nine more than another number. The sum of the larger number and twice the smaller number is 12. Find the numbers?

(15) Seven less than a number is 3. Find the number.

(16) The product of six and a number is 12. What is the number?

(17) The difference of a number and one is equal to 8. What is the number?

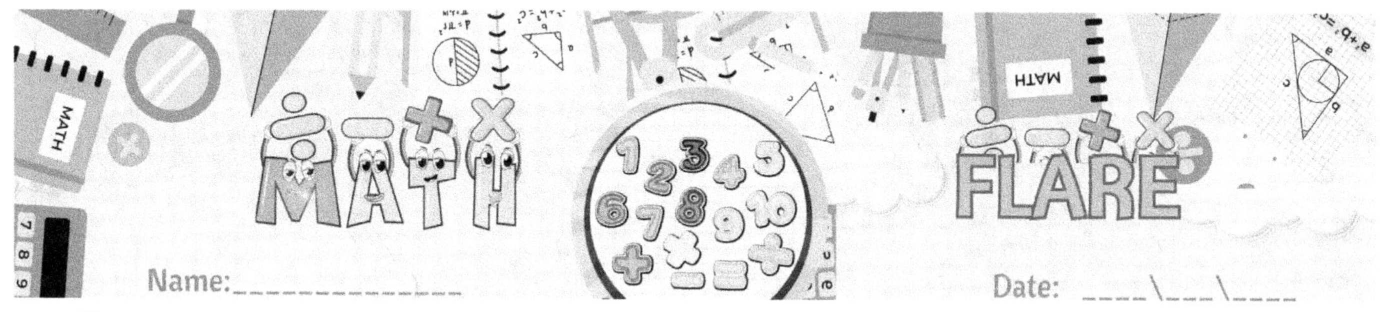

(18) Four is equal to the quotient of a number and 6. Find the number.

(19) A number diminished by 9 is 4. Find the number.

(20) The sum of a number and eight is 15. Find the number.

(21) Six times the difference of 8 minus a number is 12. What is the number?

(22) Two times a number equals 16 less than six times the number. What is the number?

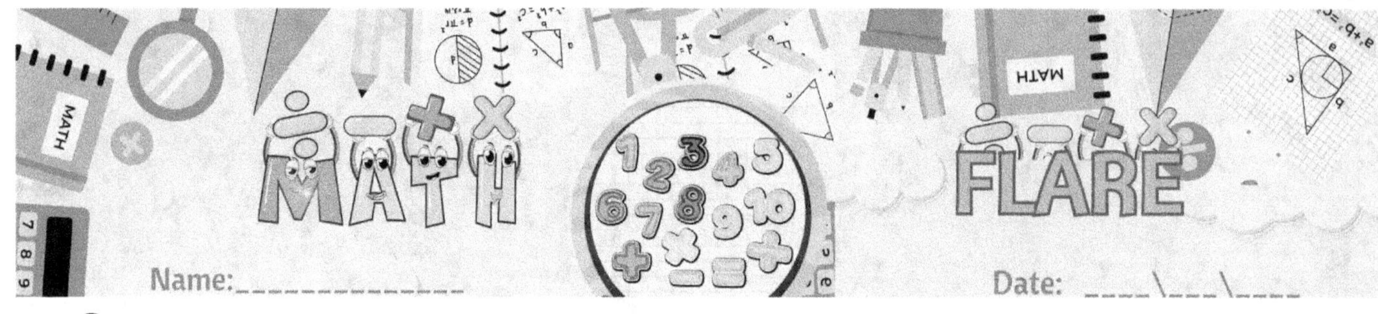

(23) Two-thirds of a number is 6. Find the number.

(24) Find two consecutive even integers such that six times the smaller decreased by the larger is 18.

(25) The difference of two numbers is 20. The larger number is 2 more than seven times the smaller number. What are the numbers?

(26) Three is equal to the quotient of a number and 6. Find the number.

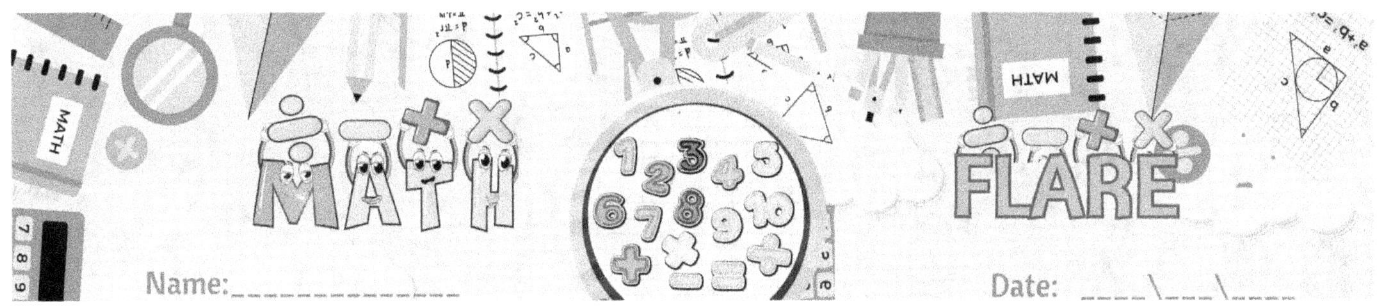

Name:________________   Date: ____________

(27) The difference of a number and five is equal to 9. What is the number?

(28) One less than three times a number is 17. Find the number.

(29) The product of two numbers is 108. One number is three less than the other. What are the numbers?

(30) A number diminished by 3 is 8. Find the number.

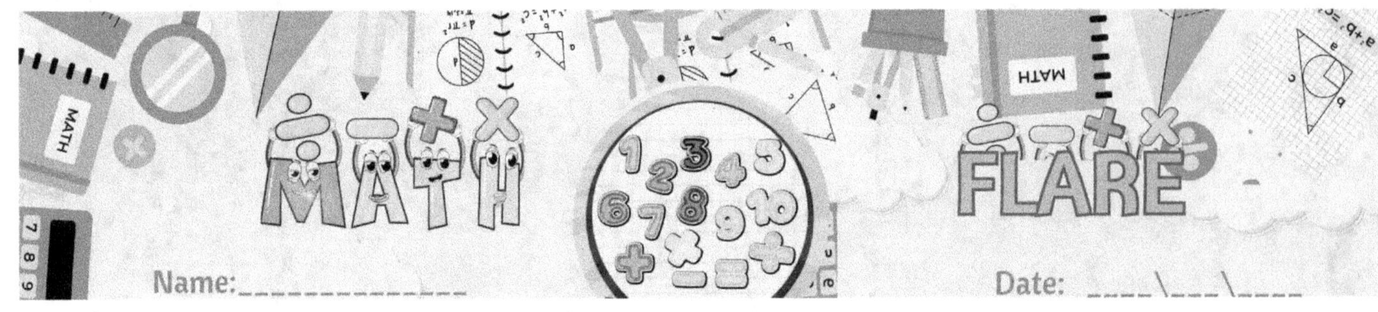

(31) The difference of two numbers is 5. The larger number is 2 more than two times the smaller number. What are the numbers?

(32) Five times a number equals 3 less than eight times the number. What is the number?

(33) Five more than eight times a number is equal to the number increased by 82. What is the number?

(34) The sum of two numbers is 20. One number is two less than the other. Find the numbers.

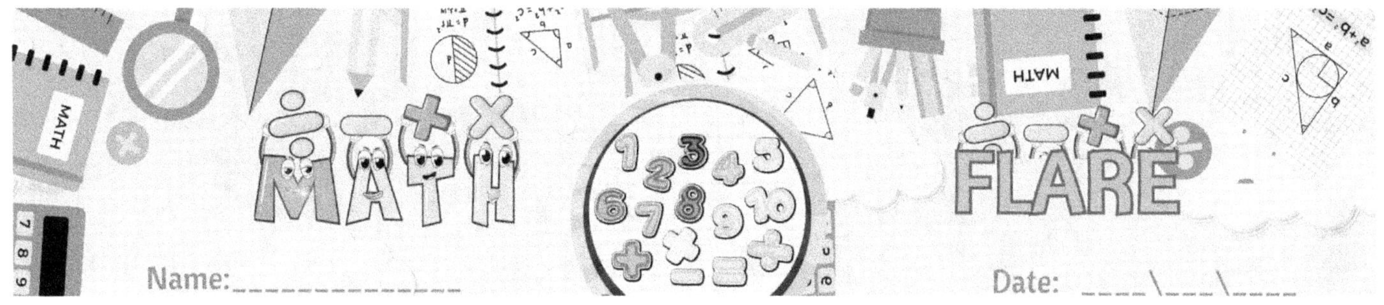

(35) The sum of three numbers is 56. The largest number is five times the smallest, and the smallest is seven less than the middle number. Find the numbers.

(36) One less than twice a number is 23. Find the number.

(37) Seven times the sum of a number and ten times the number is 154. Find the number.

(38) The quotient of a number and three increased by 4 is 11. What is the number?

(39) Eight more than a number is 16. What is the number?

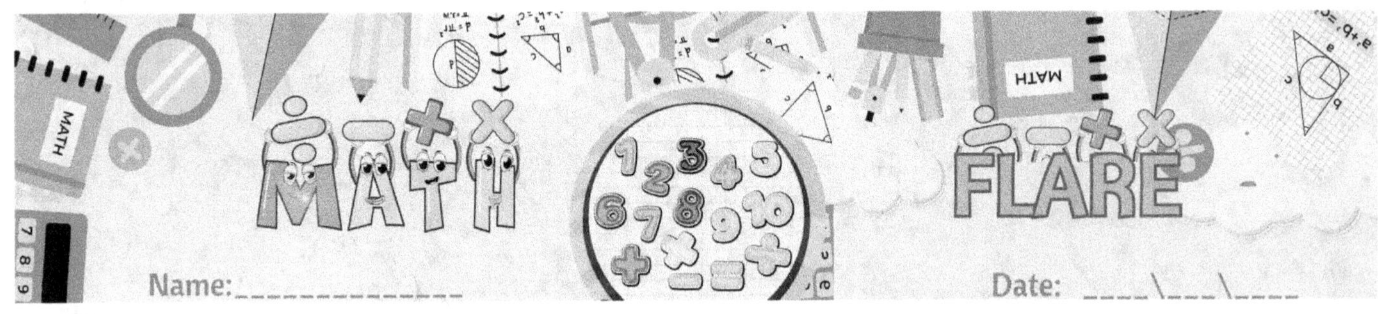

(40) Seven more than seven times a number is equal to the number increased by 37. What is the number?

(41) Four times a number is 8. What is the number?

(42) The quotient of a number and four increased by 2 is 5. What is the number?

(43) The product of two numbers is 48. One number is eight less than the other. What are the numbers?

(44) Four times a number equals 16 less than six times the number. What is the number?

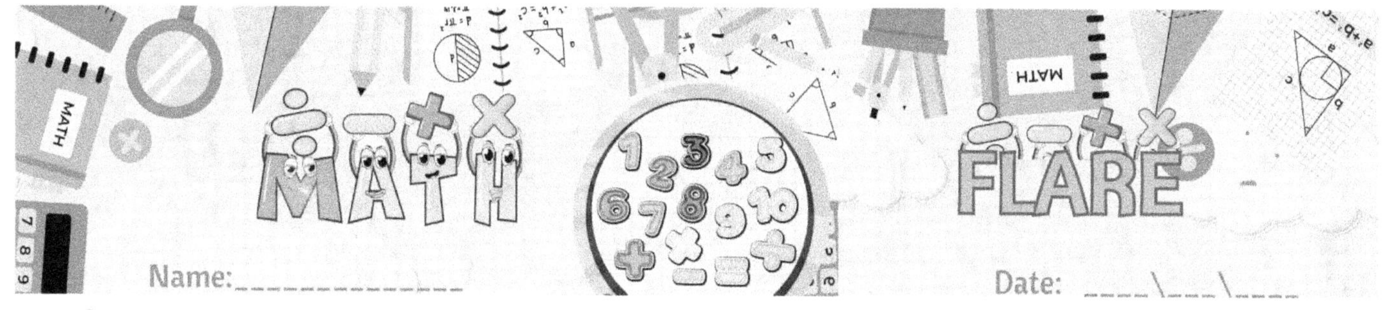

(45) Nine more than a number is 11. What is the number?

(46) Twice a number increased by 2 is 14. Find the number.

(47) Six times the difference of 19 minus a number is 54. What is the number?

(48) Ten is equal to the quotient of a number and 5. Find the number.

(49) Three times a number increased by 3 is 12. Find the number.

(50) The difference of two numbers is 9. The larger number is 3 more than two times the smaller number. What are the numbers?

(51) The sum of two numbers is 64. The larger number is seven times the smaller number. What are the numbers?

(52) The sum of two consecutive odd numbers is 12. Find the numbers.

(53) The sum of two numbers is 21. The larger number is six times the smaller number. What are the numbers?

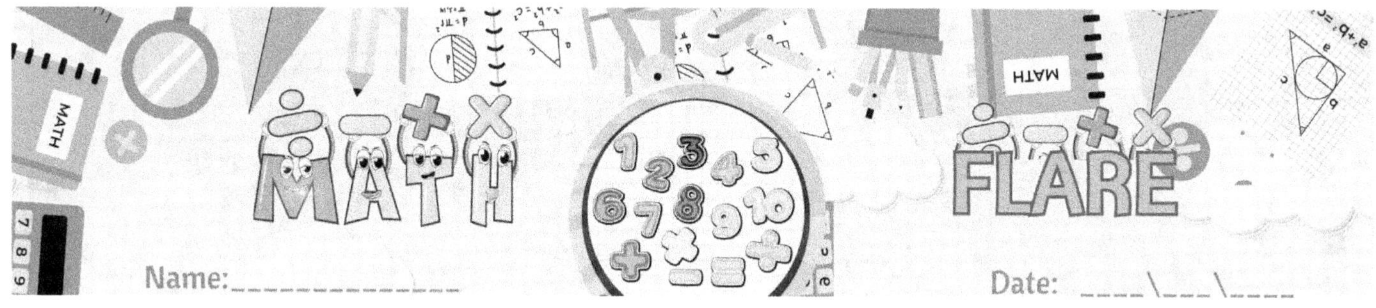

(54) Three-fourths of a number diminished by 1 is 5. Find the number.

(55) Seven less than a number is 7. Find the number.

(56) One number is nine more than another number. The sum of the larger number and twice the smaller number is 27. Find the numbers?

(57) The greater of two numbers is 3 less than seven times the smaller number. Their sum is 5. Find the numbers.

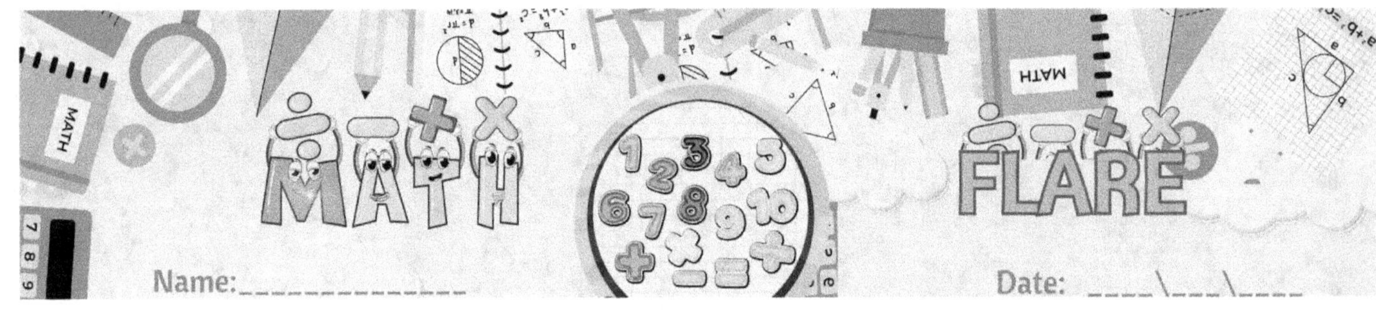

(58) One less than eight times a number is 15. Find the number.

(59) A number increased by two is 5. Find the number.

(60) One of two numbers is two-fourths of the other number. The sum of the numbers is 6. Find the numbers.

(61) A number diminished by 9 is 7. Find the number.

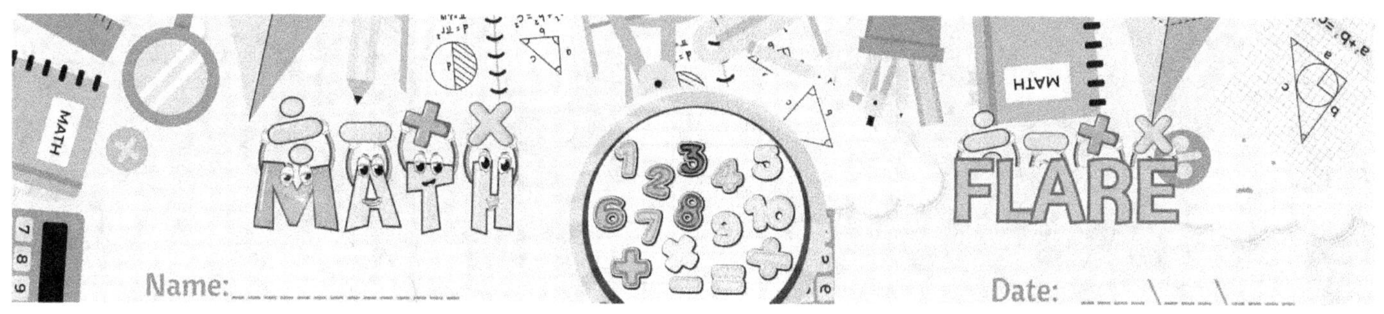

Equations (Two Sides)

Solve for the variable.

① $5z + 17 = 8 + 6z$

Subtract 6z and 17 from both sides

$5z - 6z = 8 - 17$

$-z = -9$

multiply both sides by -1

$-1 \times -z = -1 \times -9$

$z = 9$

② $71 - 3m = 5m + 7$

③ $3x + 4 = 12 - x$

④ $6 + 9x = 21 - 6x$

⑤ $9z + 5 = 45 + 4z$

⑥ $19 + x = 9 + 2x + 9$

⑦ $3 + 6x = 3x + 12$

⑧ $79 - 3m = 8m + 2$

⑨ $2k = 18 - k$

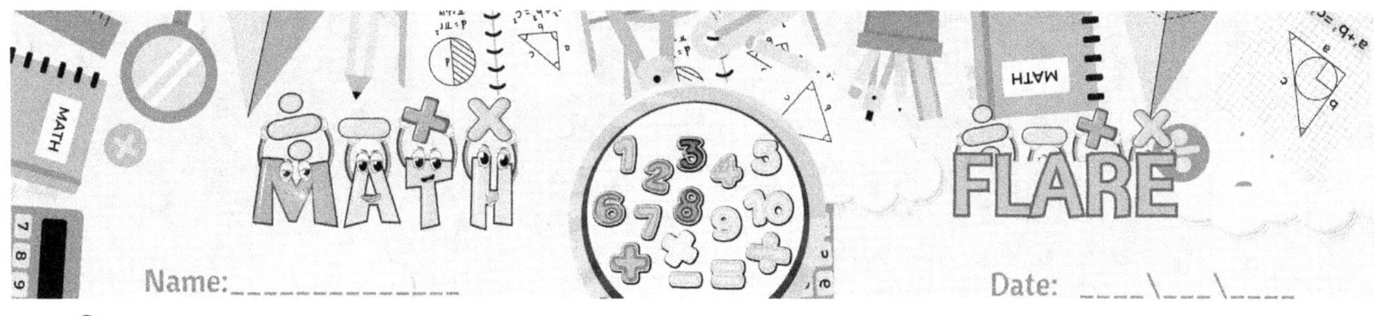

(10) $7 + 3x = 2x + 10$

(11) $20 - z = 3z + 4$

(12) $8 + y = 2y$

(13) $1 + 6m = 33 - 2m$

(14) $3z + 6 = 18 + z$

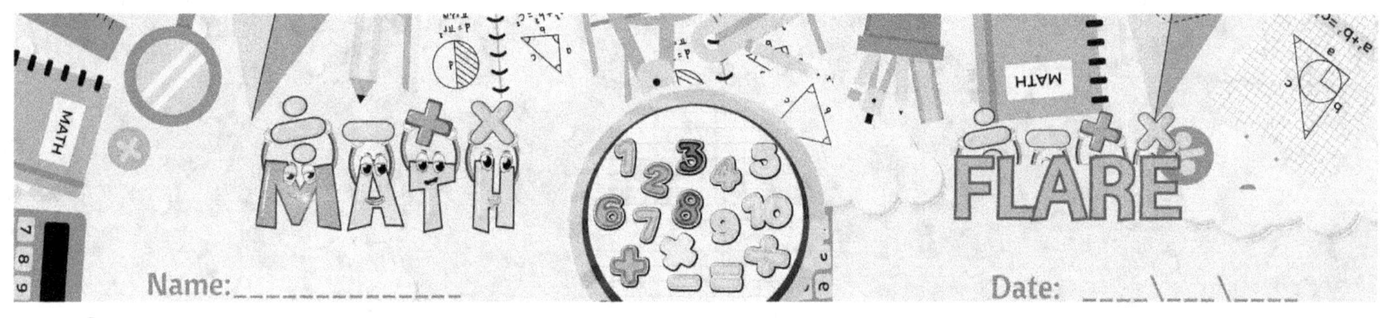

(15) 4k = 20 - k

(16) 2 + 5m + 7 = 12 + m + 1

(17) 16 - y = 1 + 2y

(18) 6 + 3z = 8 + 2z

(19) 29 - k = 8 + 2k

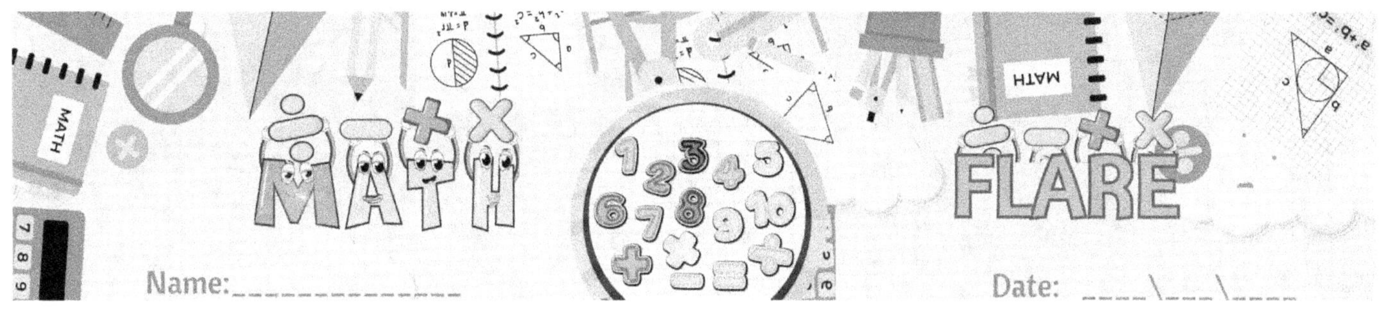

(20) $50 - y + 12 = 5 + 5y + 3$

(21) $7 + 6y + 8 = 31 + y + 4$

(22) $37 - 2k = 7 + 4k$

(23) $8 + 9m = 88 - 7m$

(24) $72 - m = 8m$

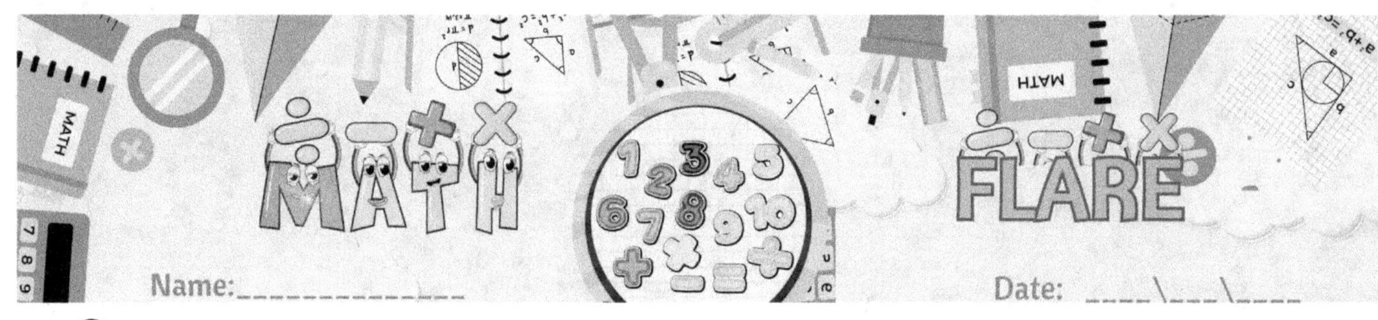

25. $7 + 4y + 9 = 36 - y$

26. $31 - 3z = 6z + 4$

27. $72 + m + -2 = 9 + 7m + 7$

28. $3 + 7x = 51 - x$

29. $53 - 6m = 9m + 8$

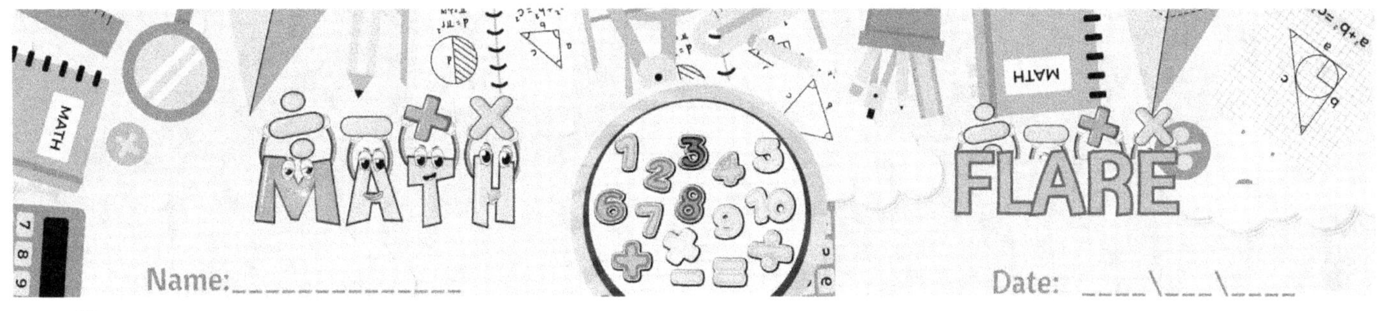

(30) $6 + m = 3m$

(31) $115 - 5m = 7m + 7$

(32) $2x = 3 - x$

(33) $7 + 2x + 4 = 35 - x$

(34) $9k + 2 = 20 + 7k$

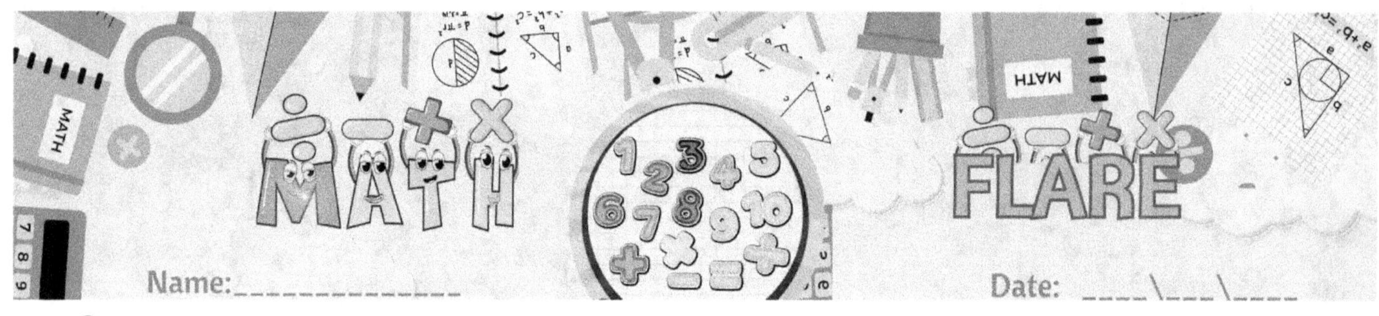

(35) 44 + y = 7y + 8

(36) 6m = 30 + m

(37) 6 + 8y = 66 − 4y

(38) 9 + 7z = 4z + 24

(39) 9y + 1 = 4 + 8y

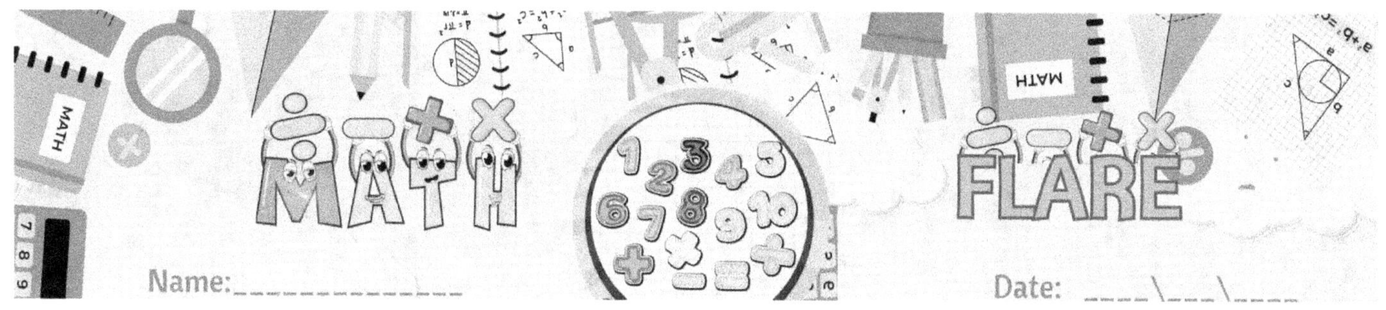

Name:_______________ Date: __________

(40) 6 + 5x + 2 = 12 − x + 8

(41) 8 + k = 1 + 5k + 3

(42) 2k = 7 + k

(43) 2 + 2z + 5 = 8 + z

(44) 4 + 8m = 74 − 6m

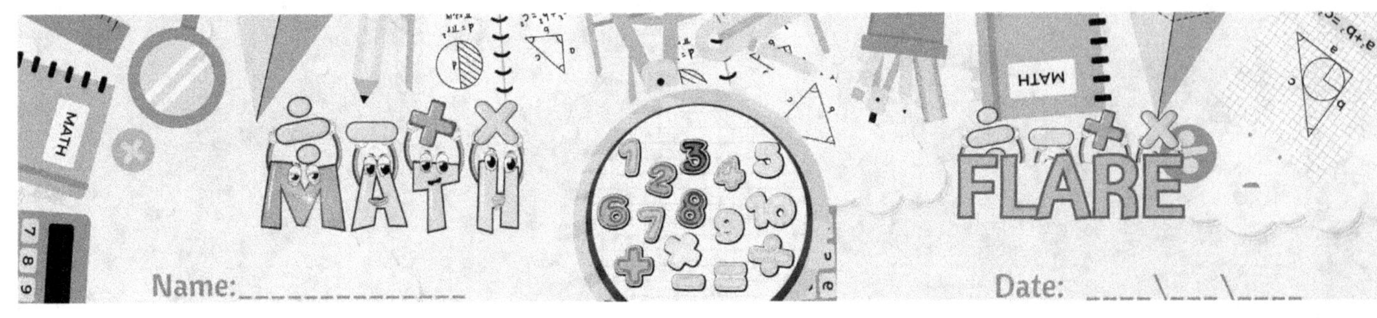

(45) 4 + z = 2z

(46) 3 + 9x = 59 + 2x

(47) 36 - m = 3 + 2m + 6

(48) 2x = 27 - x

(49) 34 - x = 2 + 7x

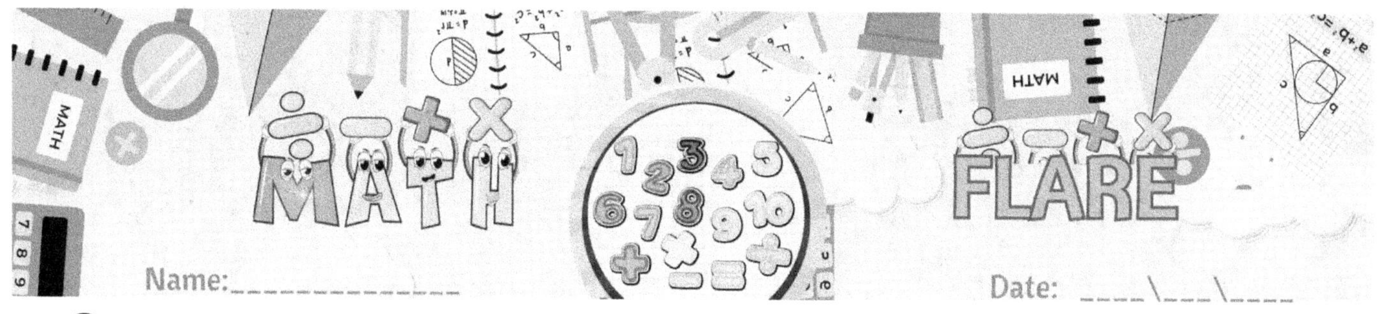

50 3z = 16 + z

51 5m + 4 = 32 + m

52 30 + z + -2 = 1 + 8z + 6

53 37 + x + 1 = 9 + 4x + 8

54 18 + m = 9 + 4m

Name:_______________   Date: ____________

(55) 18 − z = 5 + 2z + 7

(56) 9 + 2y = 27 − y

(57) 7 + 3z = 15 − z

(58) 2 + 3k = 4 + k

(59) 12 − y = 2y

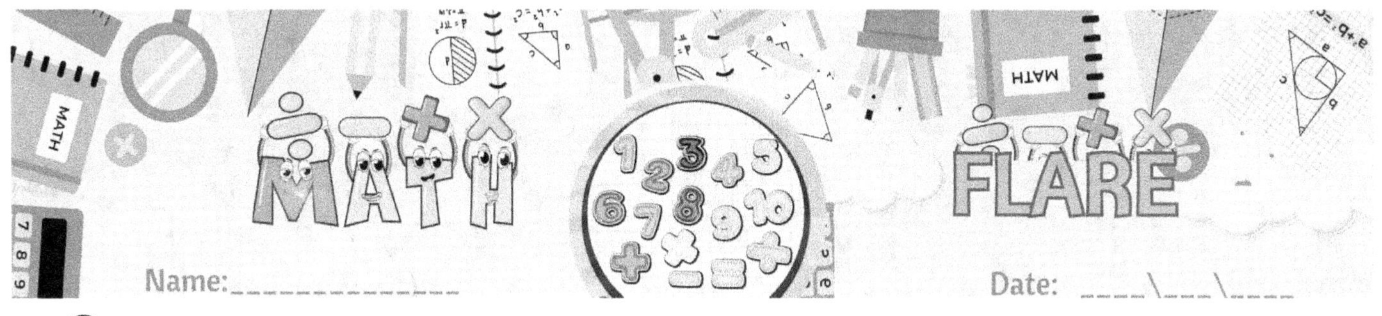

(60) $3 + 9k = 3k + 33$

(61) $12 - k + 11 = 2 + 2k + 6$

(62) $6k = 14 - k$

(63) $54 + k = 5 + 8k$

(64) $14 + z = 4z + 8$

65 $19 + m = 5 + 2m + 9$

66 $40 - 2x = 4x + 4$

67 $7k = 6 + k$

68 $16 + m = 3m$

69 $3 + 4k = 38 - k$

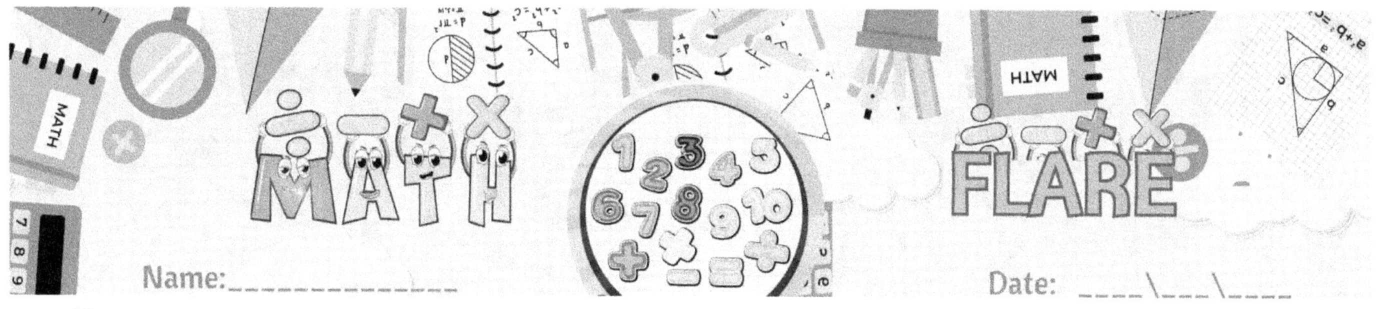

(70) $24 + 7y = 8 + 9y$

(71) $11 - x = 3 + 3x$

(72) $19 - z = 8 + 7z + 3$

(73) $81 - k = 8k$

(74) $6x + 6 = 69 - x$

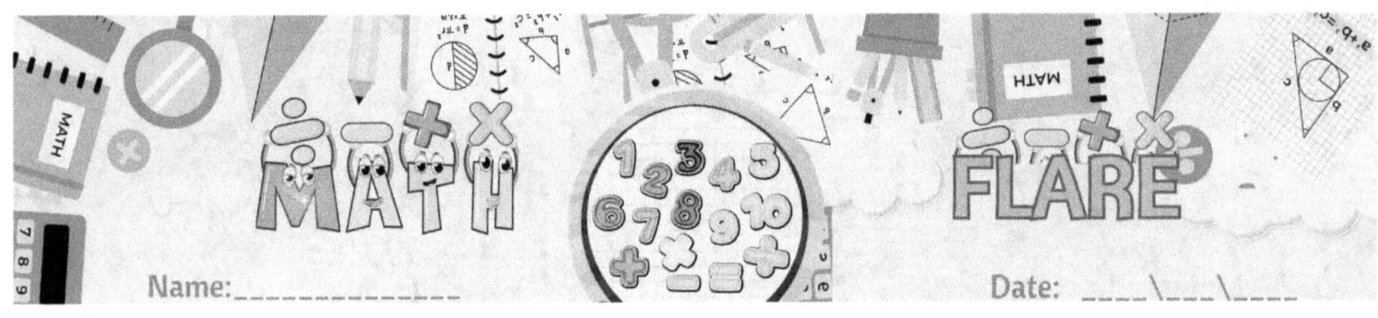

(75) $5 + 5y = 7y + 1$

(76) $2 + 8x = 56 - x$

(77) $2 + 2m + 5 = 8 - m + 8$

(78) $22 - z + 15 = 8 + 3z + 1$

(79) $2x = 6 + x$

Chapter. 02

Percentage

Percentage

Percentage is a way of expressing a number as a fraction of 100. It is commonly used to represent proportions, rates, and comparisons. The symbol "%" is used to denote percentages.

To calculate a percentage, we multiply the given number by the appropriate fraction or decimal equivalent.

How to calculate a percentage:

Convert Percentage to Decimal: If the percentage is given as a percentage value (e.g., 25%), convert it to its decimal equivalent by dividing by 100.

$$\text{For example, 25\% as a decimal is } \frac{25}{100} = 0.25$$

Multiply: Multiply the decimal equivalent of the percentage by the given number. This gives us the portion of the number that represents the percentage.

$$100 \times 0.25 = 25\%$$

Result: The result is the calculated percentage value.

For example, to calculate 25% of 80:

Convert 25% to a decimal: 25% = 0.25.

Multiply 0.25 by 80: 0.25 × 80 = 20. The result is 20.

<u>Percent Word Problems</u>

Percent word problems involve situations where percentages are used to calculate quantities or amounts. These problems often require converting percentages to decimals and then applying them to the given values.

For example:

Bella bought a pair of shoes for $90.00. If she paid an additional 90% for taxes, how much in total did she pay for the shoes?

Given:

- Bella bought a pair of shoes for $90.00.

- She paid an additional 90% for taxes.

Calculate 90% of $90:

Tax= 90% × 90

Tax= 0.90 × 90

Tax= $81

Add the tax amount to the original price:

Total cost= $90 + $81

Total cost= $171

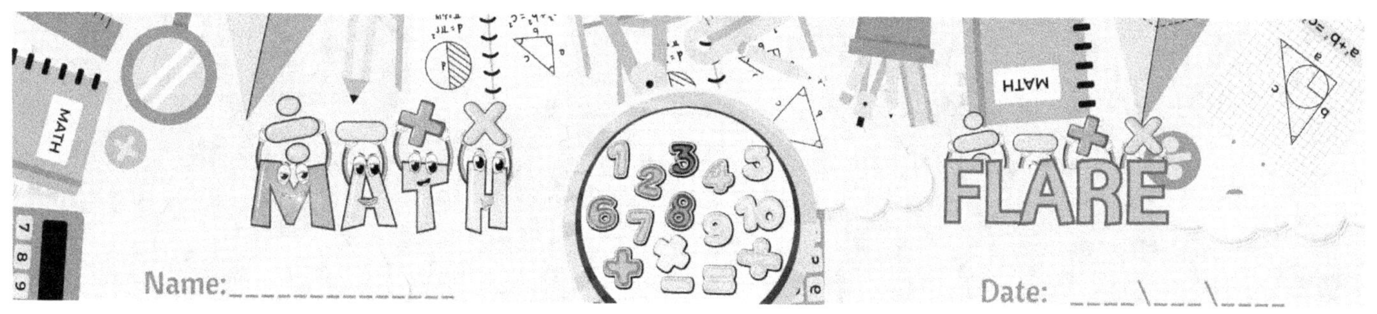

Name:_______________ Date: ____________

Percent

Calculate the given percent of each value.

① 4.8% of 61 = [2.928]
61 × 0.048

② [ ] of 60 = 29.4

③ [ ] of 3 = 0.06

④ 5.4% of 36 = [ ]

⑤ [ ] of 379 = 0.758

⑥ 38.6% of 145 = [ ]

⑦ 7.9% of [ ] = 0.474

⑧ [ ] of 760 = 4.56

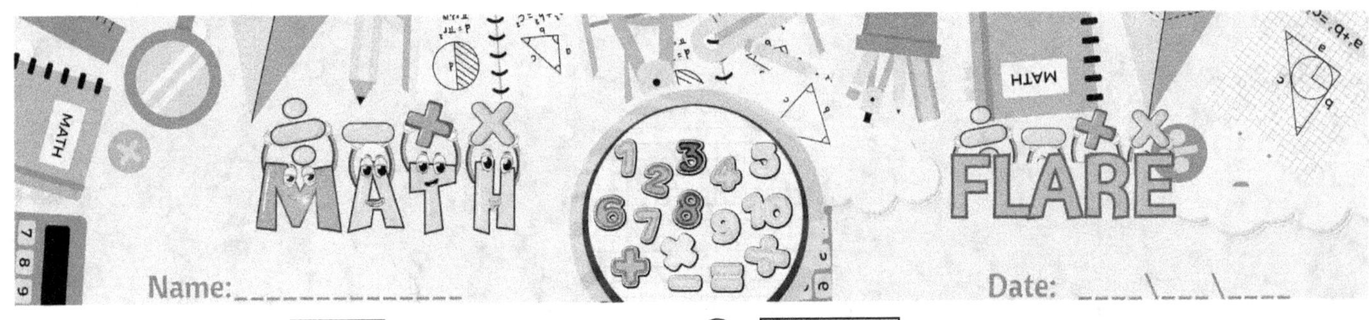

⑨ 1.7% of ☐ = 0.068

⑩ ☐ of 8 = 0.712

⑪ 42.5% of ☐ = 0.85

⑫ ☐ of 24 = 6.864

⑬ ☐ of 37 = 0.296

⑭ 0.9% of 153 = ☐

⑮ 24.6% of 9 = ☐

⑯ 0.1% of 8 = ☐

⑰ 0.8% of 68 = ☐

⑱ 0.6% of 4 = ☐

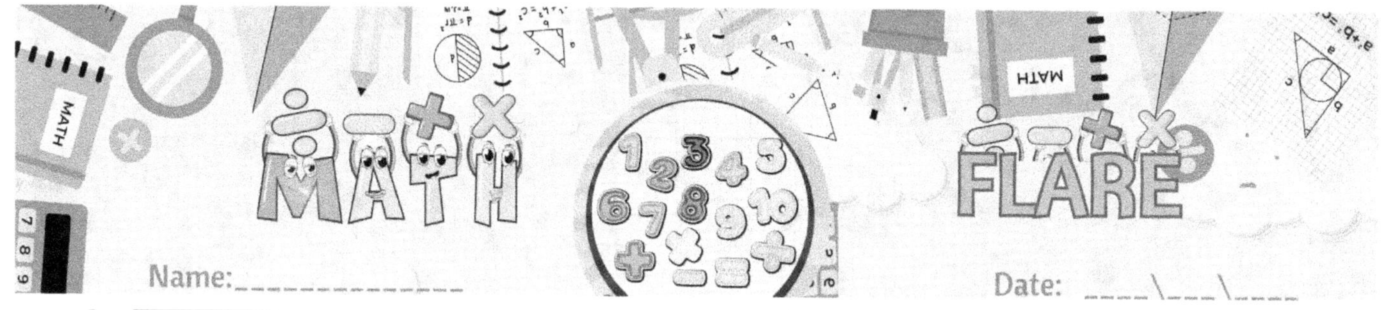

⑲ [____] of 7 = 0.035

⑳ [____] of 9 = 0.468

㉑ 27.8% of 4 = [____]

㉒ [____] of 2 = 0.172

㉓ [____] of 18 = 0.144

㉔ 9.0% of 945 = [____]

㉕ 2.3% of [____] = 7.659

㉖ 7.7% of 642 = [____]

㉗ 2.5% of [____] = 0.175

㉘ [____] of 457 = 39.302

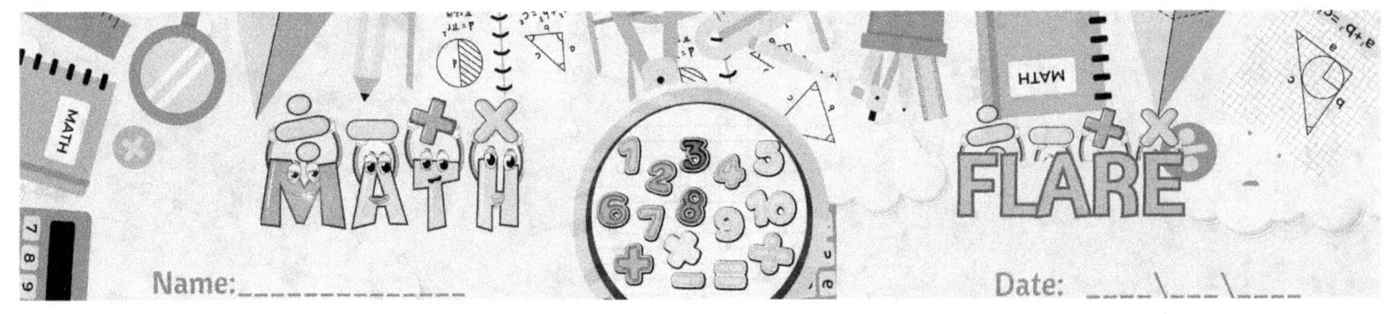

(29) 9.7% of 4 = [　　　]

(30) [　　　] of 7 = 0.476

(31) 0.5% of [　　　] = 0.235

(32) 0.9% of 8 = [　　　]

(33) [　　　] of 8 = 0.024

(34) 4.8% of [　　　] = 27.072

(35) 49.0% of 63 = [　　　]

(36) 2.0% of [　　　] = 0.76

(37) 5.4% of [　　　] = 0.108

(38) 0.2% of [　　　] = 1.382

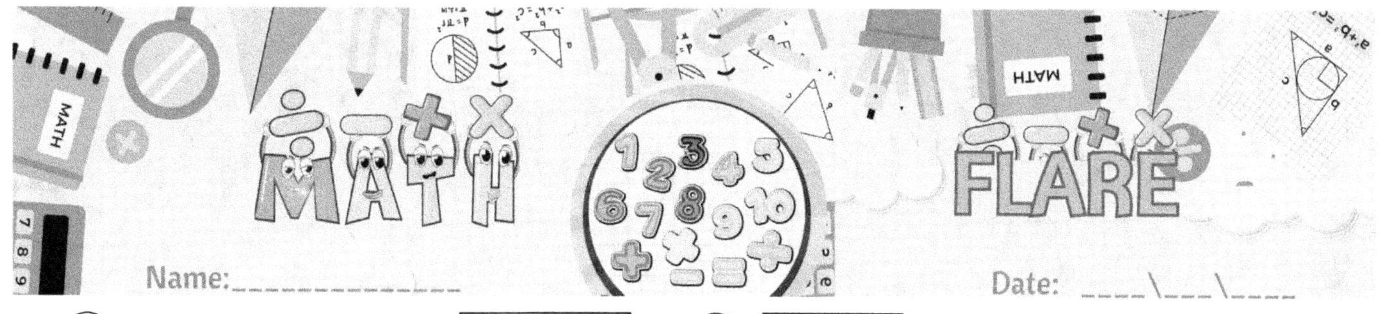

(39) 38.6% of 483 = [   ]   (40) [   ] of 32 = 2.528

(41) 0.6% of [   ] = 0.564   (42) [   ] of 1 = 0.017

(43) 8.9% of [   ] = 0.534   (44) 42.5% of 68 = [   ]

(45) 28.6% of [   ] = 218.218   (46) 0.8% of 78 = [   ]

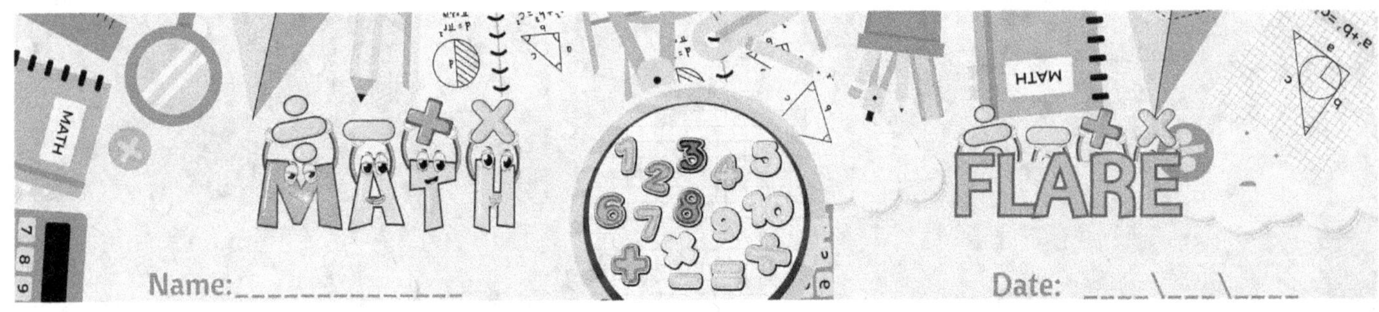

Convert: Ratio, Fraction, Percent, and Decimals

①

	Ratio	Fraction	Percent	Decimal
a.	12:15	12/15	80%	0.8
b.	1:2	1/2	50%	0.5
c.		4/15		
d.		2/6		
e.				0.714
f.				0.389
g.			50%	
h.		2/4		
i.				0.571
j.				0.583
k.				1
l.				0.158
m.		3/7		
n.		13/15		
o.				0.438

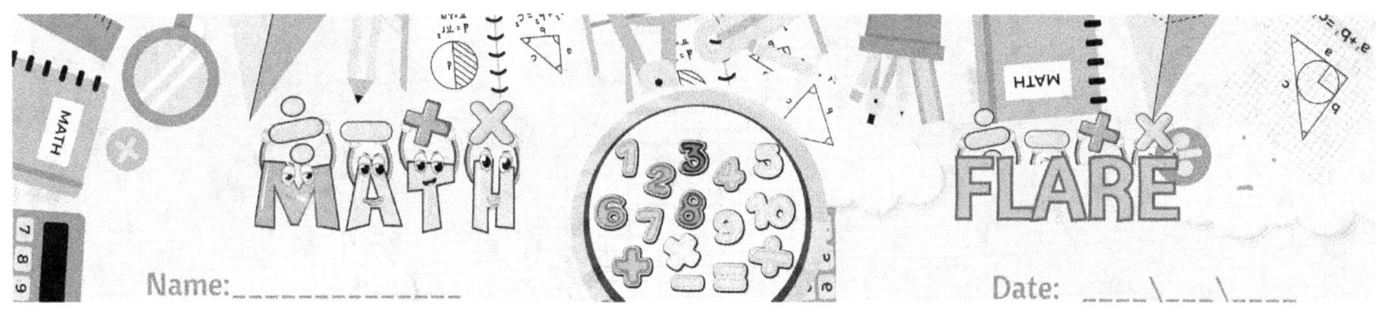

②

	Ratio	Fraction	Percent	Decimal
a.			83.3%	
b.	18:20			
c.			63.2%	
d.		3/7		
e.		13/13		
f.	1:2			
g.	2:16			
h.				0.4
i.				0.053
j.				0.067
k.	1:4			
l.	14:16			
m.		8/18		
n.				0.538
o.			47.1%	

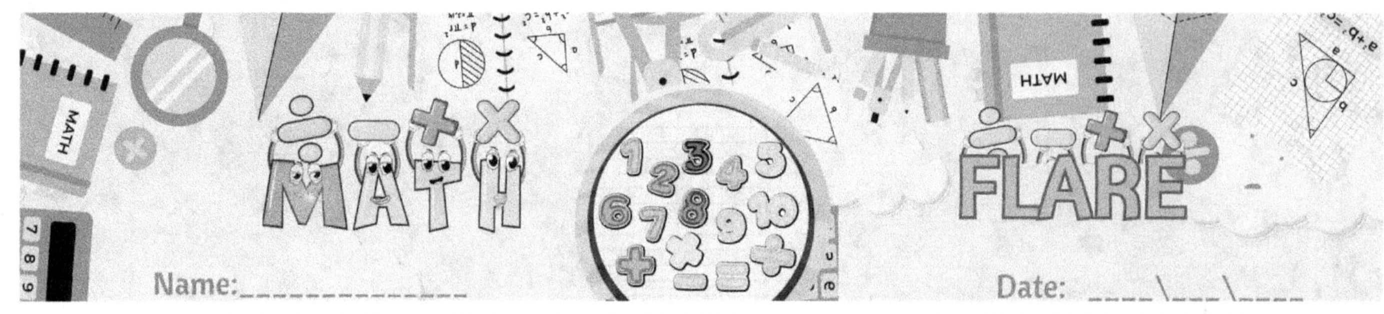

③

	Ratio	Fraction	Percent	Decimal
a.		2/2		
b.	4:10			
c.			80%	
d.	1:4			
e.	3:19			
f.		13/17		
g.				0.25
h.	14:20			
i.				0.333
j.				0.2
k.				0.938
l.	3:8			
m.	5:7			
n.			68.8%	
o.		1/18		

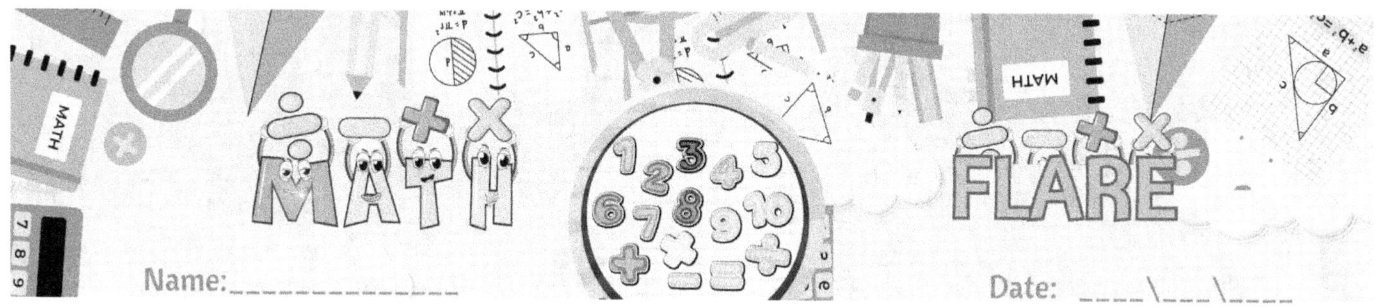

Name:_______________   Date: ____________

④

	Ratio	Fraction	Percent	Decimal
a.	3:4			
b.				1
c.		9/13		
d.			14.3%	
e.				0.364
f.		4/6		
g.	6:19			
h.			68.8%	
i.	4:16			
j.	2:4			
k.		1/2		
l.				0.278
m.			30%	
n.				0.25
o.				0.333

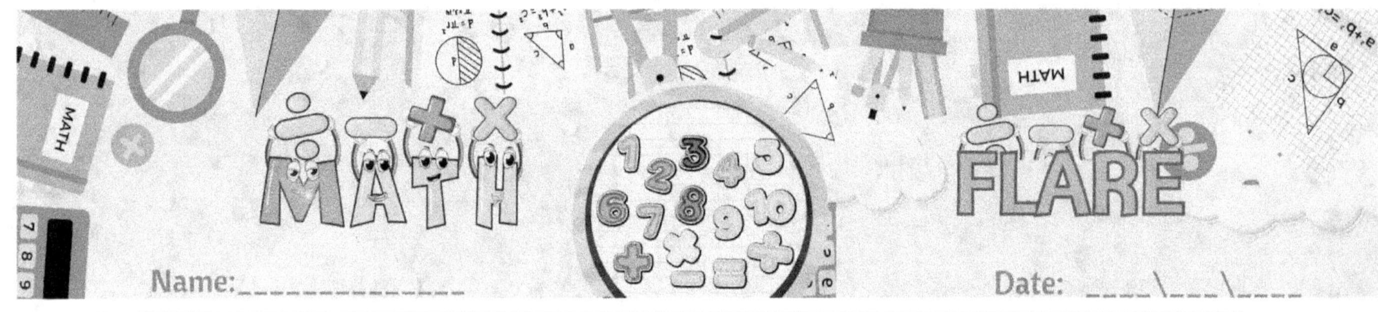

⑤

	Ratio	Fraction	Percent	Decimal
a.		7/18		
b.		2/6		
c.				0.333
d.				0.5
e.		1/8		
f.		1/1		
g.			60%	
h.	15:18			
i.	10:16			
j.	1:18			
k.		3/18		
l.			26.3%	
m.	2:3			
n.			53.3%	
o.			43.8%	

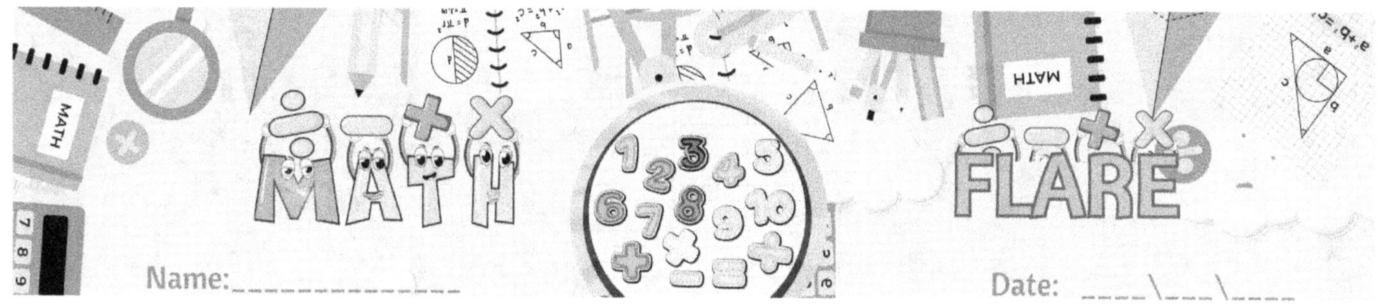

Word Problems: Percent

① Piper bought a book for $100.00. If she paid an additional 1% for sales tax, how much in total did she pay for the book?

Sales tax = 1% of $100
= $100 × 0.01
= $1

Total amount paid = $100 + $1 = $101

② A school has a total of 80 teachers. If 85% of them are men, how many female teachers are there?

③ A classroom has 85 students, of which 20% are girls. How many boys are in the classroom?

④ If the number 100 is decreased by 19%, what is the value of the new number?

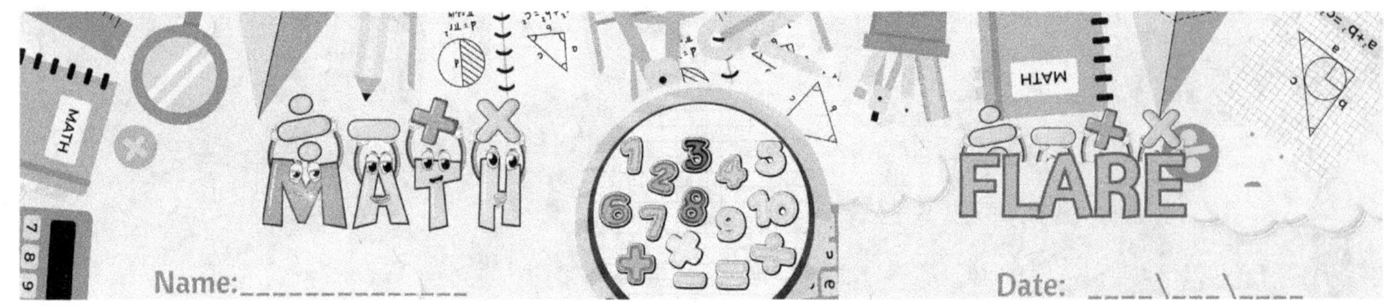

Name:________________   Date: ____________

⑤ Reagan bought a bag for $95.00. If she paid an additional 20% for sales tax, how much in total did she pay for the bag?

⑥ In a class of 25 students, 32% of them are in the Math Club. How many students are in the Math Club?

⑦ Miles buys computers for $20.00 to sell them in market. If he wants to earn 5% profit. What must be the selling price of computers?

⑧ Chase bought a bicycle that cost $70.00 when it was new. If he eventually sold it for 20% of the original cost, how much was it sold for?

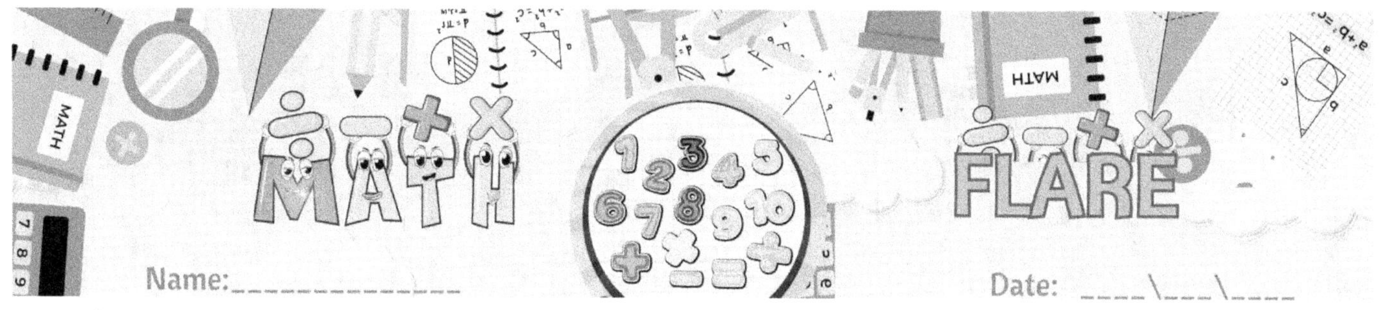

⑨ In a class of 50 students, 8% are girls. How many are girls?

⑩ A teacher gave a math test with 25 questions. If a student got 8% questions correct, how many questions were correct?

⑪ If the number 45 is increased by 20%, what is the value of the new number?

⑫ A store has 10 books. If 20% of them are sold at the end of the day, how many books are sold?

⑬ In a survey of 20 people, 5% said they prefer cats over dogs. How many people prefer cats?

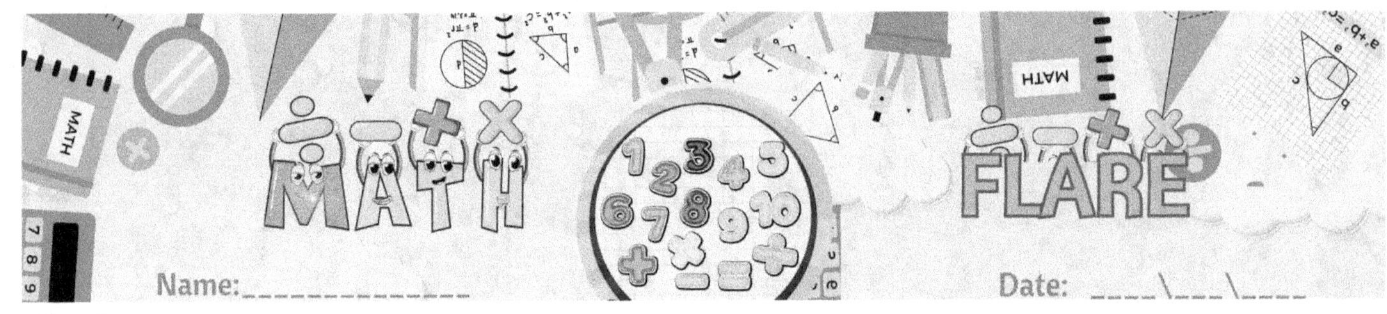

⑭ Roman had 40 apples. He gave away 20% of them. How many did he have left?

⑮ Robert earned $100.00 for a week's work. If he paid 1% of it in taxes how much did he pay in taxes?

⑯ A company wants to increase its revenue by 8%. If its current revenue is $25.00 million, what should be its new revenue?

⑰ A store increases the prices of all items by 8%. If the bananas originally costs $100.00, what is the sale price?

⑱ A school has a total of 5 teachers. If 20% of them are men, how many male teachers are there?

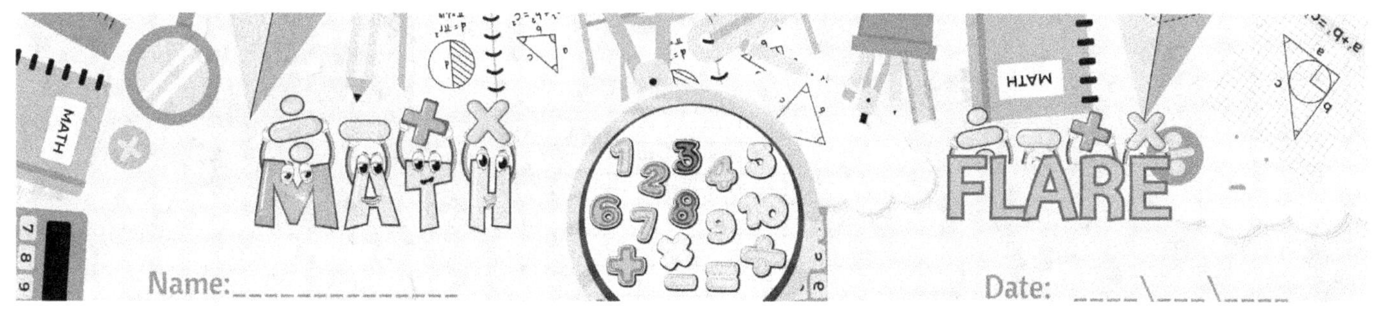

(19) A school has 25 students. If 8% of them play tennis, how many students play tennis?

(20) A store offers a 20% discount on all items. If Aaliyah buys phones originally priced at $5.00, how much money did she save?

(21) A school has 50 students. If 42% of them play football, how many students play football?

(22) In a basket of 100 flowers, 24% are red flowers . How many are red flowers?

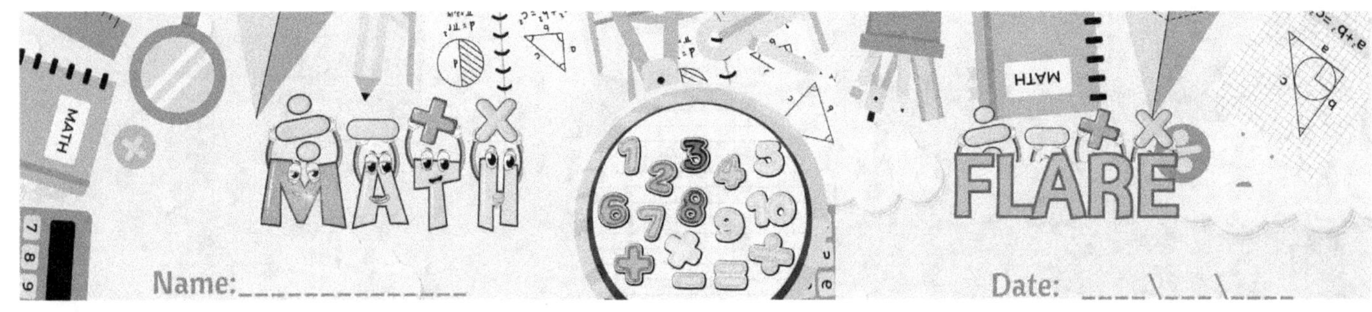

(23) A store is having a sale where everything is 20% off. The folders originally priced at $65.00 is now on sale. How much is the new price of folders now?

(24) A store offers 20% discount on all products. If the original price of pens was 90, what is the sales price?

(25) A school has 50 students. If 18% of them play baseball, how many students play baseball?

(26) A store offers 35% discount on all products. If the sale price of thermometers was 40, what was the original price?

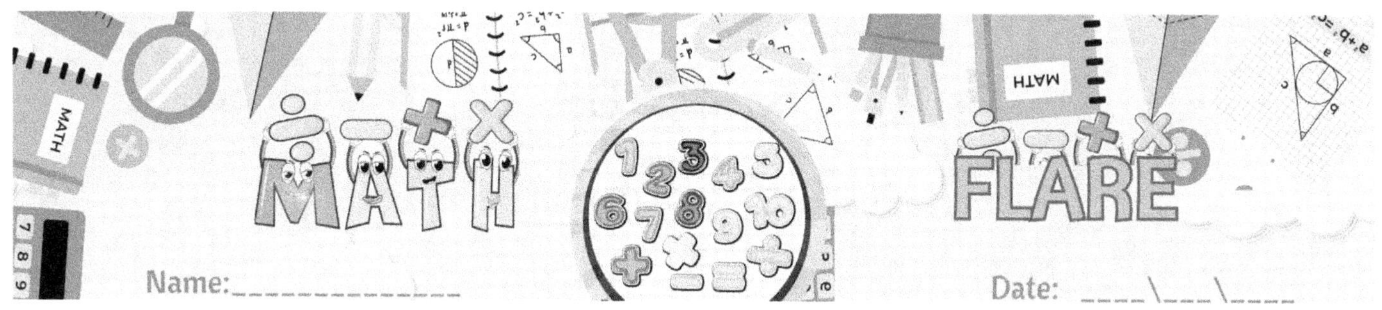

27. Eva bought a shoes for $10.00. If she paid an additional 20% for sales tax, how much in total did she pay for the shoes?

28. Ellie bought a camera for $20.00. If she paid an additional 35% for sales tax, how much in total did she pay for the camera?

29. In a survey of 55 people, 20% said they preferred android OS. How many people preferred android OS?

30. Levi's monthly sales of mirrors was $55.00. If he earned 20% of profit, what was his profit?

Chapter. 03

Linear Equation

A linear equation is an algebraic equation that represents a straight line when graphed on a coordinate plane. It consists of variables raised to the power of 1 (i.e., no exponents higher than 1) and constant coefficients.

The general form of a linear equation in one variable x is:

$$ax + b = 0$$

Where a and b are constants, and x is the variable.

Let's solve the linear equation:

$$-2x + 9 = 5$$

- **Isolate the variable term:** We want to isolate the term containing x on one side of the equation. To do this, we'll move the constant term to the other side. Subtract 9 from both sides:

$$-2x + 9 - 9 = 5 - 9$$

$$-2x = -4$$

- **Divide by the coefficient of the variable:** To solve for x, divide both sides by the coefficient of x, which is -2:

$$\frac{-2x}{-2} = \frac{-4}{-2}$$

$$x = 2$$

<u>Slop from Two Points</u>

The slope between two points on a Cartesian coordinate system is a measure of the steepness of the line connecting those points. It's calculated by finding the change in the y-coordinates divided by the change in the x-coordinates.

- The coordinates of the first point as $(x_1, y_1) = (2, -30)$.

- The coordinates of the second point as $(x_2, y_2) = (-5, 40)$.

The formula to calculate the slope (m) between two points:

$$\frac{y_2 - y_1}{x_2 - x_1}$$

$$= \frac{40 - (-30)}{-5 - 2} = \frac{70}{-7}$$

$$\text{Slope} = -10$$

<u>Plot Lines</u>

To plot the lines using the given points, we'll first locate each point on the coordinate plane, and then connect the points to form the lines. Let's plot each line one by one:

A = (-6, -3)	B = (0, 3)
C = (-4, -1)	D = (1, 4)
E = (4, 7)	F = (2, 5)

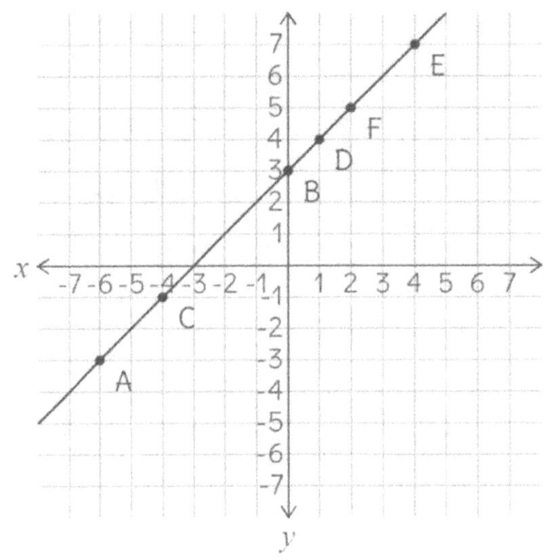

Graphing Linear Equation

Graphing a linear equation involves plotting the points that satisfy the equation on a coordinate plane and connecting them to form a straight line. Linear equations are equations of the form $y = mx + b$, where m represents the slope of the line, and b represents the y-intercept, the point where the line intersects the y-axis.

To graph a linear equation:

1. Identify the slope (m) and y-intercept (b) from the equation.

2. Plot the y-intercept $(0, b)$) as a point on the y-axis.

3. Use the slope to find additional points on the line. The slope represents the change in y for every unit change in x.

4. Connect the points to form a straight line.

For example, to graph the equation:

$$y = \frac{9}{4}x - 8$$

1. **Identify the slope and y-intercept:** The slope is $\frac{9}{4}$, and the y-intercept is -8.

MathFlare - Math Workbook 8th and 9th Grade

2. **Plot the y-intercept:** Plot the point (0,−8).

3. **Use the slope to plot additional points:** the slop is $\frac{9}{4}$ to find another point. we will move up 9 units and 4 units to the right from the y-intercept to find another point.

4. **Draw the line:** Once we have at least two points, we can draw a straight line.

We can continue this process to plot more points and extend the line further if needed.

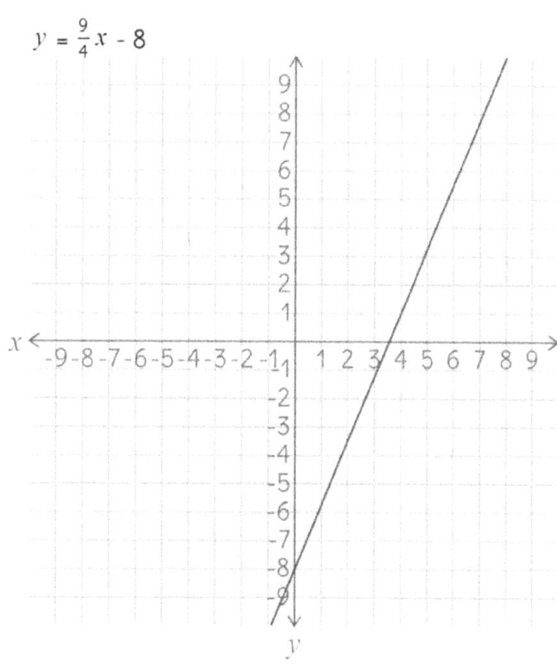

System of Equations

A system of equations is a collection of two or more equations involving the same set of variables. The solution to a system of equations is the set of values for the variables that satisfy all the equations simultaneously.

Solving by Elimination:

To solve a system of equations by elimination, we manipulate the equations to eliminate one of the variables.

Given the system:

$$4x + 5y = 6$$

$$10x + 6y = 8$$

Step 1: Multiply each equation by a constant such that the coefficients of one of the variables become equal or multiples of each other.

Let's try to eliminate the variable x.

- Multiply the first equation by 5 and the second equation by -2:

$$20x + 25y = 30$$

$$-20x - 12y = -16$$

Step 2: Add the two equations together to eliminate the variable x.

$$(20x - 20x) + (25y - 12y) = 30 - 16$$

$$13y = 14$$

$$y = \frac{14}{13} = 1.077$$

Step 3: Solve for y:

Step 4: Substitute the value of y into one of the original equations to solve for x. Let's use the first equation:

$$4x + 5(\frac{14}{13}) = 6$$

$$4x + \frac{70}{13} = 6$$

$$4x = 6 - \frac{70}{13}$$

$$4x = \frac{78 - 70}{13}$$

$$4x = \frac{8}{13}$$

$$X = \frac{2}{13} = 0.154$$

the solution to the system of equations is x =0.154 and y = 1.077.

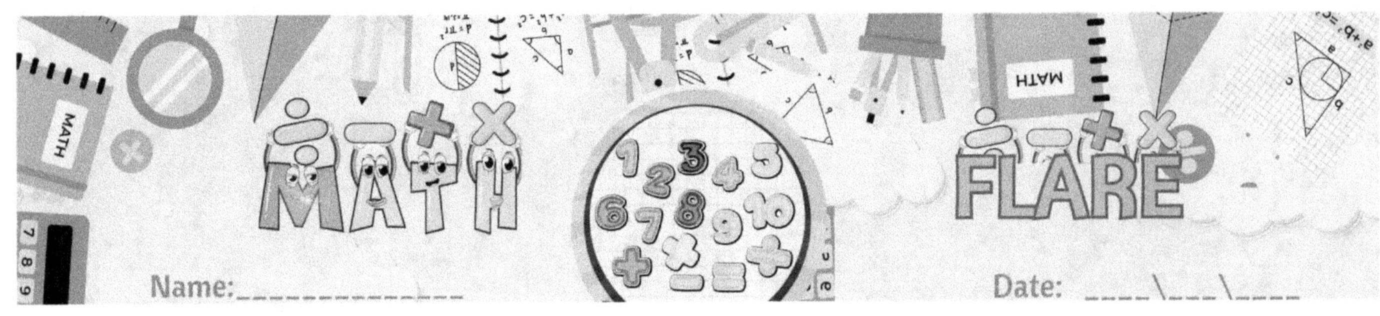

Linear Equations

Find the value of x.

① 9x + -10 = -37

  add 10 to both sides

  9x-10+10 = -37+10

  9x = -27

  divide both sides by 9

  $$\frac{9x}{9} = \frac{-27}{9} \qquad x = -3$$

② -6x + -4 = 38

③ -7x + 3 = 73

④ -8x + -9 = 47

⑤ -7x + -5 = -26

⑥ 9x + -1 = 8

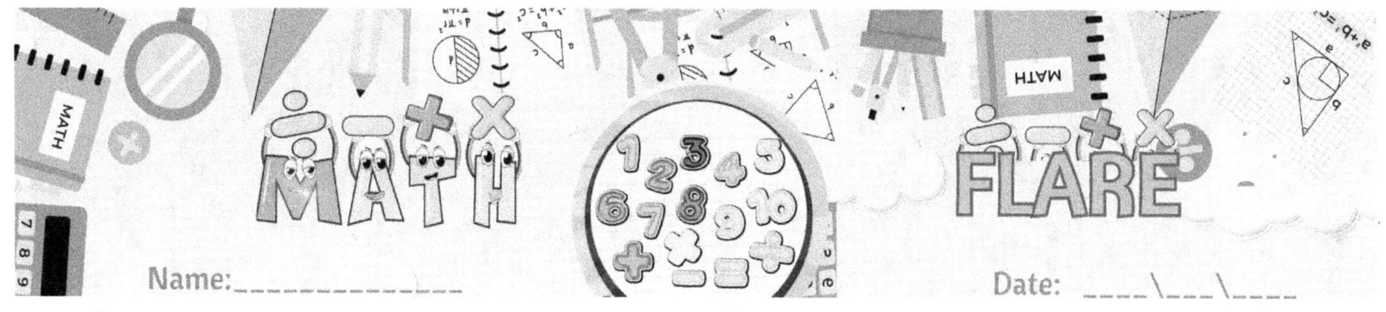

⑦ -2x + -4 = -12

⑧ -6x + -7 = -25

⑨ -8x + -5 = 75

⑩ 3x + -4 = 23

⑪ -6x + -3 = 21

⑫ 7x + 4 = -38

⑬ -6x + -4 = 14

⑭ 5x + 3 = 13

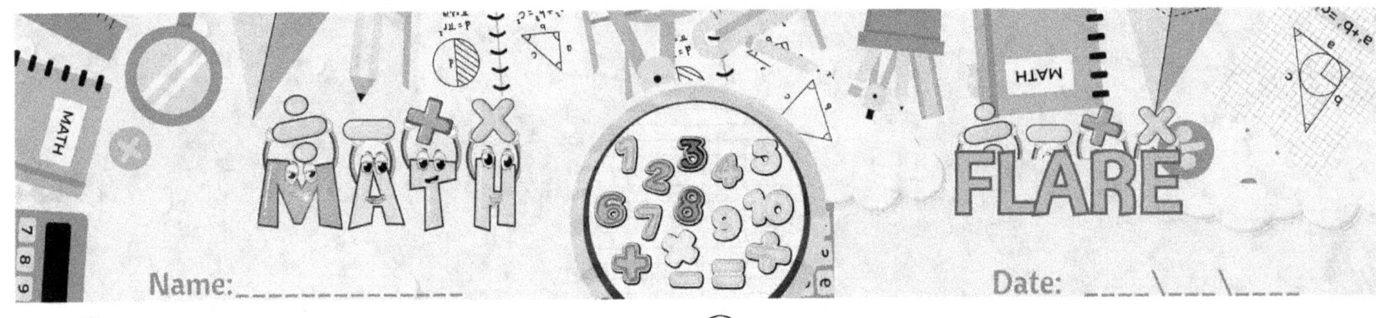

(15) $-7x + 7 = -49$

(16) $3x + -2 = -14$

(17) $8x + 5 = 13$

(18) $-8x + -1 = 23$

(19) $9x + -8 = 64$

(20) $9x + 6 = -75$

(21) $-4x + 2 = 10$

(22) $7x + 10 = -46$

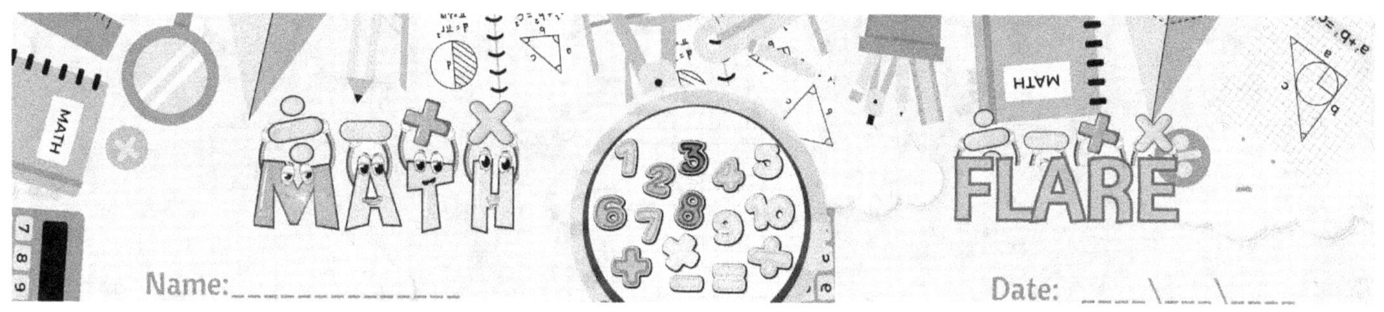

Slope from Two Points

Find the slope of the line passing through two points.

① (-9, -48) and (-9, -48)

② (2, -30) and (-5, 40)

$$\text{Slope} = \frac{y2 - y1}{x2 - x1}$$

$$= \frac{40 - (-30)}{-5 - 2} = \frac{70}{-7}$$

$$\text{Slope} = -10$$

③ (-7, 80) and (9, -80)

④ (-3, 10) and (8, -12)

⑤ (3, 13) and (10, 34)

⑥ (3, -9) and (6, -18)

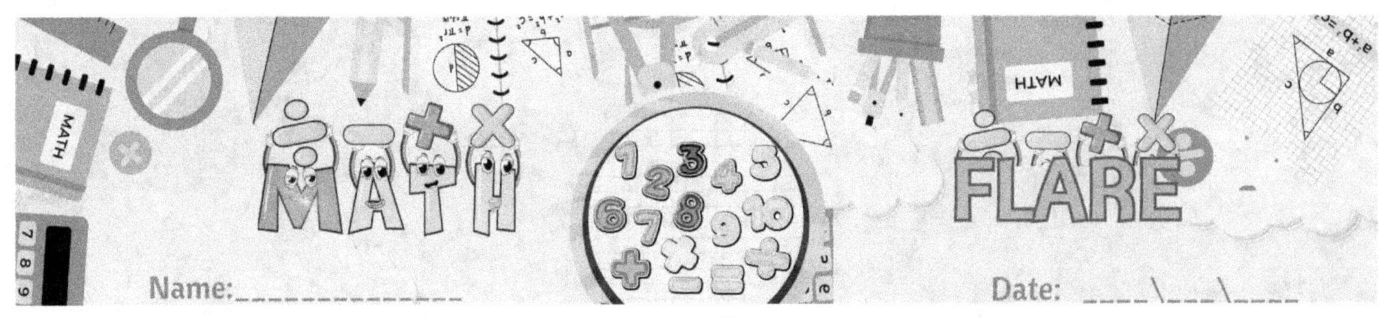

⑦ (4, 25) and (-4, -15)

⑧ (-9, 33) and (-7, 27)

⑨ (7, 66) and (-2, -6)

⑩ (10, 39) and (-9, -37)

⑪ (4, -14) and (0, -6)

⑫ (-10, -37) and (2, -1)

⑬ (0, 0) and (-9, -27)

⑭ (-8, 49) and (-8, 49)

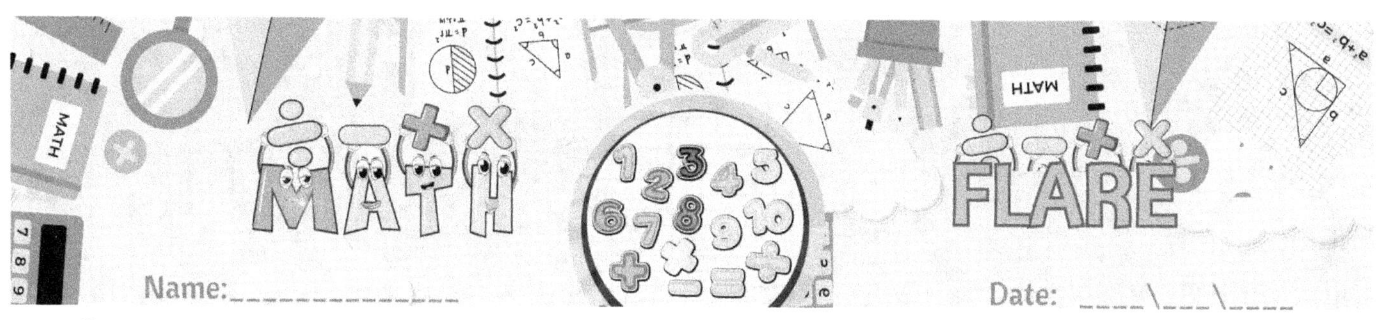

⑮ (-3, 11) and (-1, 9)

⑯ (-7, -23) and (-3, -15)

⑰ (3, 24) and (-4, -11)

⑱ (7, 49) and (4, 31)

⑲ (5, 48) and (-2, -22)

⑳ (0, 1) and (-3, -17)

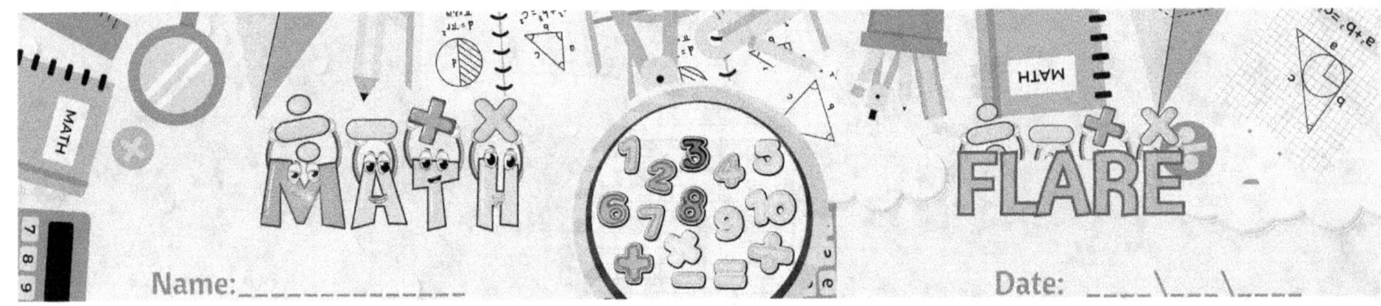

Plotting Lines
Plot and draw the lines.

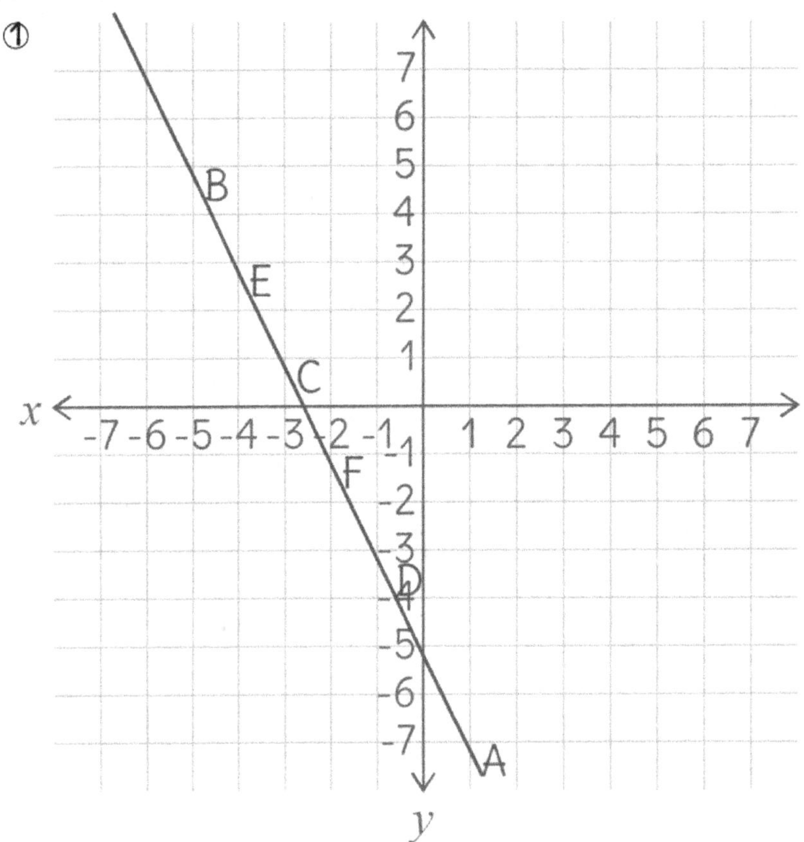

A = (1, -7)　　　　B = (-5, 5)

C = (-3, 1)　　　　D = (-1, -3)

E = (-4, 3)　　　　F = (-2, -1)

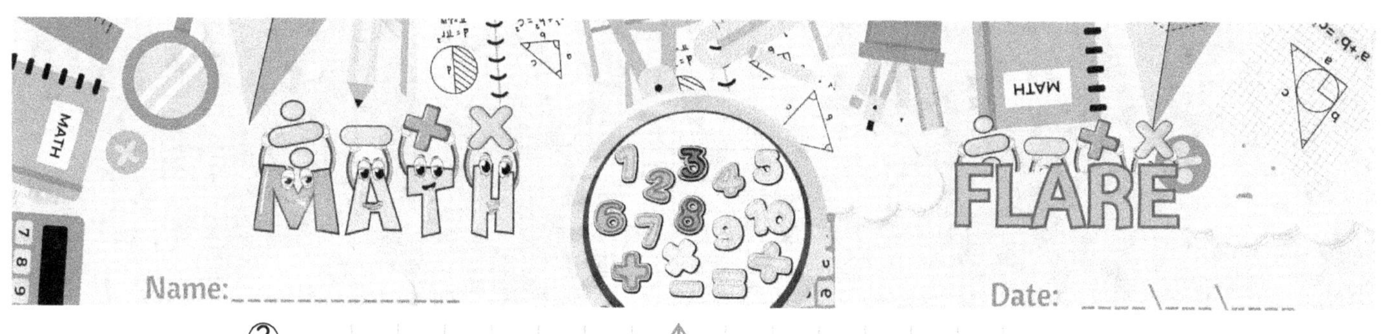

② 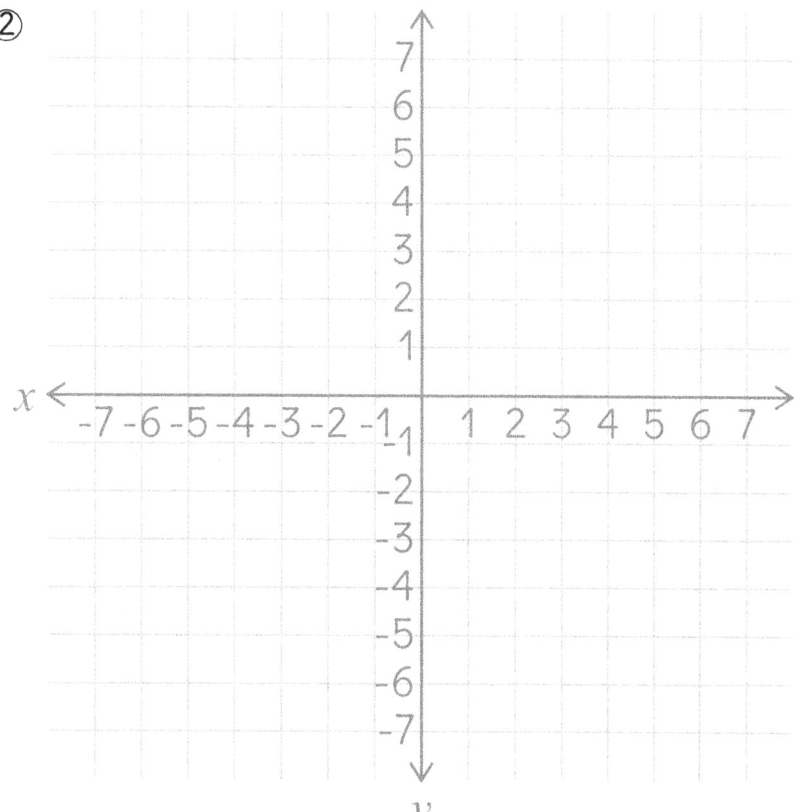

A = (-6, -6)   B = (2, -2)

C = (0, -3)   D = (-2, -4)

E = (-4, -5)   F = (6, 0)

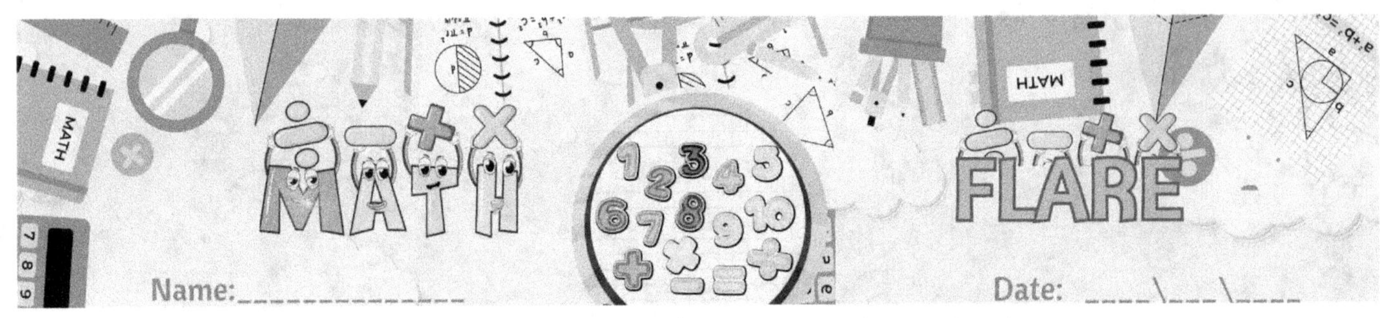

③

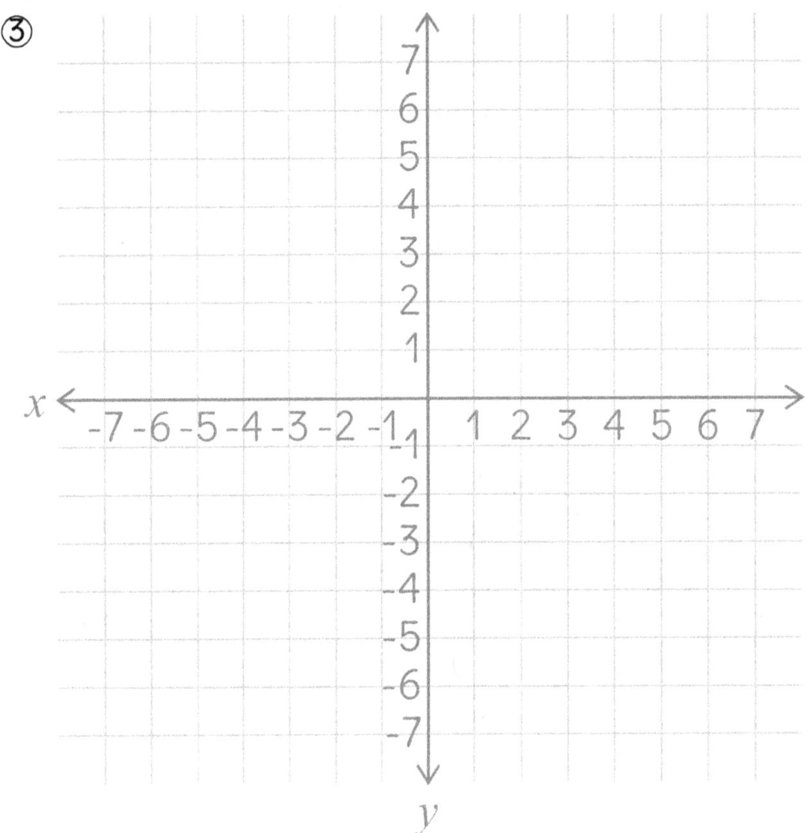

A = (3, 6)   B = (-2, 1)

C = (2, 5)   D = (-4, -1)

E = (-7, -4)   F = (-6, -3)

Name:_________________   Date: ____________

④

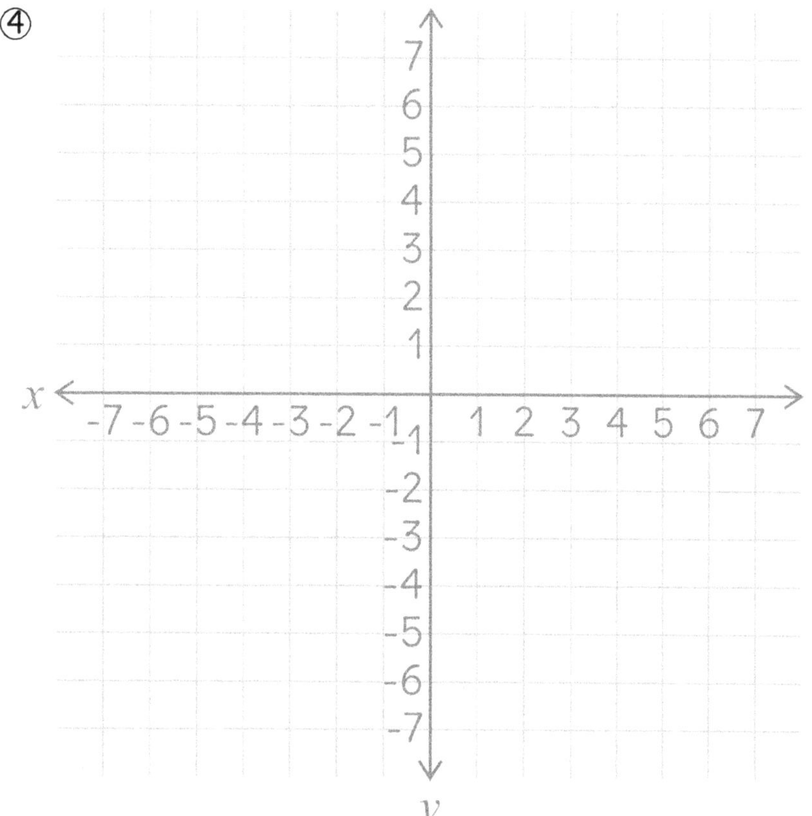

A = (-3, 1)   B = (5, -7)

C = (-7, 5)   D = (-5, 3)

E = (3, -5)   F = (2, -4)

⑤

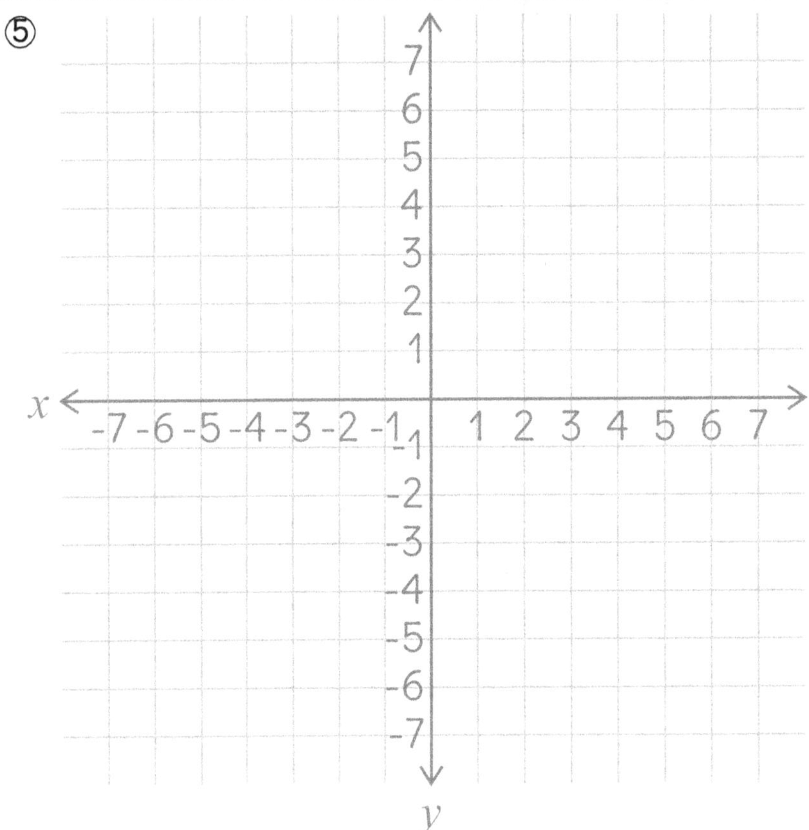

A = (0, -4)   B = (1, -6)

C = (-2, 0)   D = (-1, -2)

E = (-5, 6)   F = (-4, 4)

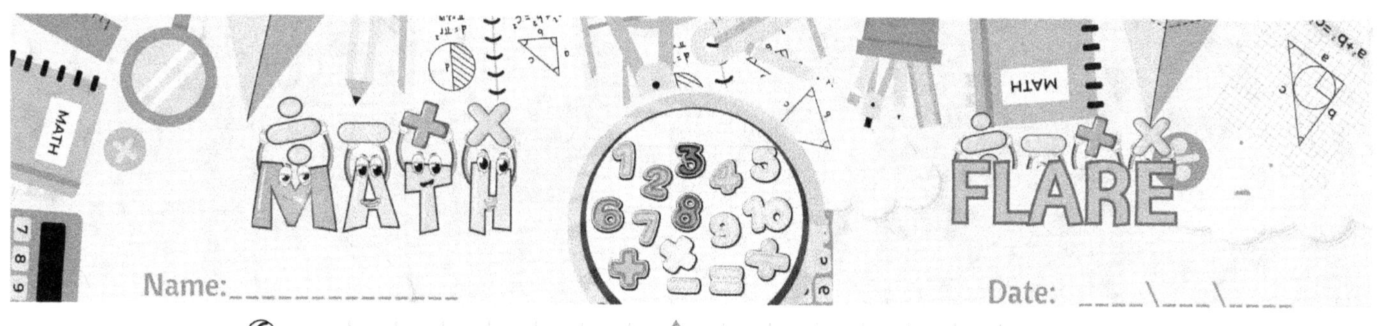

⑥

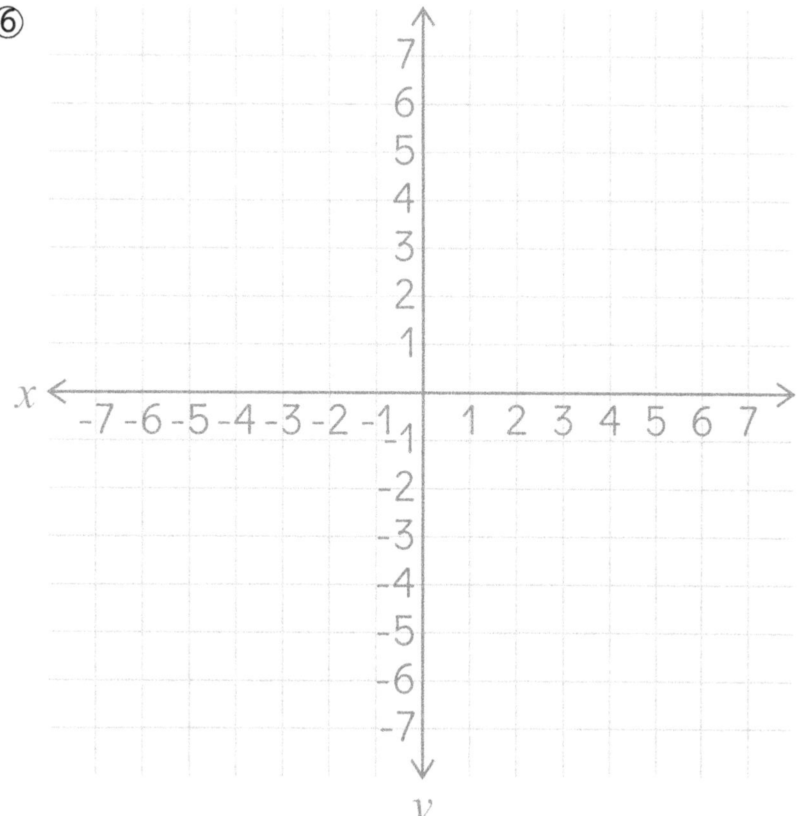

A = (-7, -3)   B = (-2, 2)

C = (2, 6)   D = (-6, -2)

E = (-4, 0)   F = (-5, -1)

⑦

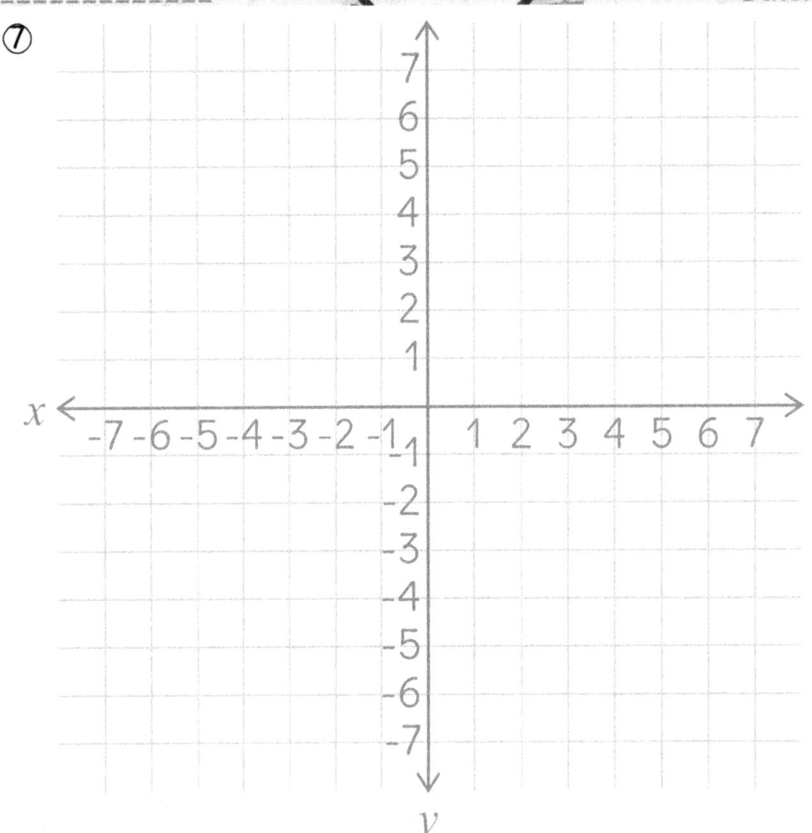

A = (4, -3)   B = (3, -2)

C = (1, 0)   D = (-2, 3)

E = (-6, 7)   F = (-4, 5)

⑧

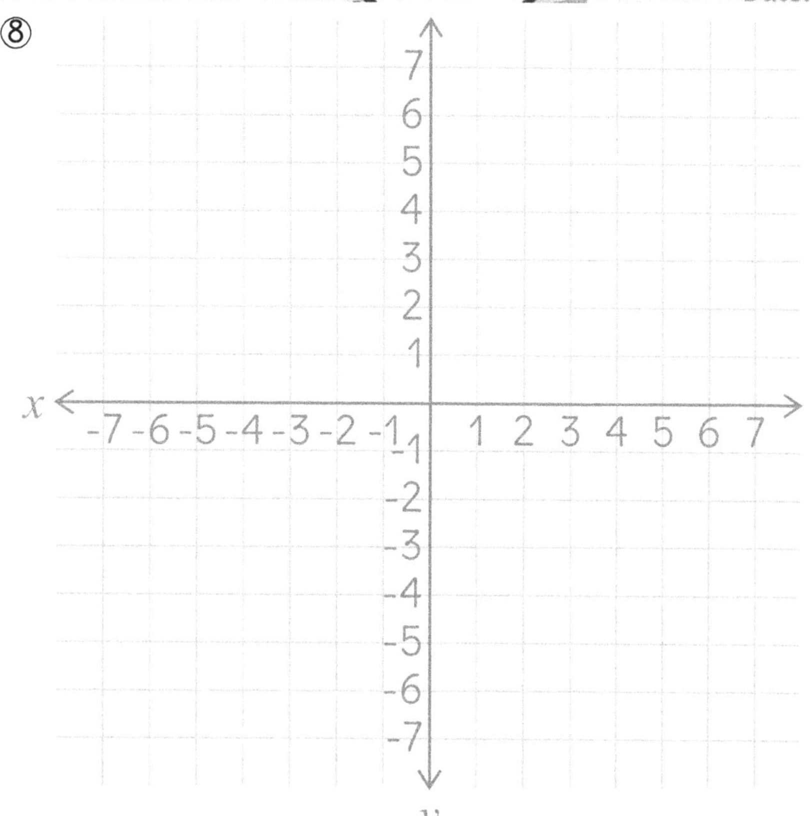

A = (7, 6)   B = (-3, -4)

C = (3, 2)   D = (-6, -7)

E = (-2, -3)   F = (-1, -2)

⑨

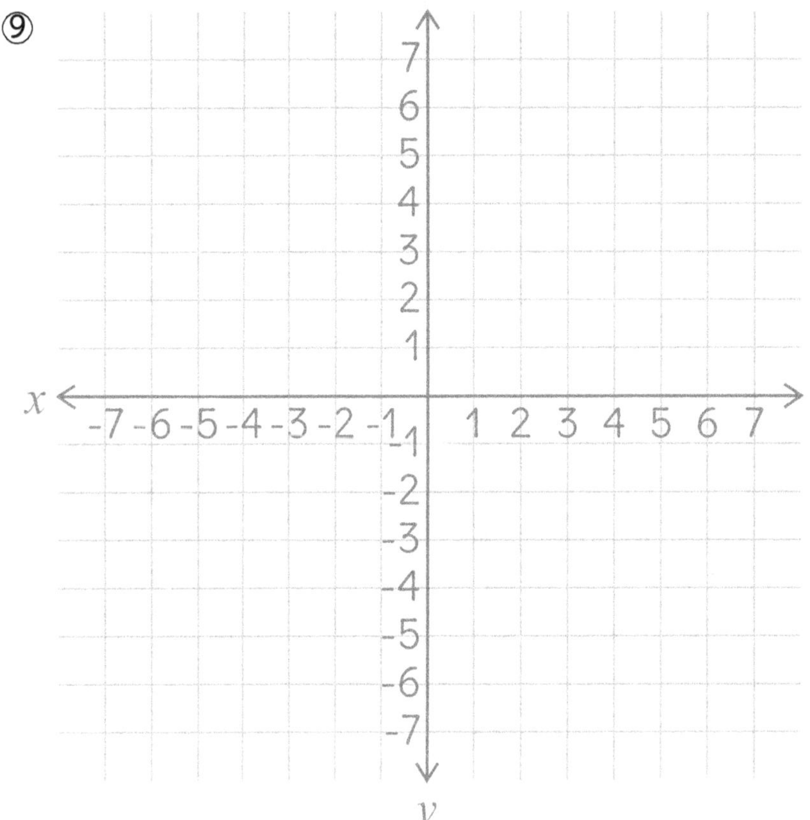

A = (-4, 4)   B = (7, 4)

C = (5, 4)   D = (-6, 4)

E = (-1, 4)   F = (0, 4)

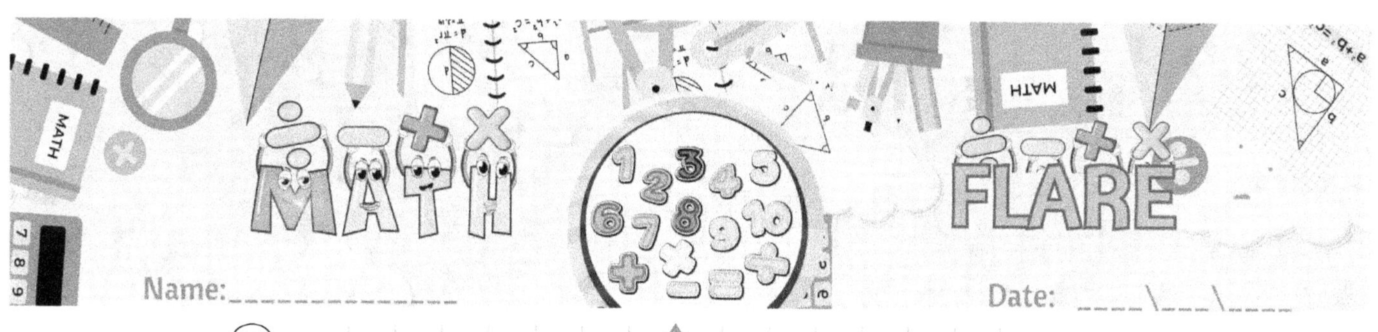

(10)

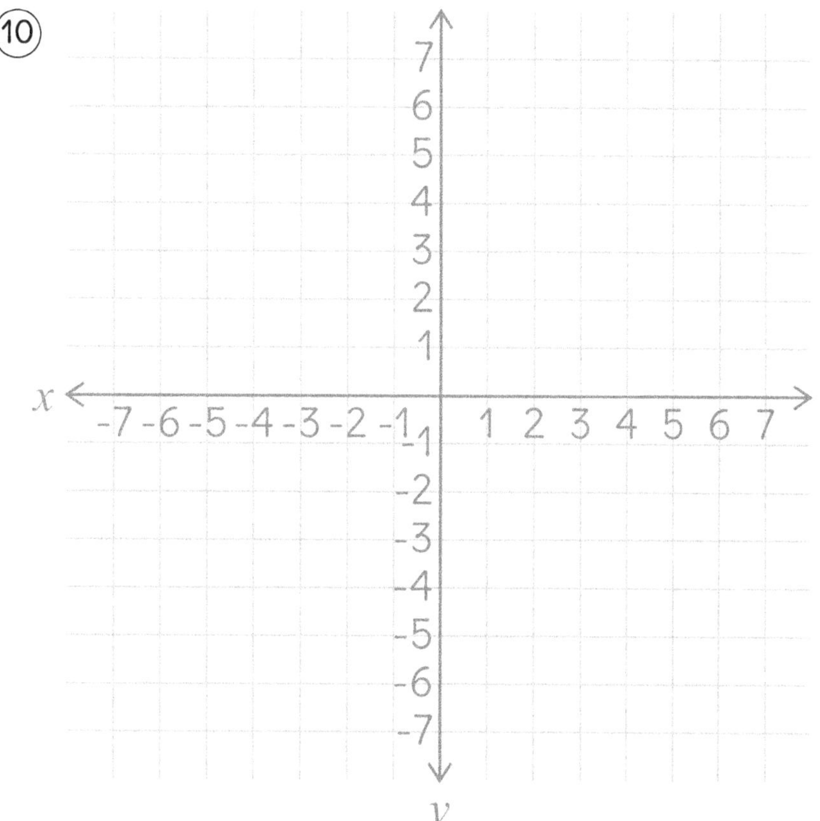

A = (-6, 5)   B = (2, 1)

C = (4, 0)   D = (6, -1)

E = (-4, 4)   F = (-2, 3)

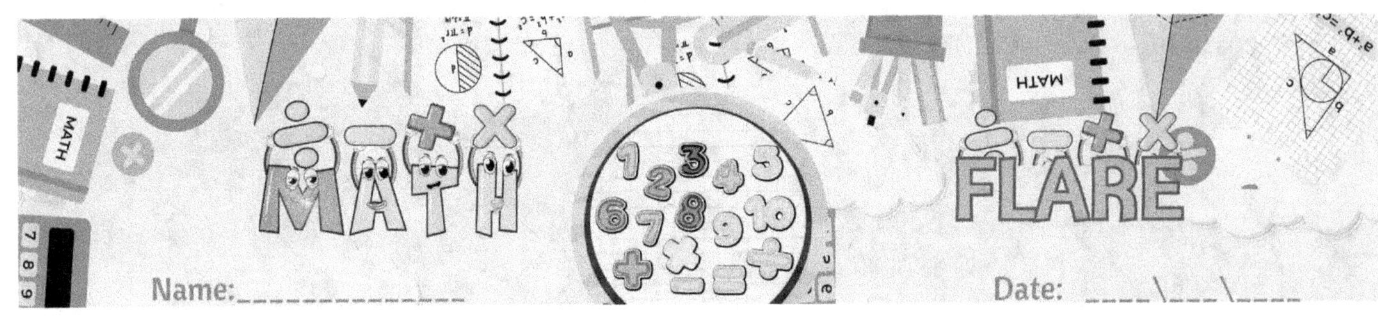

Graphing Linear Equations

① $y = \dfrac{11}{4}x + 4$

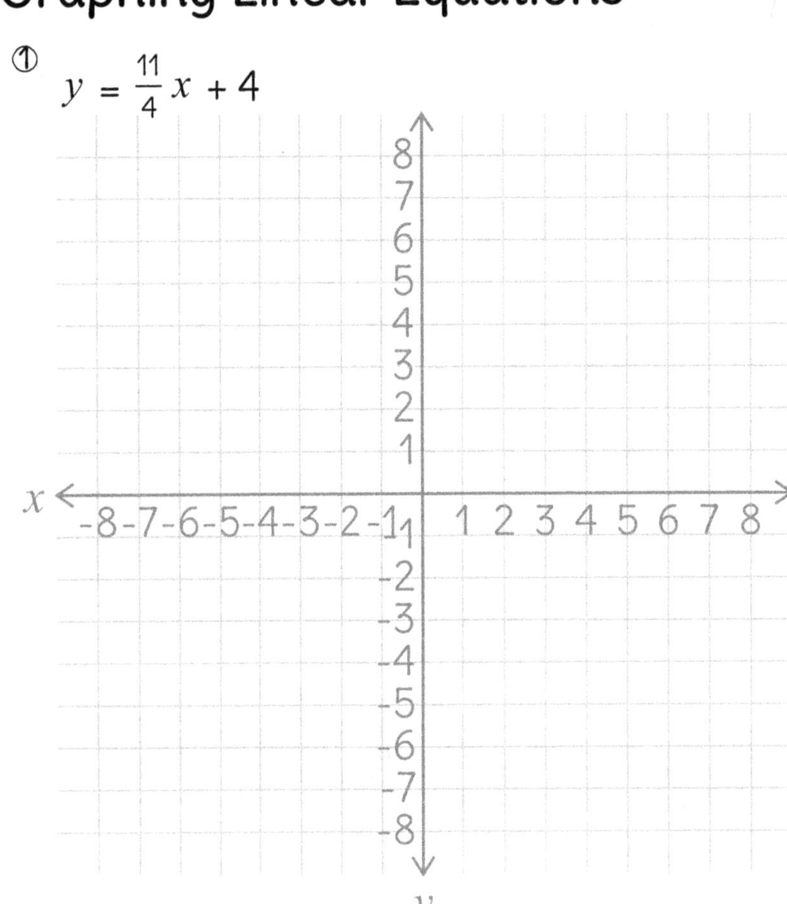

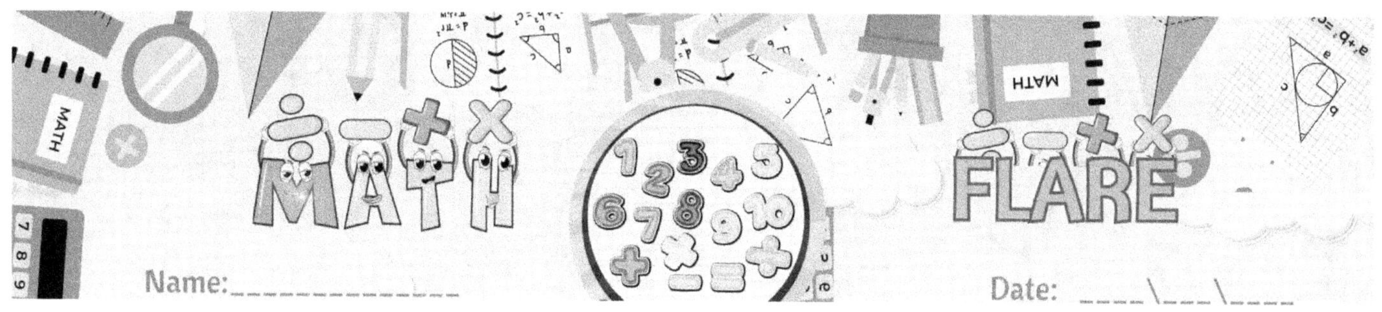

② $y = \dfrac{5}{4}x + 5$

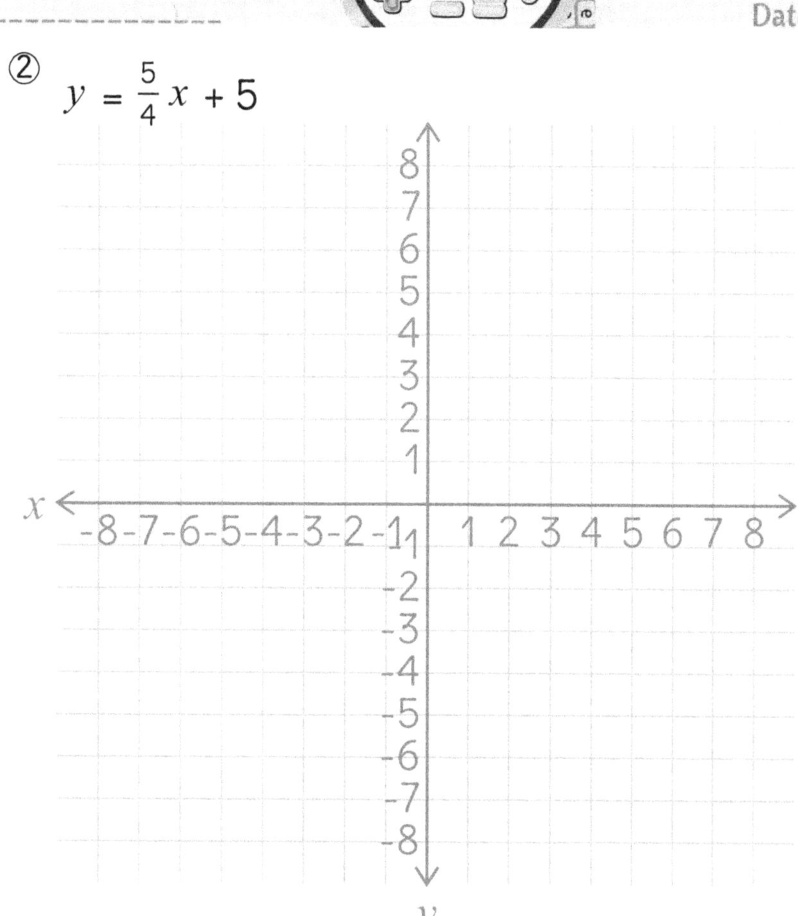

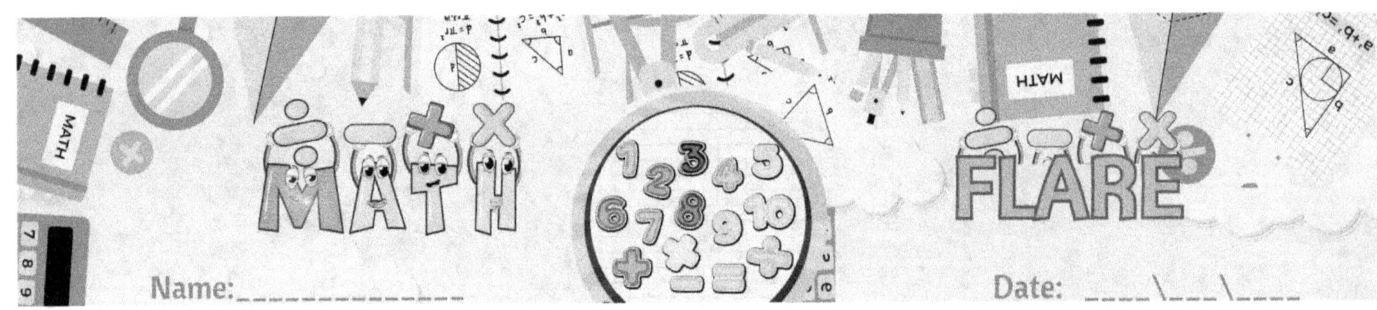

Name: _______________________ Date: _____ \ ____ \ _____

③ $x = 4$

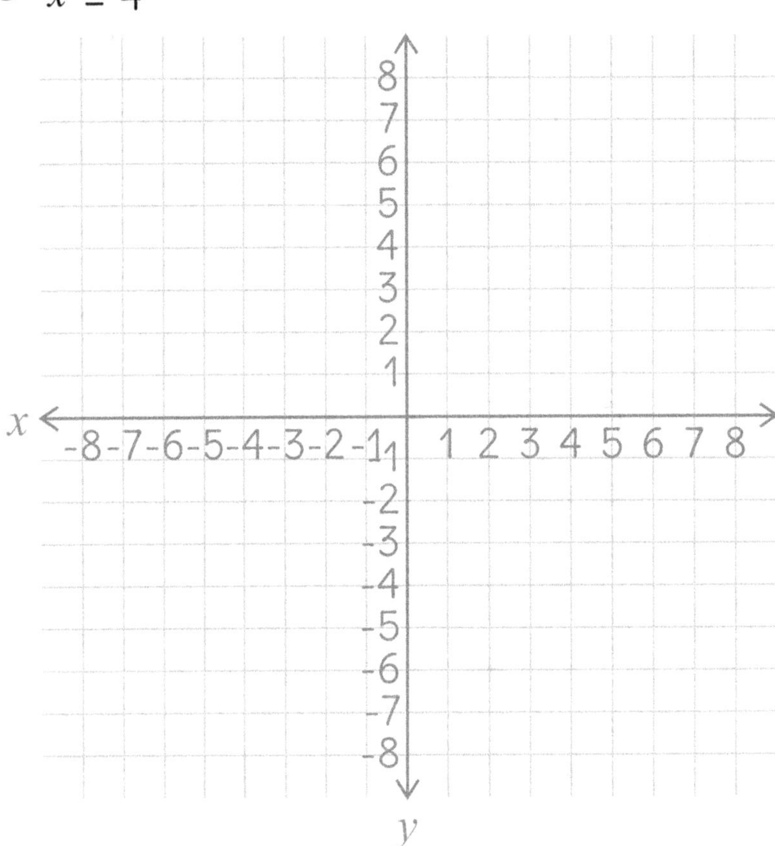

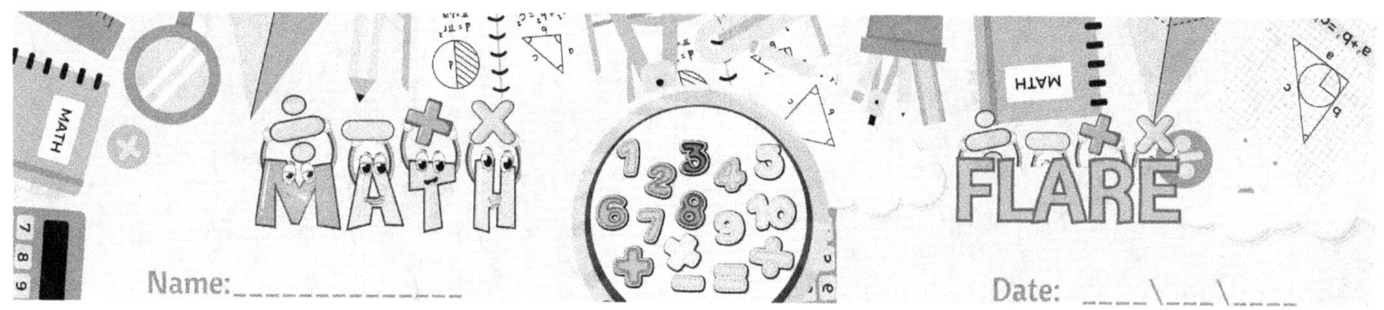

④ $x = -5$

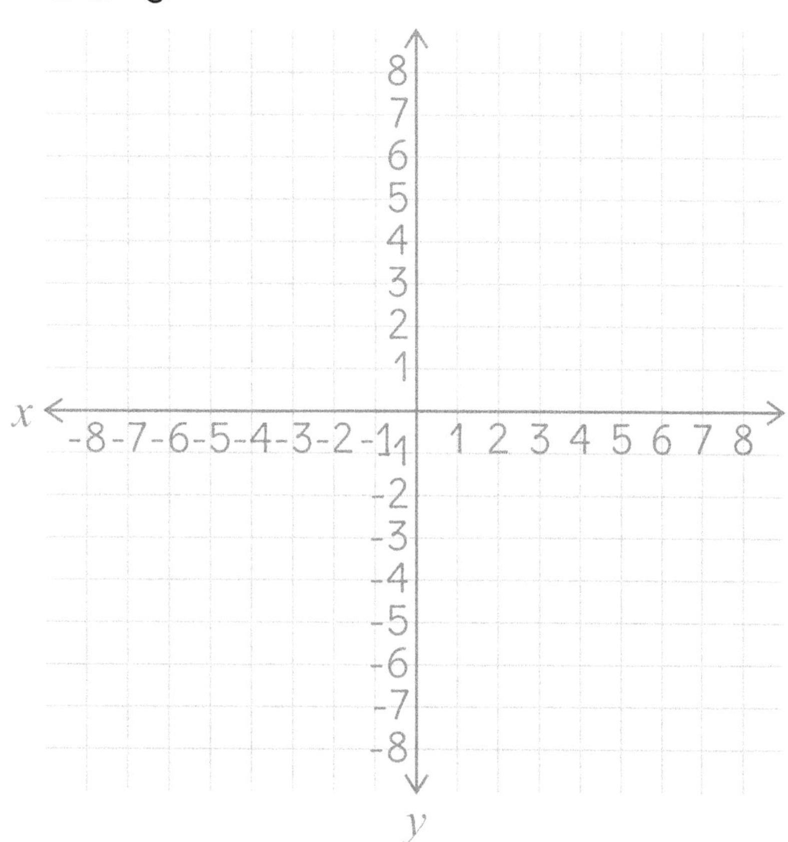

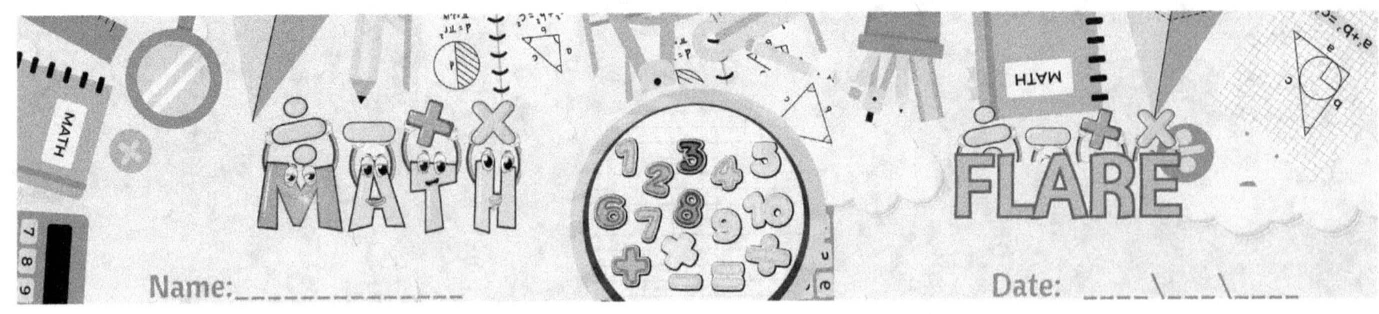

⑤ $y = \dfrac{-3}{4}x + 6$

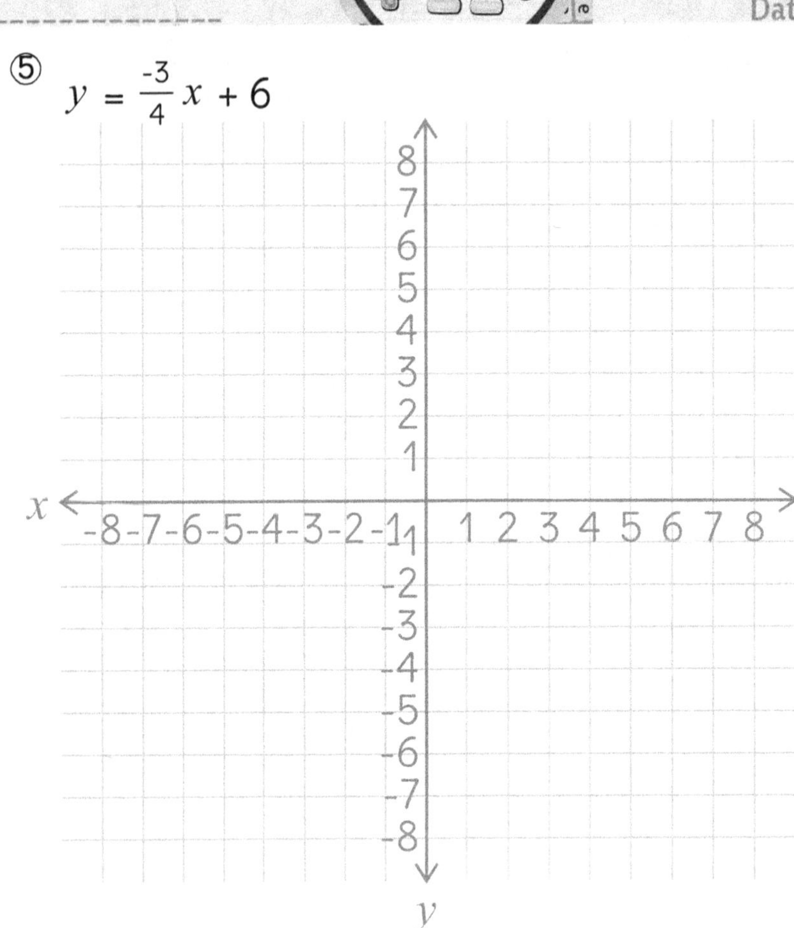

Name:________________   Date: ______________

⑥ $y = -3x + 4$

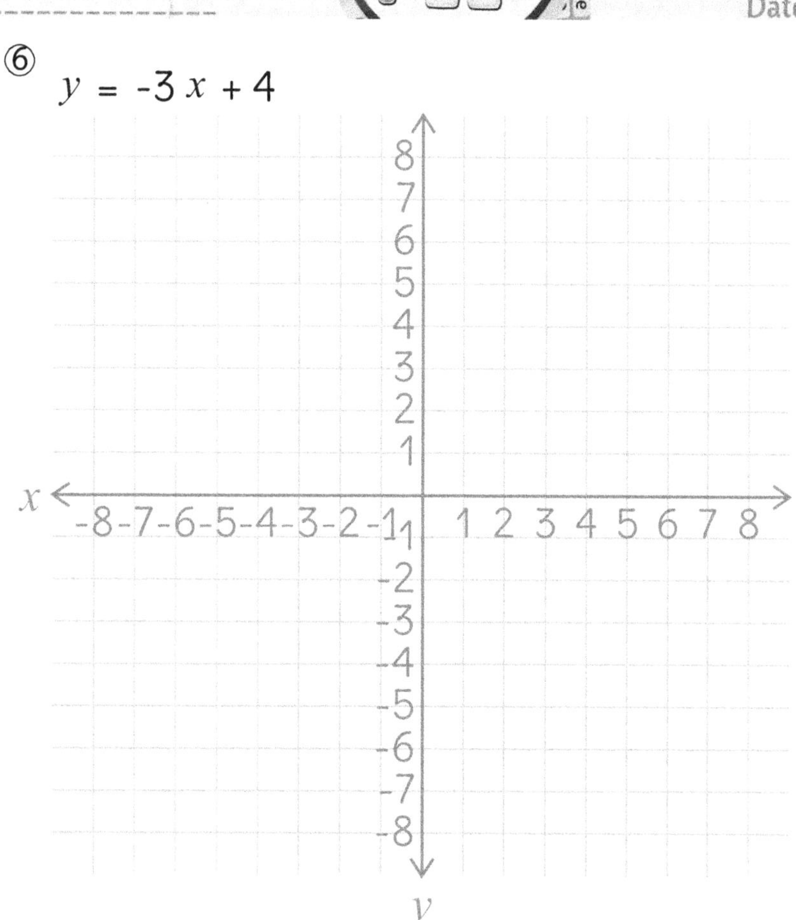

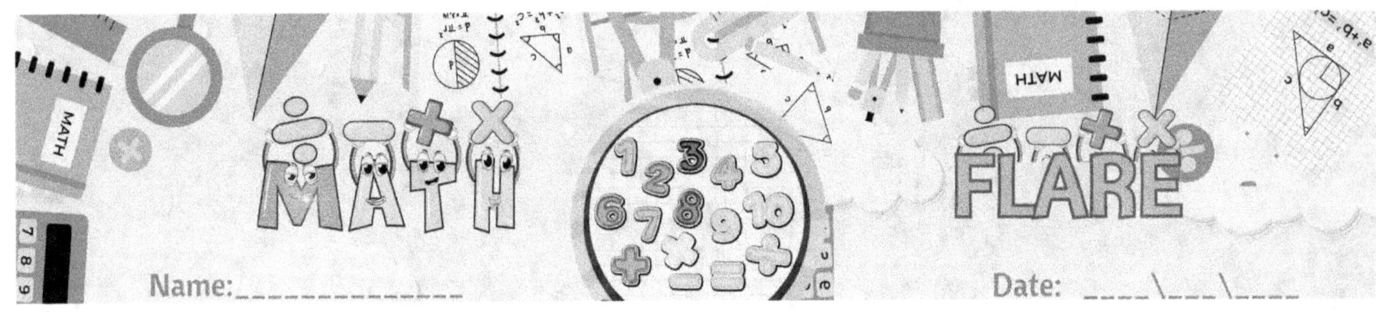

① $y = 3x + 7$

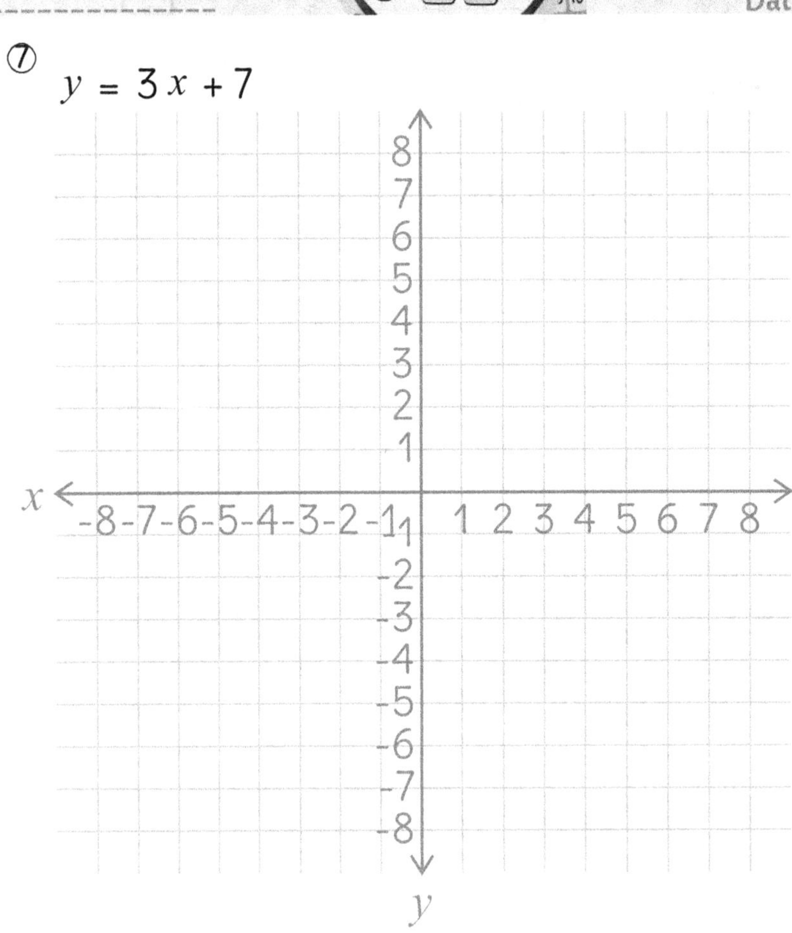

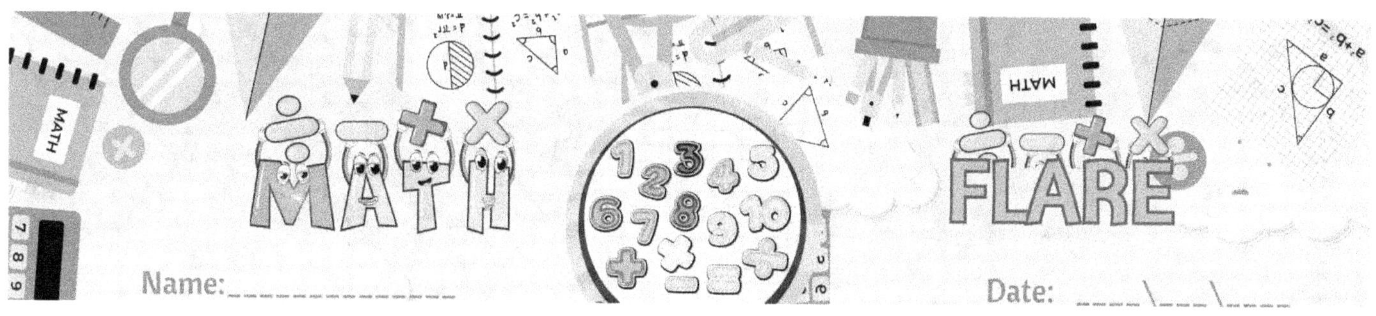

Name:____________________   Date: _______________

⑧ $y = -x + 4$

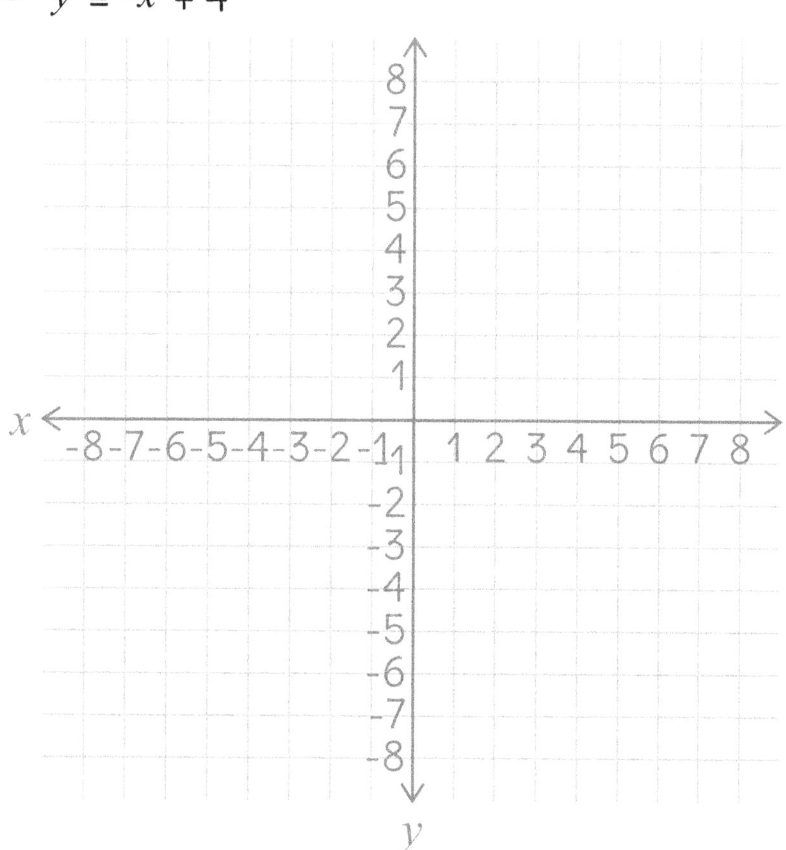

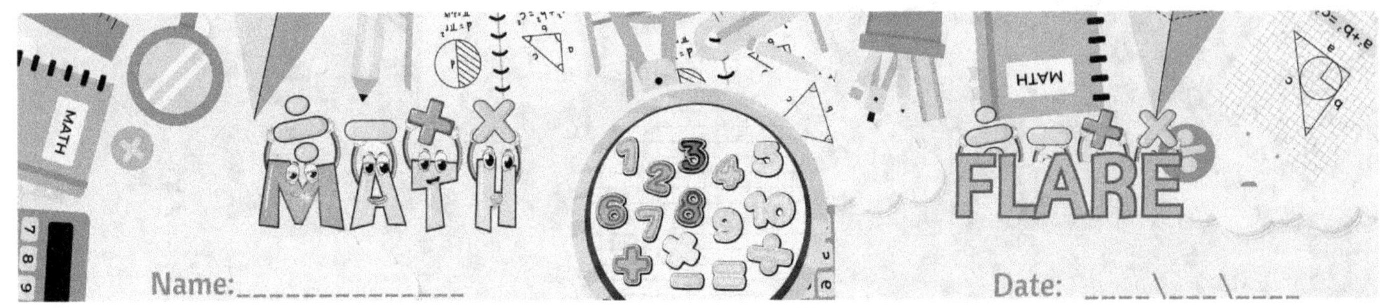

⑨ $y = -2x + 4$

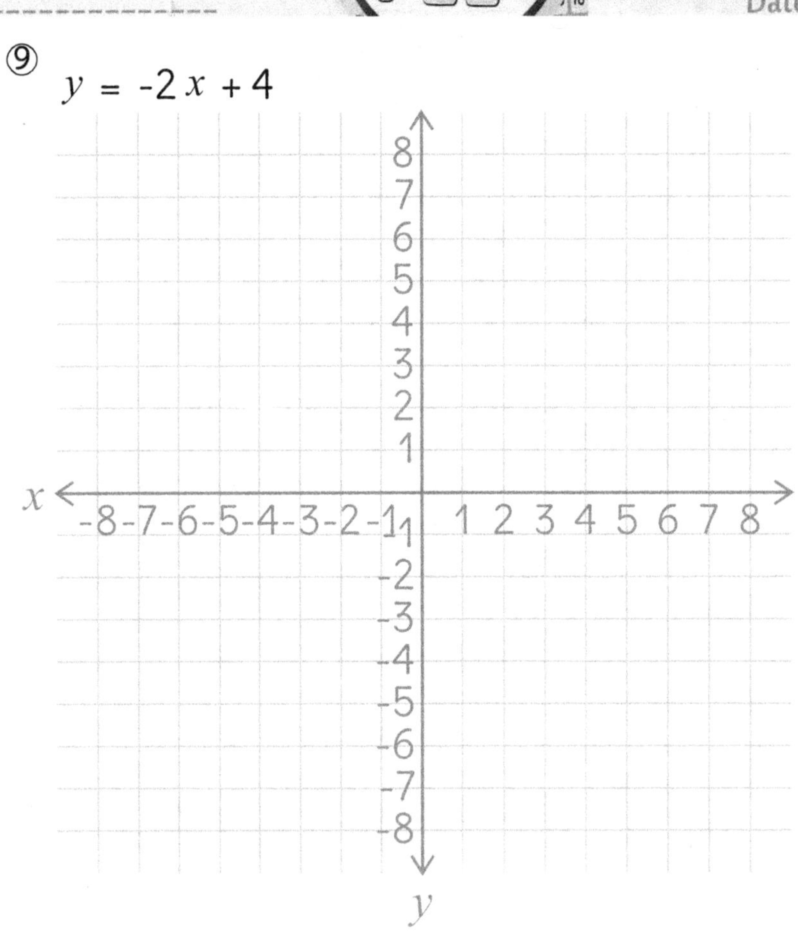

(10) $y = \dfrac{7}{4}x - 6$

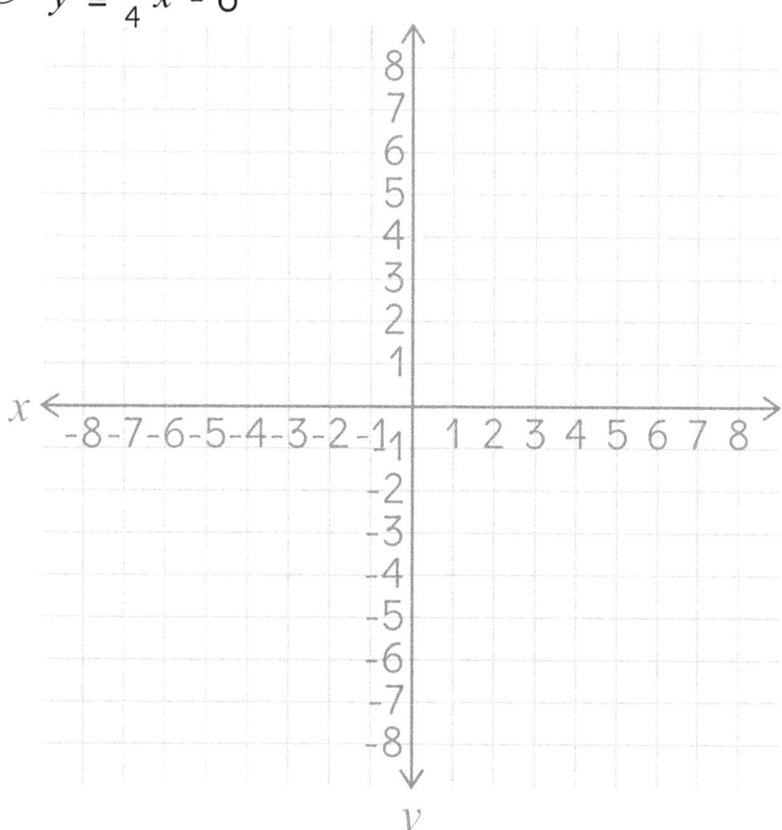

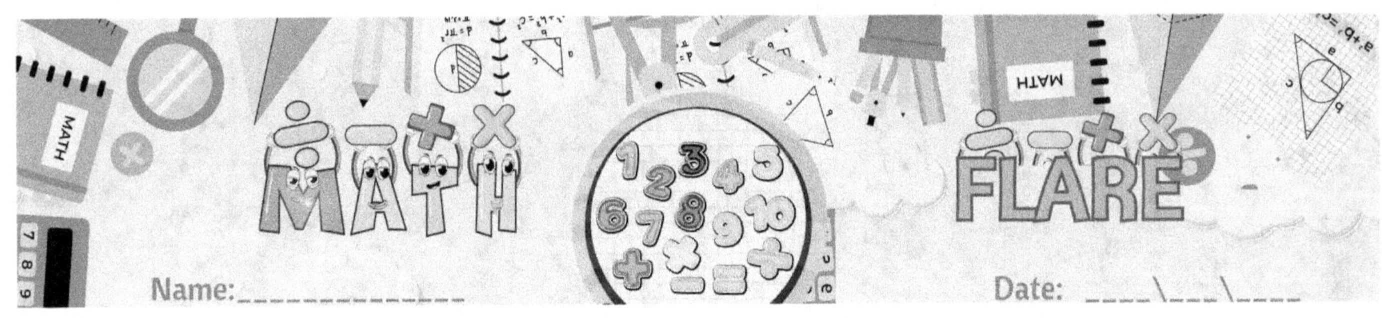

System of Equations

Solve either by Elimination or Substitution method

① 4x + 5y = 6
10x + 6y = 8

x = 0.154   y = 1.077

② 6x + 8y = 1
3x + 10y = 4

③ 6x + 2y = 4
6x + 7y = 7

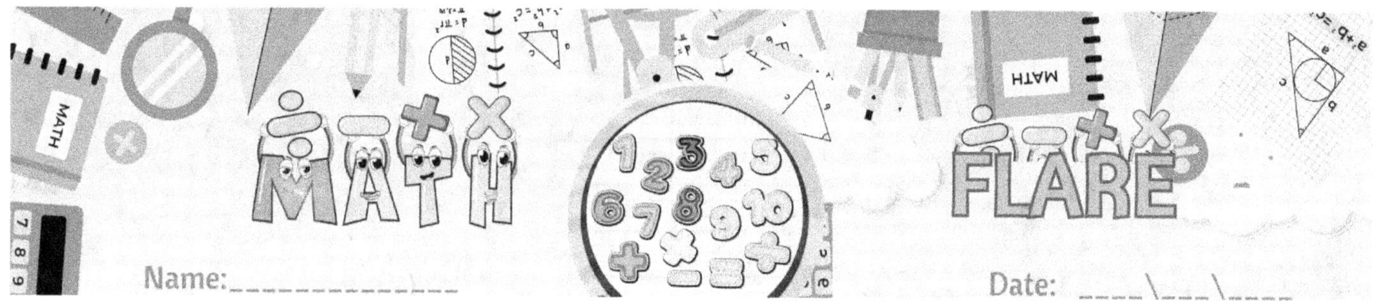

Name:_______________

Date: __________

④ 5x + 3y = 5
4x + 10y = 10

⑤ 7x + 7y = 3
x + 7y = 6

⑥ 10x + 5y = 10
10x + 9y = 2

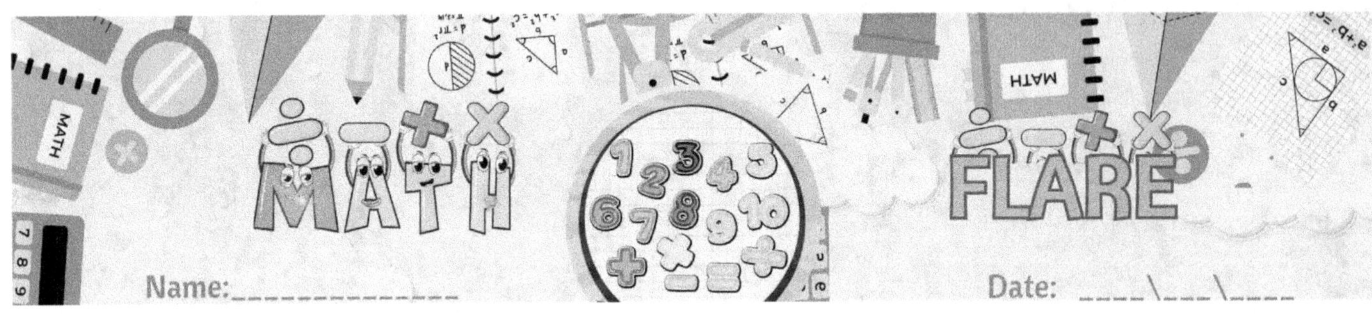

⑦ 4x + 10y = 8
6x + 6y = 6

⑧ 10x + 10y = 4
2x + 9y = 10

⑨ 3x + 7y = 10
2x + 2y = 7

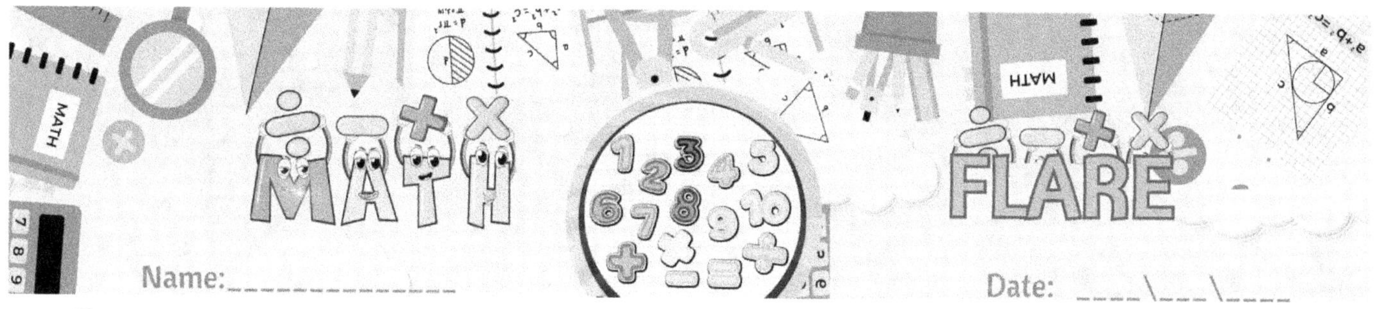

⑩ $9x + 7y = 9$
$4x + 8y = 7$

⑪ $10x + 8y = 1$
$6x + 10y = 7$

⑫ $10x + 5y = 3$
$2x + 2y = 10$

⑬ x + 8y = 7
2x + 8y = 7

⑭ 5x + 7y = 9
6x + 2y = 10

⑮ 9x + 2y = 4
7x + 1y = 3

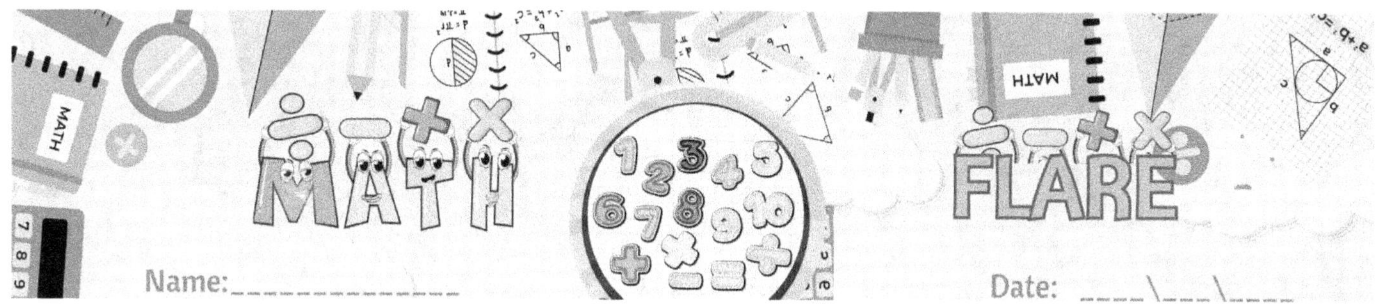

Name:_________________   Date: ____________

16 $6x + 7y = 2$
    $x + 3y = 5$

17 $8x + 9y = 6$
    $3x + 10y = 8$

18 $2x + 1y = 6$
    $x + 6y = 1$

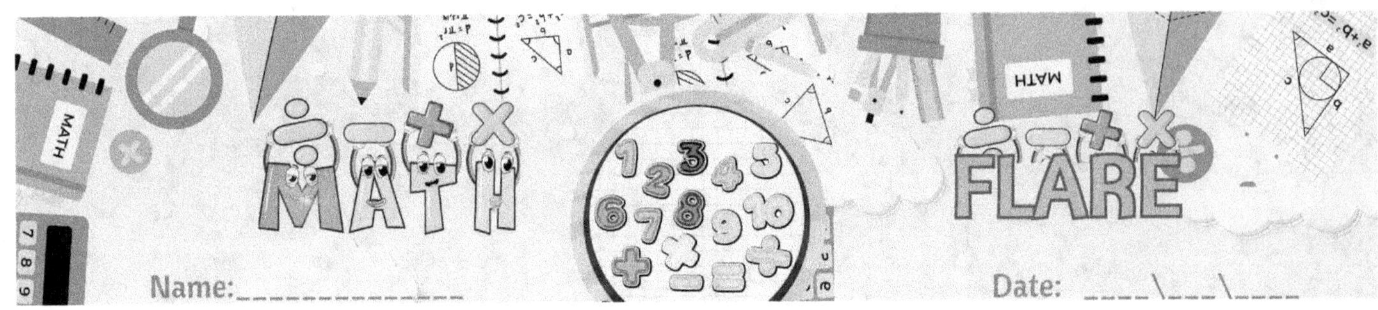

(19) $6x + 6y = 5$
$4x + 5y = 4$

(20) $7x + 2y = 3$
$7x + 7y = 10$

(21) $3x + 5y = 10$
$5x + 4y = 5$

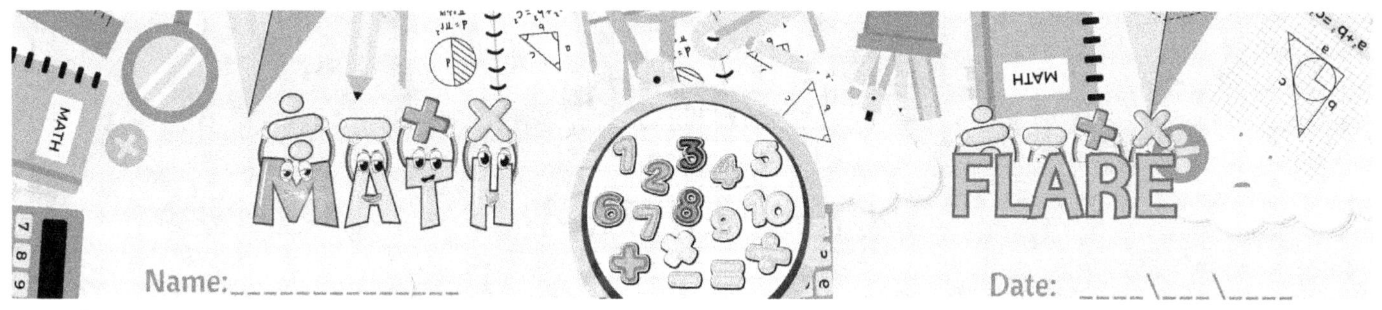

22) $3x + 5y = 1$
$7x + 6y = 1$

23) $6x + 6y = 3$
$2x + 7y = 6$

24) $6x + 10y = 6$
$5x + 6y = 3$

Chapter. 04

Cartesian Plane

Cartesian Coordinates

The Cartesian Coordinate System, also known as the x-y plane, provides a method for representing points on a graph using two perpendicular lines: the x-axis and the y-axis. At their intersection, denoted by the letter "O", lies the origin.

To plot a point on this system, we use coordinates, consisting of two numbers. The first number represents the horizontal movement from the origin (x-coordinate), while the second number represents the vertical movement (y-coordinate). These coordinates are written as an ordered pair (x, y).

For instance, let's plot these coordinates:

$$A = (1, 3) \quad B = (5, 0) \quad C = (8, 6)$$

$$D = (9, 5) \quad E = (1, 9) \quad F = (3, 1)$$

$$G = (0, 8) \quad H = (4, 6) \quad I = (4, 9)$$

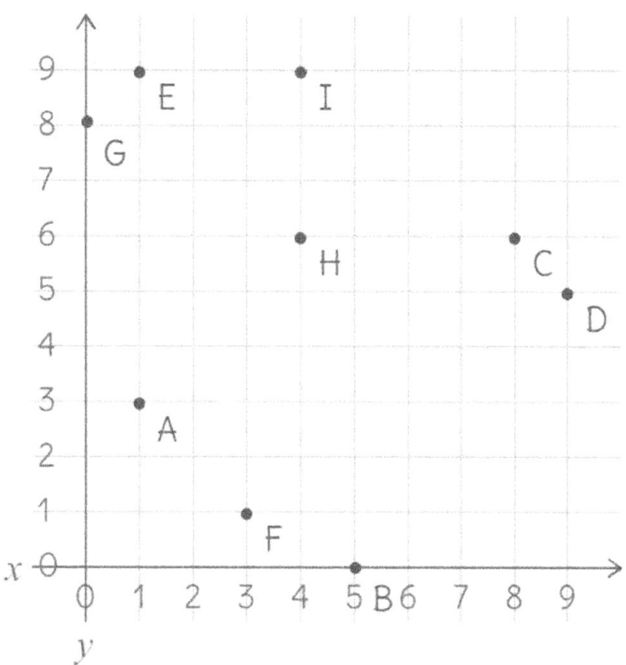

Cartesian Coordinates (Four Quadrants)

In a Cartesian coordinate system with four quadrants, there are two perpendicular number lines intersecting at the origin (0,0), dividing the plane into four quadrants.

To plot a point in this Cartesian coordinate system, we use an ordered pair (x, y), where x represents the distance from the y-axis, and y represents the distance from the x-axis.

For instance, let's plot these coordinates:

$$A = (-4, 1) \quad B = (2, 1) \quad C = (4, 2)$$

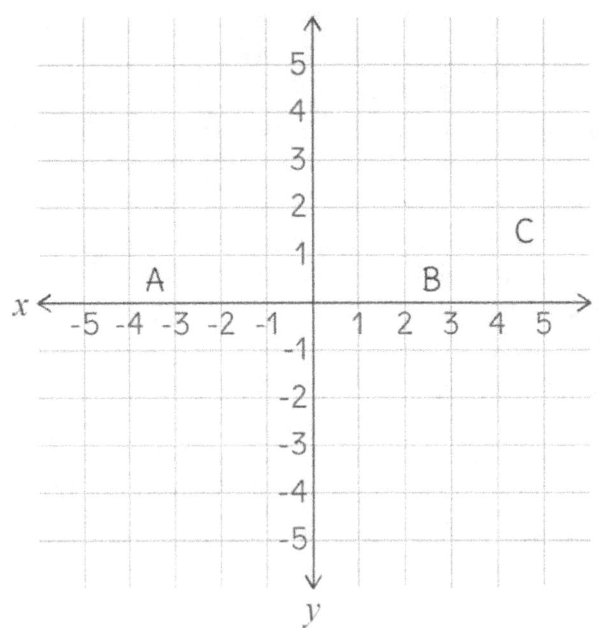

5
4
3
2
1
C
A
B
x
-5 -4 -3 -2 -1
1 2 3 4 5
-1
-2
-3
-4
-5
y

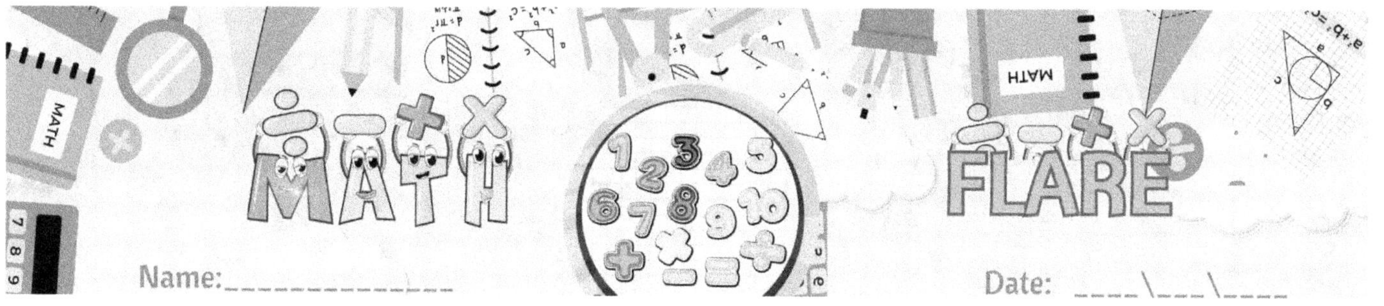

Cartesian Coordinates

Plot the points.

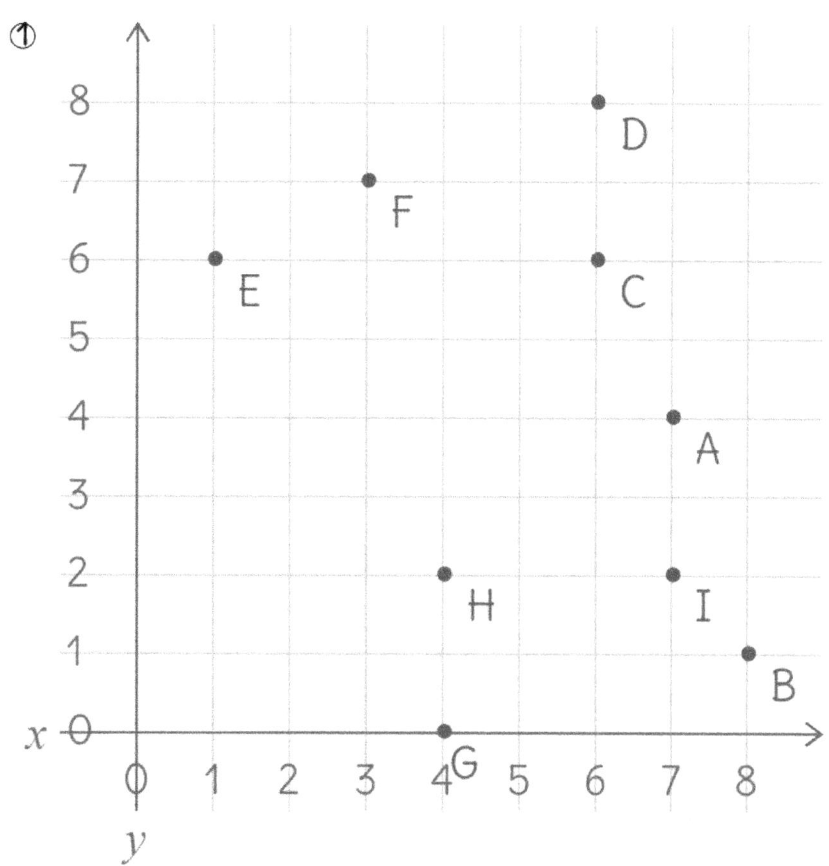

A = (7, 4)   B = (8, 1)   C = (6, 6)

D = (6, 8)   E = (1, 6)   F = (3, 7)

G = (4, 0)   H = (4, 2)   I = (7, 2)

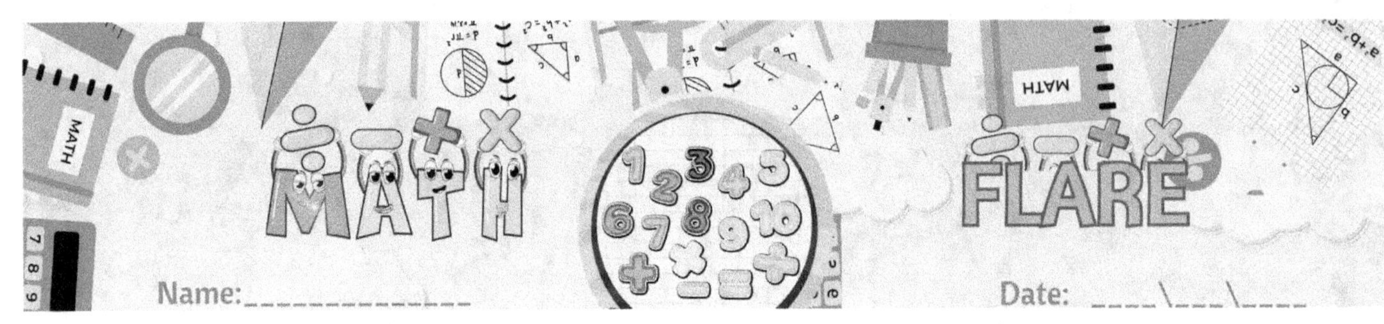

② 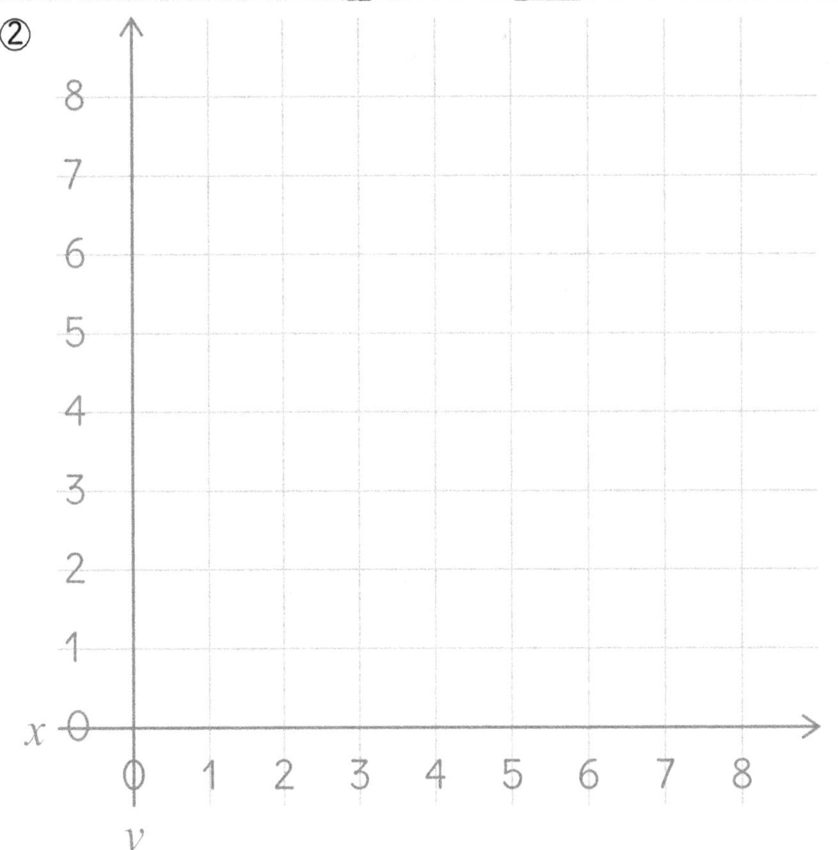

A = (8, 2)   B = (3, 7)   C = (4, 6)

D = (1, 6)   E = (8, 7)   F = (6, 1)

G = (5, 5)   H = (3, 2)   I = (7, 4)

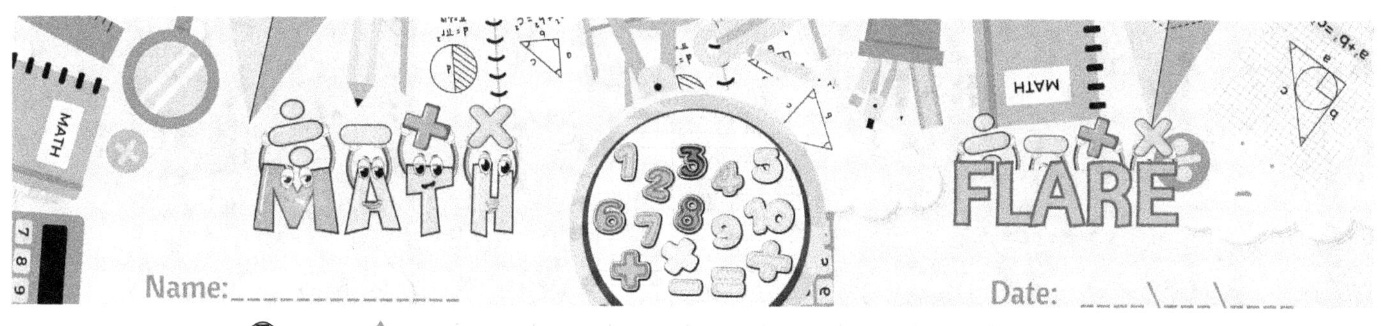

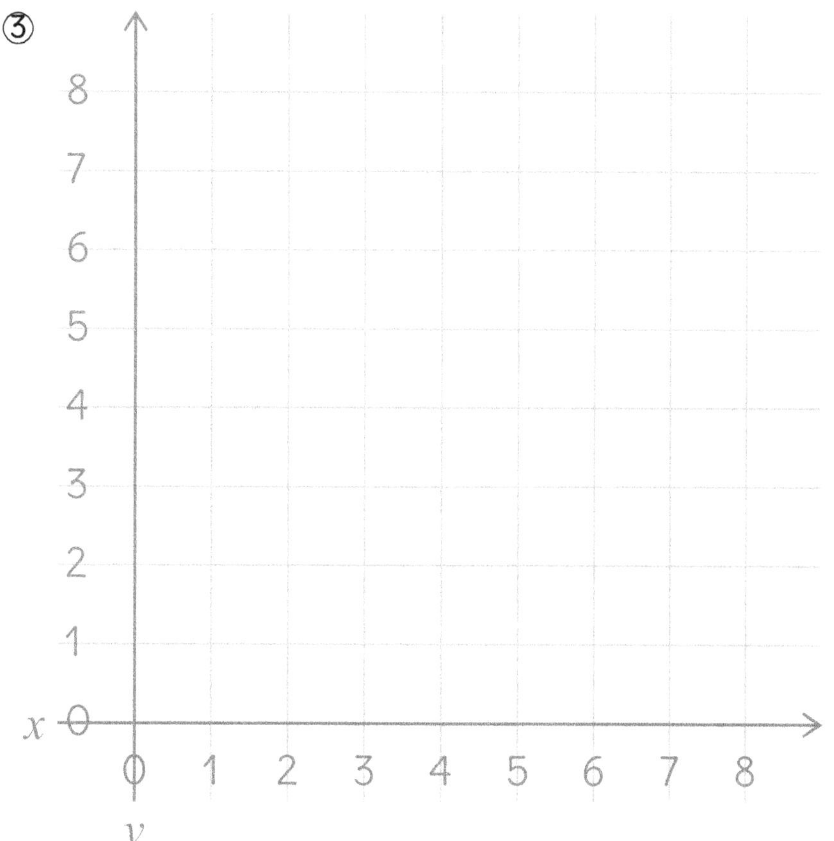

③

A = (2, 6)   B = (2, 3)   C = (6, 7)

D = (2, 8)   E = (3, 0)   F = (4, 5)

G = (1, 6)   H = (7, 8)   I = (4, 8)

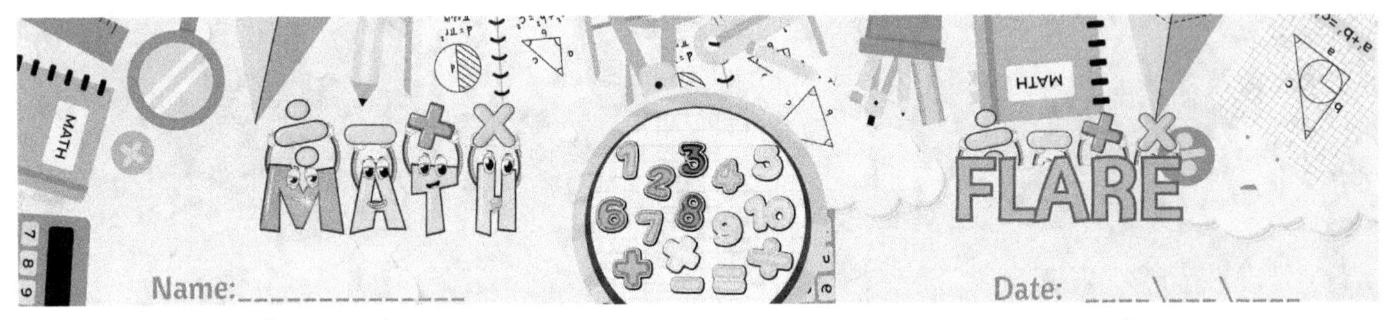

④

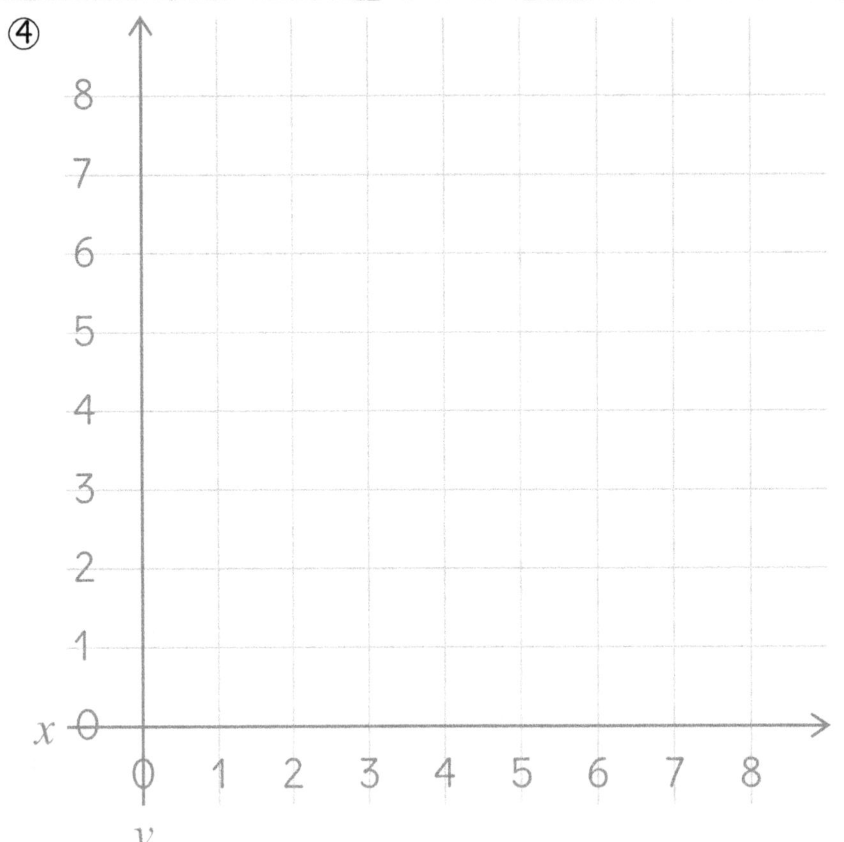

A = (4, 5)   B = (4, 0)   C = (3, 0)

D = (7, 1)   E = (5, 7)   F = (7, 0)

G = (5, 2)   H = (5, 6)   I = (5, 1)

⑤

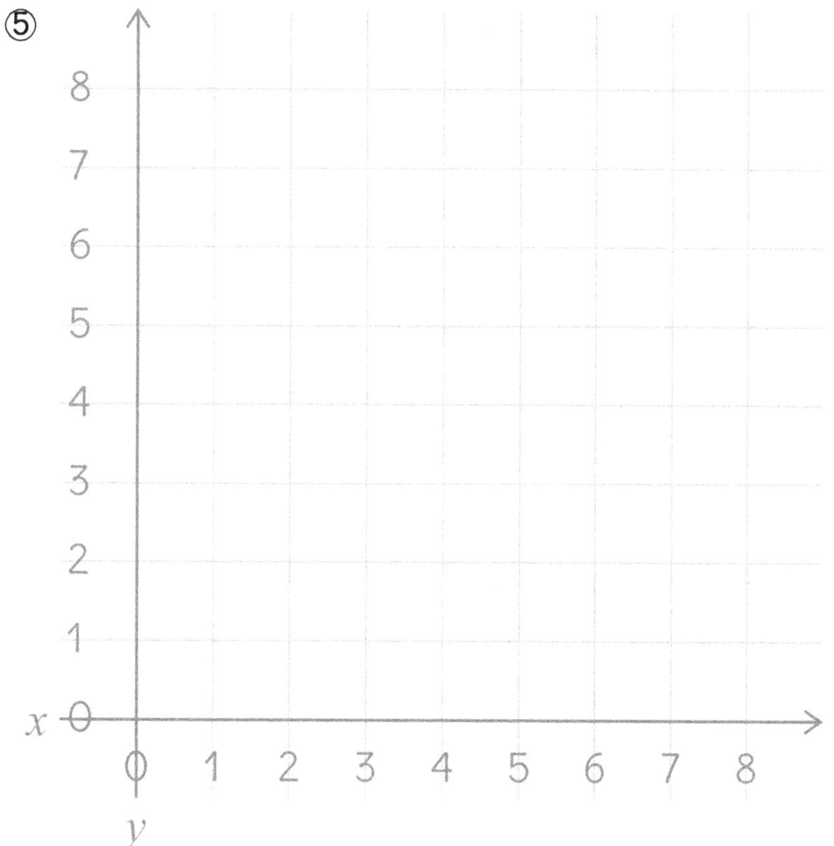

A = (0, 3)   B = (1, 0)   C = (8, 1)

D = (5, 6)   E = (4, 4)   F = (7, 2)

G = (7, 3)   H = (6, 3)   I = (4, 7)

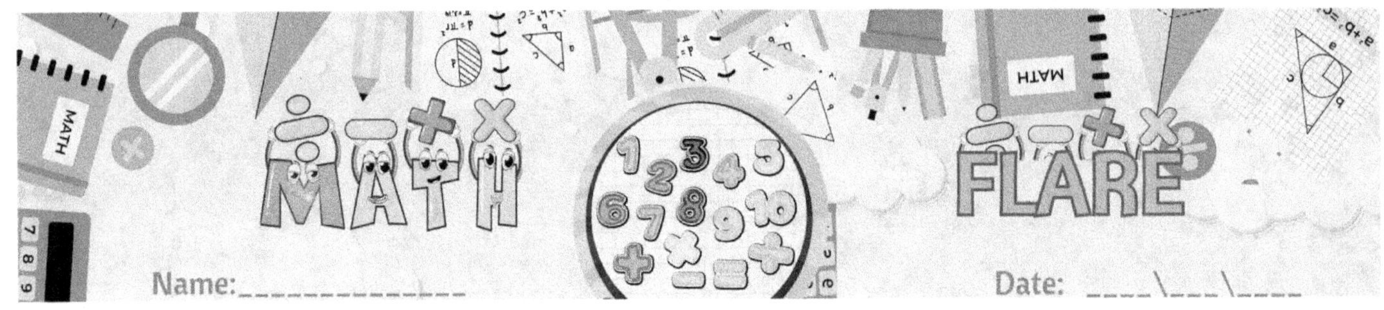

Cartesian Coordinates

Plot the points.

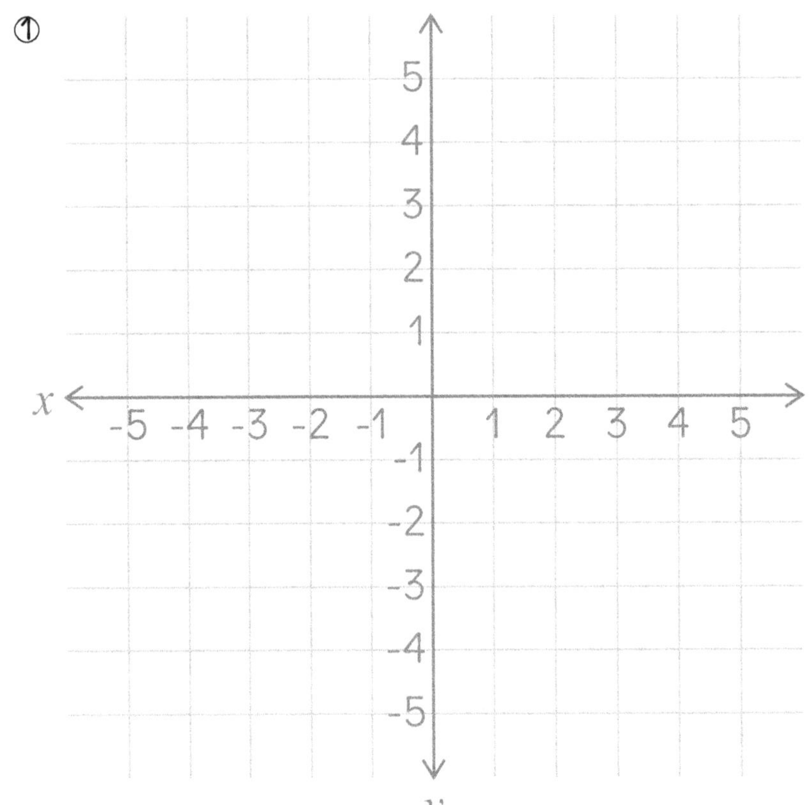

A = (2, -3)   B = (-2, -3)   C = (1, 2)

D = (-3, -1)   E = (-5, -1)   F = (0, -3)

G = (-4, 0)   H = (-4, 2)   I = (4, -4)

②

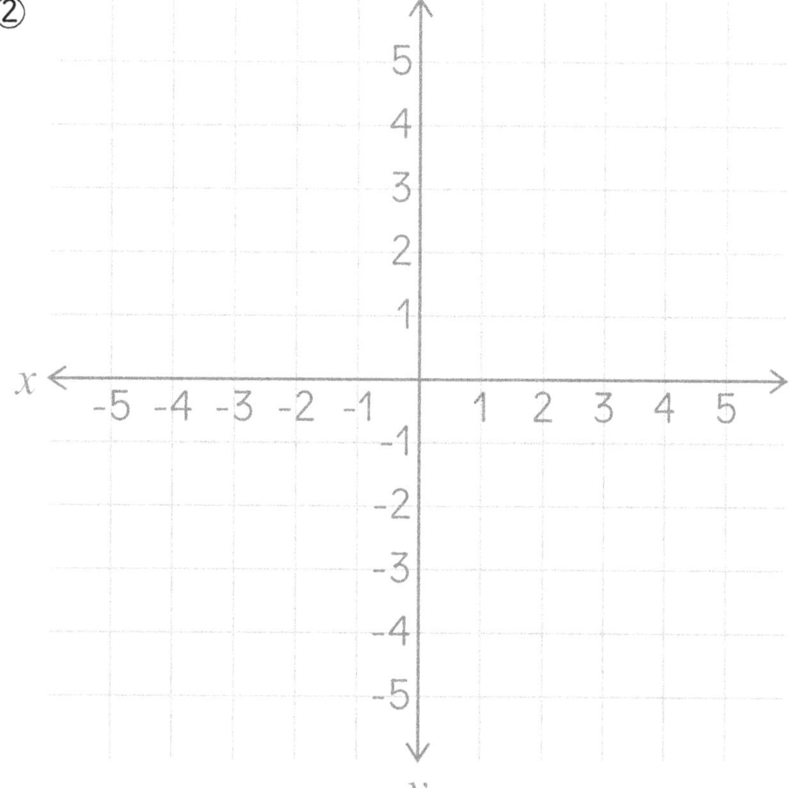

A = (2, 0)   B = (3, -1)   C = (-1, 2)

D = (1, -2)   E = (-2, -2)   F = (5, -1)

G = (-3, -3)   H = (2, 2)   I = (-5, -1)

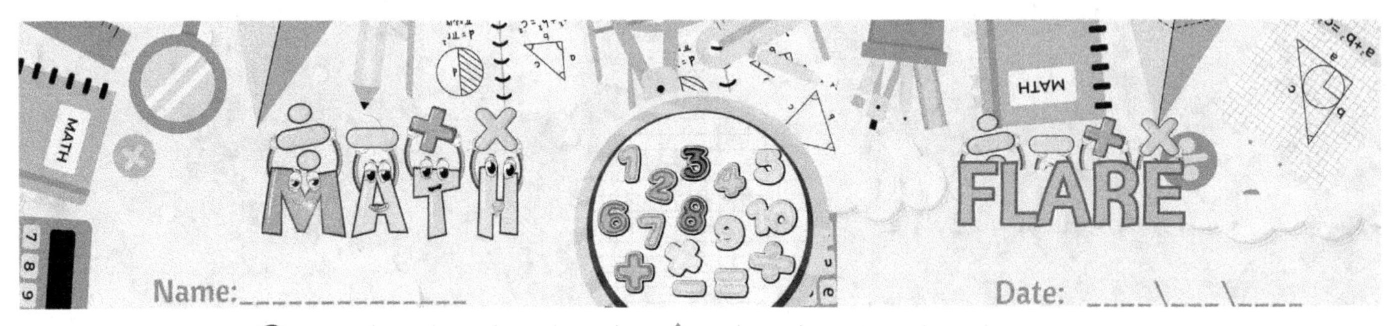

③

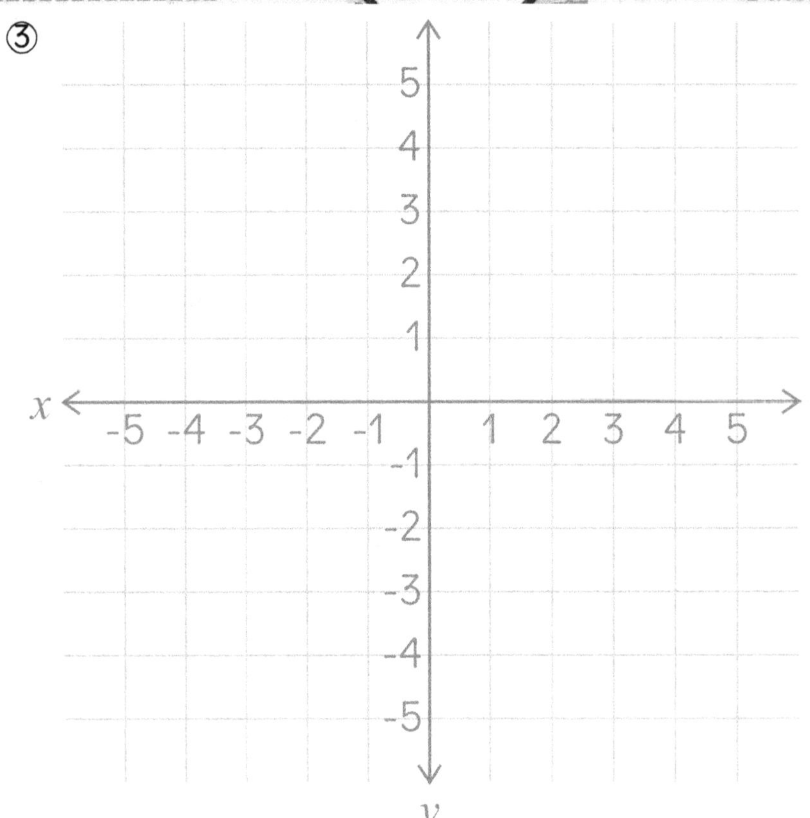

A = (4, 4)   B = (3, 0)   C = (3, -1)

D = (-5, -4)   E = (-3, -3)   F = (-1, -2)

G = (-3, -4)   H = (0, 2)   I = (2, -5)

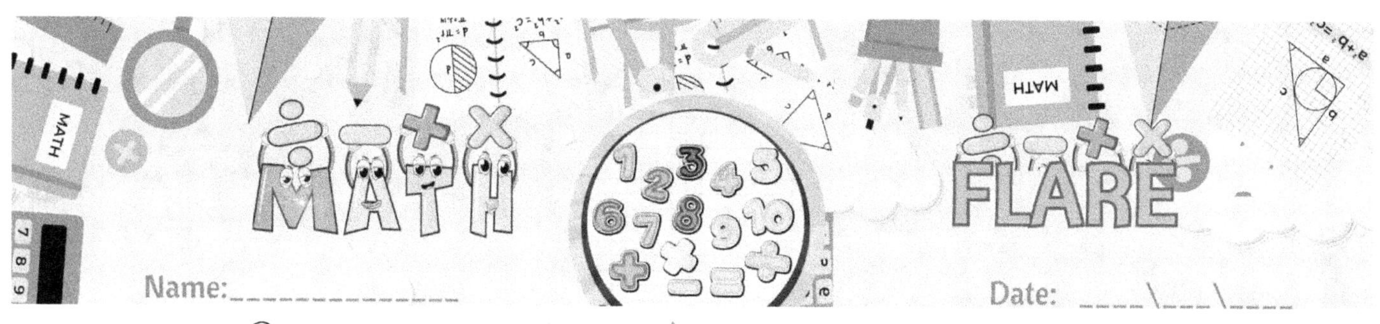

④

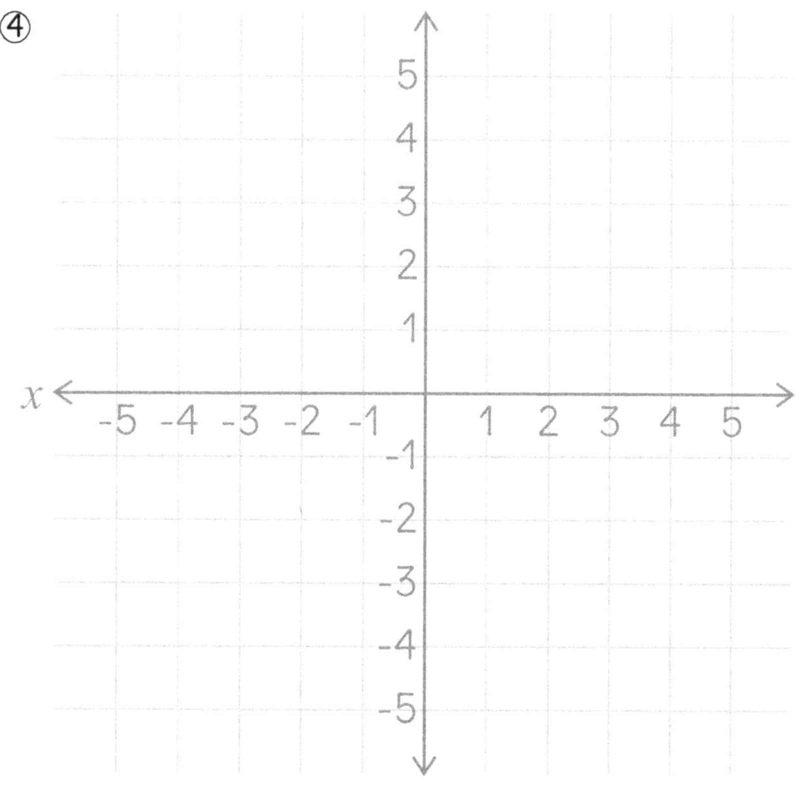

A = (-4, -2)   B = (3, 1)   C = (1, -2)

D = (-2, 5)   E = (0, 2)   F = (-3, -3)

G = (0, -1)   H = (4, -5)   I = (-2, -3)

⑤

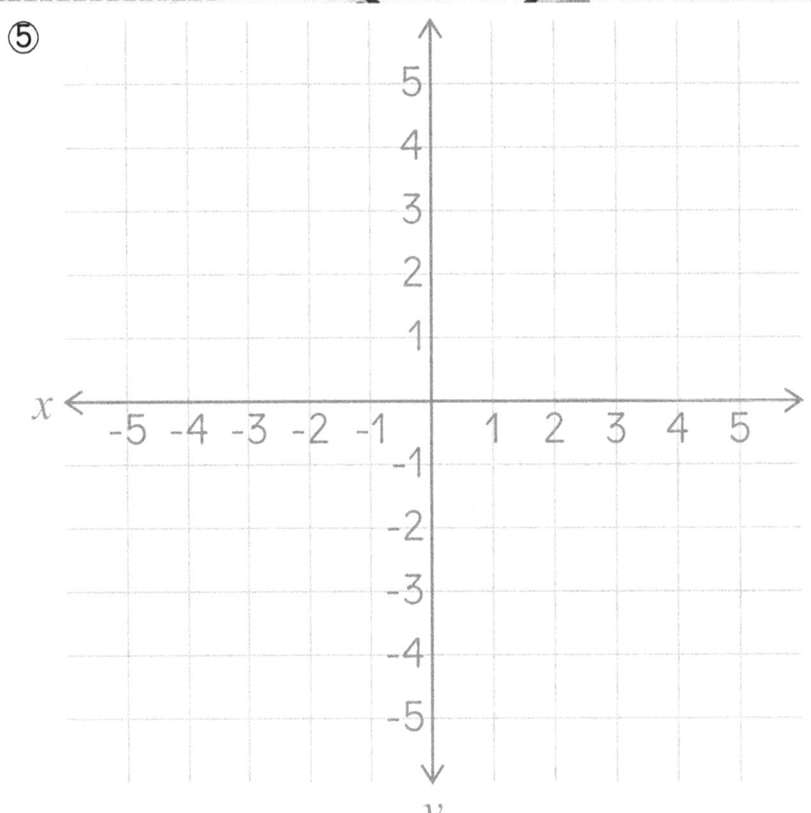

A = (3, -2)   B = (-1, -2)   C = (0, -1)

D = (4, 5)   E = (-5, 3)   F = (5, 1)

G = (1, 2)   H = (1, -2)   I = (-3, 0)

Chapter. 05

Geometry

Area and Perimeter

The area of a shape represents the amount of space it occupies. The perimeter of a shape is the total distance around its outer edge.

Area of Rectangle

For a square, since all four sides are equal, we only need to know the length of one side to find its area. We can calculate the area of a square by multiplying the length of one side by itself (squared). So, if the length of one side of the square is 's', then the area (A) is given by:

$$A = s \times s$$

4 in

4 in

$$A = 4 \times 4$$

$$A = 16$$

Perimeter of Rectangle

For a square, since all four sides are equal, we can find the perimeter by adding up the lengths of all four sides. If 's' represents the length of one side, then the perimeter (P) is given by:

$$P = 4 \times s$$

$$P = 4 \times 4$$

$$P = 16$$

Area of Triangle:

The area of a triangle represents the amount of space enclosed within its three sides. The formula for calculating the area of a triangle depends on the type of triangle. For a general triangle, we use the formula:

$$A = \frac{1}{2} \times base \times height$$

Where:

- A represents the area of the triangle.

- The base is the length of any one side of the triangle.

- The height is the perpendicular distance from the base to the opposite vertex.

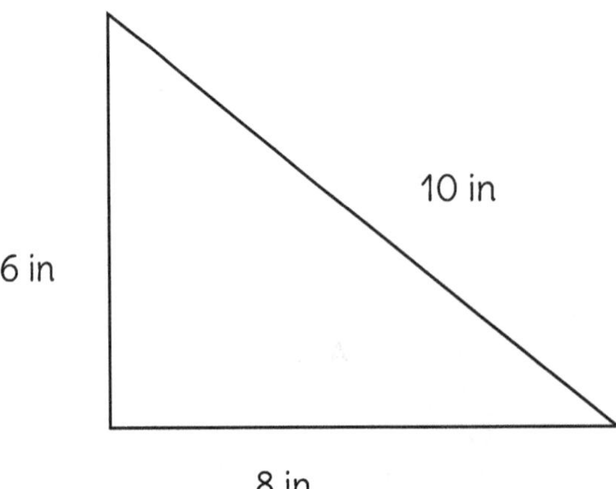

$$A = \frac{1}{2} \times base \times height$$

$$A = \frac{1}{2} \times 6 \times 8$$

$$A = \frac{1}{2} \times 48$$

$$A = 24$$

Perimeter of Triangle:

The perimeter of a triangle is the total length of its three sides. To find the perimeter, we simply add the lengths of all three sides together:

$$P = side1 + side2 + side3$$

$$P = 6 + 8 + 10$$

$$P = 24$$

Equilateral Triangle

An equilateral triangle is a triangle in which all three sides are equal in length. To find the area and perimeter of an equilateral triangle, we can use the following formulas:

- Area (A): $\frac{\sqrt{3}}{4} \times a^2$ where a is the length of one side of the equilateral triangle.

- Perimeter (P): $P = 3a$ where a is the length of one side of the equilateral triangle.

Let's solve a problem:

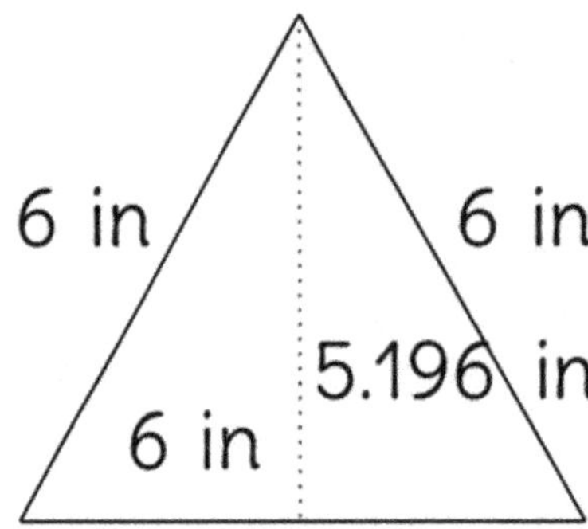

Area of Equilateral Triangle:

$$\text{Area (A): } \frac{\sqrt{3}}{4} \times (6)^2$$

$$\text{Area (A): } \frac{\sqrt{3}}{4} \times 36$$

$$\text{Area (A): } \frac{36\sqrt{3}}{4}$$

$$\text{Area (A): } \frac{36(1.73)}{4}$$

$$\text{Area (A): } \frac{62.35}{4}$$

$$\text{Area (A): } 15.59 \text{ in}^2$$

Perimeter of Equilateral Triangle:

$$P = 3a$$

$$P = 3(6) = 18$$

MathFlare - Math Workbook 8th and 9th Grade

Isosceles Triangle

An isosceles triangle is a triangle with at least two sides of equal length. The angles opposite the equal sides are also equal.

Area of Isosceles Triangle

$$A = \frac{1}{2} \times base \times height$$

$$A = \frac{1}{2} \times 8 \times 8$$

$$A = \frac{1}{2} \times 64$$

$$A = 32$$

Perimeter of Isosceles Triangle

The perimeter of a triangle is the total length of its three sides. To find the perimeter, we simply add the lengths of all three sides together:

$$P = side1 + side2 + side3$$

$$P = 9 + 9 + 8$$

$$P = 26$$

Scalene Triangle

A scalene triangle is a triangle with no equal sides and no equal angles. The formula for finding various properties of a scalene triangle is as follows:

Area (A): The area of a scalene triangle can be calculated using Heron's formula, which is given by:

$$A = \sqrt{s(s-a)(s-b)(s-c)}$$

where s is the semi-perimeter of the triangle,

and a, b, and c are the lengths of its three sides.

Perimeter (P): The perimeter of a scalene triangle is the sum of the lengths of its three sides.

$$P = side1 + side2 + side3$$

Let's find the Area and Perimeter of a Scalene Triangle:

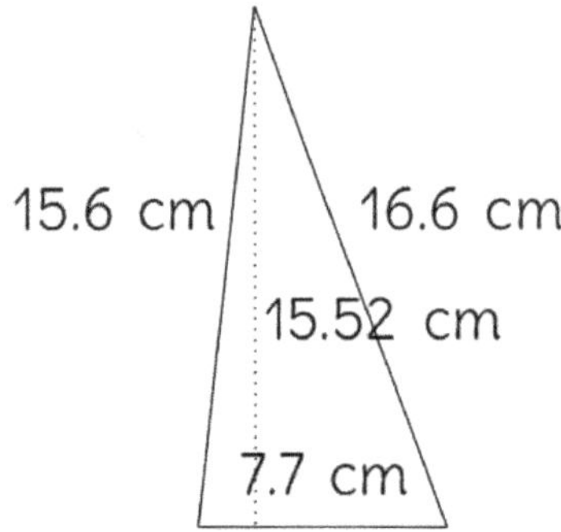

Area (A): First, we calculate the semi-perimeter (s):

$$S = \frac{a+b+c}{2} = \frac{15.6 + 16.6 + 7.7}{2} = \frac{39.8}{2} = 19.9 \text{ cm}$$

Heron's formula to find the area:

$$A = \sqrt{s(s-a)(s-b)(s-c)}$$

$$A = \sqrt{19.9\,(19.9-15.6)\,(19.9-16.6)\,(19.9-7.7)}$$

$$A = \sqrt{19.9 \times 4.3 \times 3.3 \times 12.2}$$

$$A = \sqrt{3445} \approx 59$$

Perimeter (P):

$$P = side1 + side2 + side3$$

$$P = 15.6 + 16.6 + 7.7$$

$$P = 39.8$$

Area and Perimeter of an L-shape

The L-shaped figure typically consists of two rectangles joined together to form an L-shape. To find the area and perimeter of an L-shaped figure, we will need to calculate the areas and perimeters of each rectangle and then combine them.

Area=Area of Rectangle 1 + Area of Rectangle 2

Perimeter=Perimeter of Rectangle 1 + Perimeter of Rectangle 2

Let's find the Area and Perimeter of an L-shape:

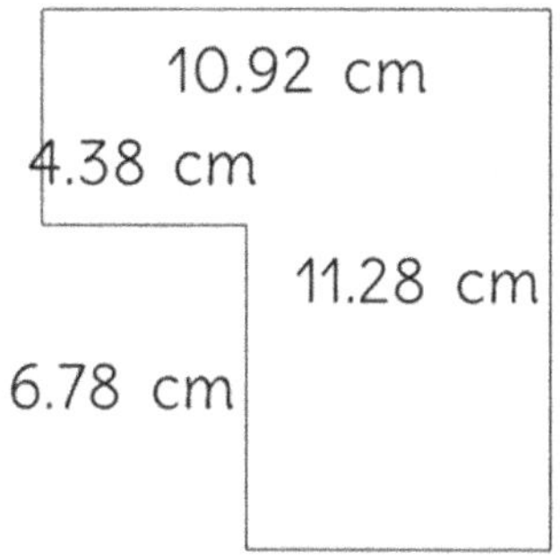

Area of L-Shape

$$\text{Area 1} = 4.38 \times 4.5 = 19.7 \text{ cm}^2$$

$$\text{Area 2} = 11.28 \times 6.54 = 73.7 \text{ cm}^2$$

$$\text{Area} = 19.7 + 73.7$$

$$\text{Area} = 93.481 \text{ cm}^2$$

Perimeter of L-Shape

$$P = 11.28 + 6.54 + 6.78 + 4.38 + 4.5 + 10.92$$

$$P = 44.4 \text{ cm}$$

Area and Perimeter of U-shape

U-shape is basically composed of three rectangles, we'll need to calculate the area and perimeter of each rectangle separately and then sum them up.

Area of the U-shape:

The total area (A) of the U-shape is the sum of the areas of the three rectangles:

$$A = A1 + A2 + A3$$

Perimeter of the U-shape: The total perimeter (P) of the U-shape is the sum of the perimeters of the three rectangles:

$$P = P1 + P2 + P3$$

Let's find the area and perimeter of the following U-shape:

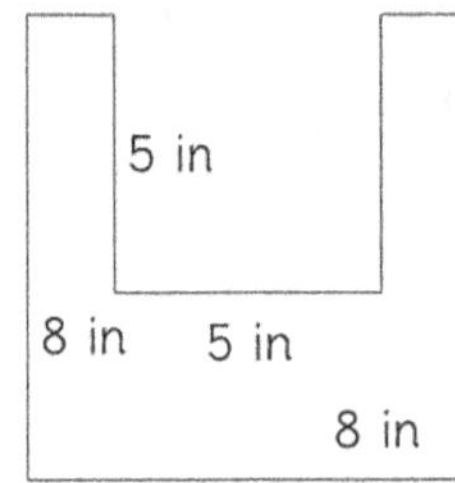

Area:

$$A1 = 8 \times 1.5 = 12 + A2 = 3 \times 5 = 15 + A3 = 8 \times 1.5 = 12$$

$$= 12 + 15 + 12$$

$$= 39 \text{ in}^2$$

Perimeter:

$$2 \times 8 + 2 \times 5 + 2 \times 8$$

$$= 16 + 10 + 16$$

$$= 42$$

Area and Perimeter of T-shape

The T-shape consists of two rectangles joined together to form a T-like structure.

Area of the T-shape:

To find the total area of the T-shape, we need to calculate the areas of both rectangles and then add them together.

$$\text{Area of Rectangle 1} = \text{Length} \times \text{Width}$$

$$\text{Area of Rectangle 2} = \text{Length} \times \text{Width}$$

$$\text{Total Area} = \text{Area of Rectangle 1} + \text{Area of Rectangle 2}$$

The perimeter of the T-shape is the sum of the perimeters of the two rectangles, minus the length of the overlapping side:

$$\text{Perimeter} = 2(l1+w1) + 2(l2+w2) - (w1-w2)$$

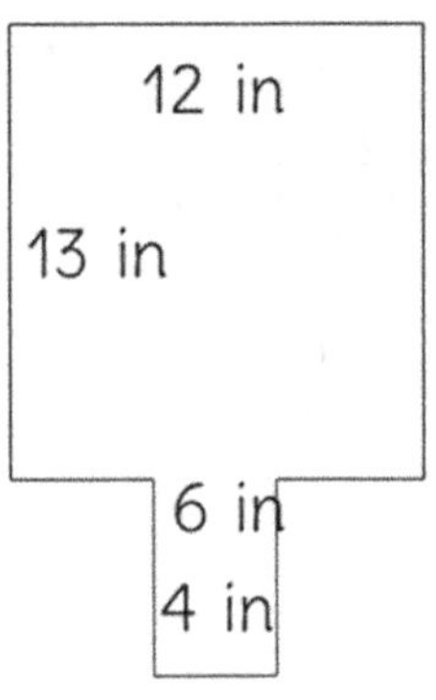

Area= 12 × 13 + 6 × 4

Area= 156 + 24

Area= 180 in²

Perimeter= 2(12+13) +2(6+4) – (12-4)

Perimeter=2(25) + 2(10) – 8

Perimeter= 50 + 20 – 8

Perimeter= 62 in²

Area and Perimeter of Parallelogram

A parallelogram is a four-sided polygon with opposite sides that are parallel and equal in length. To find the area and perimeter of a parallelogram, we use specific formulas based on its dimensions.

For example:

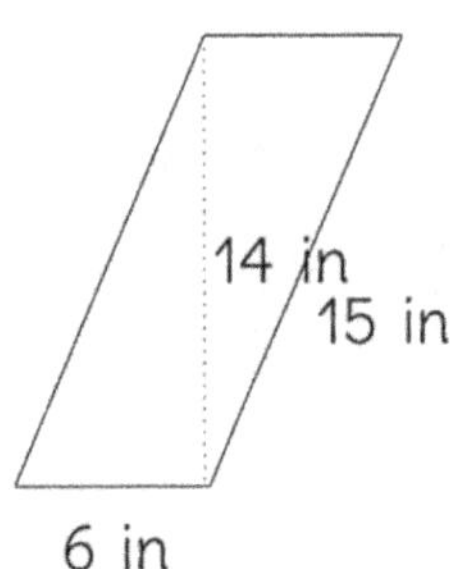

Let's denote:

- The length of one side of the parallelogram as $a = 15$.

- The length of an adjacent side (parallel to a) $b = 6$.

- The height of the parallelogram (perpendicular distance between the two parallel sides) as $h=14$

Area of Parallelogram

$$\text{Area} = \text{Base} \times \text{Height}$$

$$\text{Area} = 6 \times 14$$

$$\text{Area} = 84$$

Perimeter of Parallelogram

$$2(a + b)$$

$$= 2(15+6)$$

$$= 2(21)$$

$$= 42$$

Area and Perimeter of Trapezoids

A trapezoid is a quadrilateral with at least one pair of parallel sides. To find the area and perimeter of a trapezoid, we use specific formulas based on its dimensions.

For example:

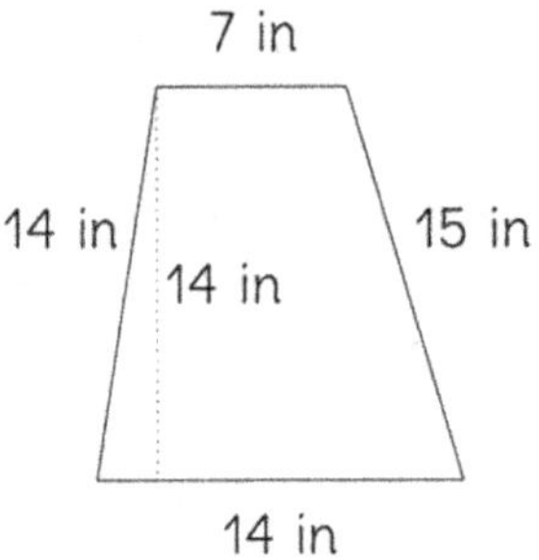

Let's denote:

- The lengths of the parallel sides of the trapezoid as $a = 7$ and $b = 14$.

- The lengths of the non-parallel sides as $c = 14$ and $d = 15$.

- The height of the trapezoid (the perpendicular distance between the parallel sides) as $h=14$.

Area of the Trapezoid:

The area of a trapezoid is given by the formula:

$$\text{Area} = \frac{1}{2} \times \text{Height} \times (\text{Sum of the lengths of the parallel sides})$$

$$\text{Area} = \frac{1}{2} \times h \times (a + b)$$

$$\text{Area} = \frac{1}{2} \times 14 \times (7 + 14)$$

$$\text{Area} = \frac{1}{2} \times 14 \times 21$$

$$\text{Area} = 147 \text{ in}^2$$

Perimeter of the Trapezoid:

$$\text{Perimeter} = 7 + 14 + 14 + 15$$

$$= 50 \text{ in}^2$$

Pythagorean Theorem

The Pythagorean Theorem is a fundamental principle in geometry that relates the lengths of the sides of a right triangle. It states that in any right triangle, the square of the length of the hypotenuse (the side opposite the right angle) is equal to the sum of the squares of the lengths of the other two sides.

$$a2 + b2 = c2$$

Let's use the Pythagorean Theorem to find the length of the hypotenuse (c) when $a=44$ and $b=78$.

$$c^2 = 44^2 + 78^2$$
$$c^2 = 1936 + 6084$$
$$c^2 = 8020$$
$$c = \sqrt{8020}$$
$$c \approx 89.554$$

Volume and surface Area

Volume refers to the amount of space occupied by a three-dimensional object. For shapes like cubes or rectangular prisms, we calculate volume by multiplying their length, width, and height.

To find the volume V of a rectangular prism, we use the formula:

$$Volume = length \; x \; width \; x \; height$$

Surface Area represents the total area covering all the faces of a three-dimensional object. For shapes like cubes or rectangular prisms, we find the surface area by summing the areas of all its faces.

The formula for surface area SA of a cube or rectangular prism is:

$$Surface\ Area\ =\ 2lw\ +\ 2lh\ +\ 2wh$$

Where: l is the length, w is the width, and h is the height of the object.

For example: Let's find the Volume and Surface Area of following rectangular prisms:

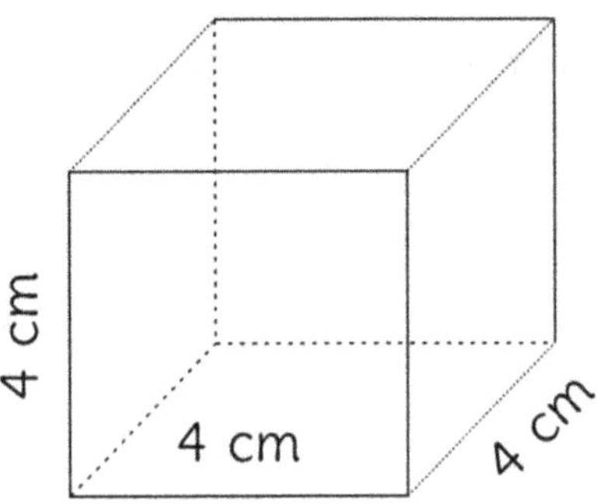

$$Volume\ =\ length\ \times\ width\ \times\ height$$

$$= 4 \times 4 \times 4$$

$$= 64\ cm^2$$

$$Surface\ Area\ =\ 2lw\ +\ 2lh\ +\ 2wh$$

$$= 2(4 \times 4) + 2(4 \times 4) + 2(4 \times 4)$$

$$= 32 + 32 + 32$$

$$= 96\ cm2$$

Different 3D objects have unique formulas for finding their volume and surface area. Here are some common ones:

1. Cube:

    - Volume: $V = s^3$ (where s is the length of one side of the cube)

    - Surface area: $SA = 6s^2$

2. **Sphere:**

   - Volume: $V = (\frac{4}{3})\pi r^3$ (where r is the radius of the sphere)

   - Surface area: $SA = 4\pi r^2$

3. **Cone:**

   - Volume: $V = (\frac{1}{3})\pi r^2 h$ (where r is the radius of the base and h is the height of the cone)

   - Surface area: $SA = \pi r^2 + \pi r \sqrt{(r^2 + h^2)}$

4. **Cylinder:**

   - Volume: $V = \pi r^2 h$ (where r is the radius of the base and h is the height of the cylinder)

   - Surface area: $SA = 2\pi r^2 + 2\pi rh$

5. **Pyramid:**

   - Volume: $V = (\frac{1}{3})Bh$ (where B is the area of the base and h is the height of the pyramid)

   - Surface area: $SA = B + \frac{1}{2}Pl$ (where P is the perimeter of the base and l is the slant height of the pyramid)

Area and Perimeter

① 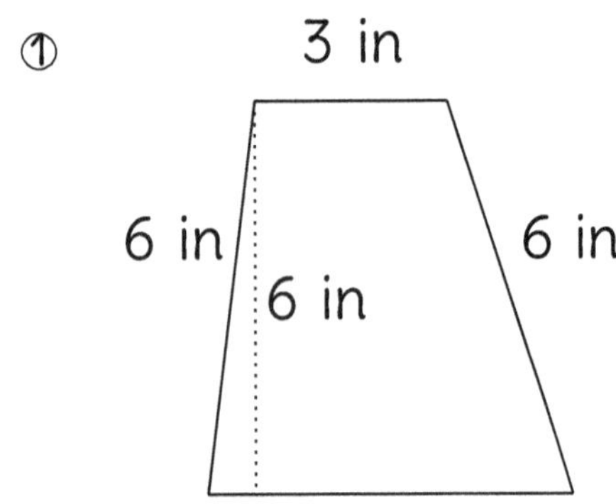

② 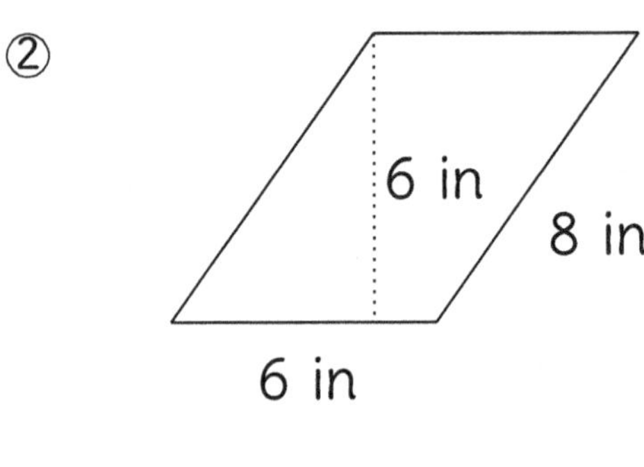

③

④ 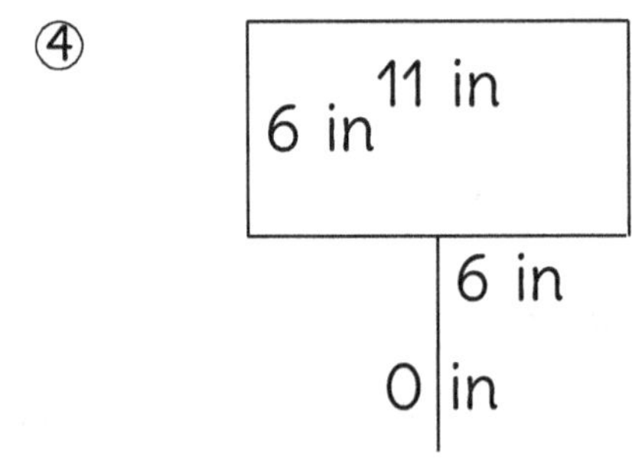

Name:
Date:

⑤

15 in
10 in
11 in
11 in
8 in

⑥

16 in
16 in
14.83 in
12 in

⑦

5 in
12 in
5 in
0 in

⑧

7 in
7 in
7 in
6.062 in

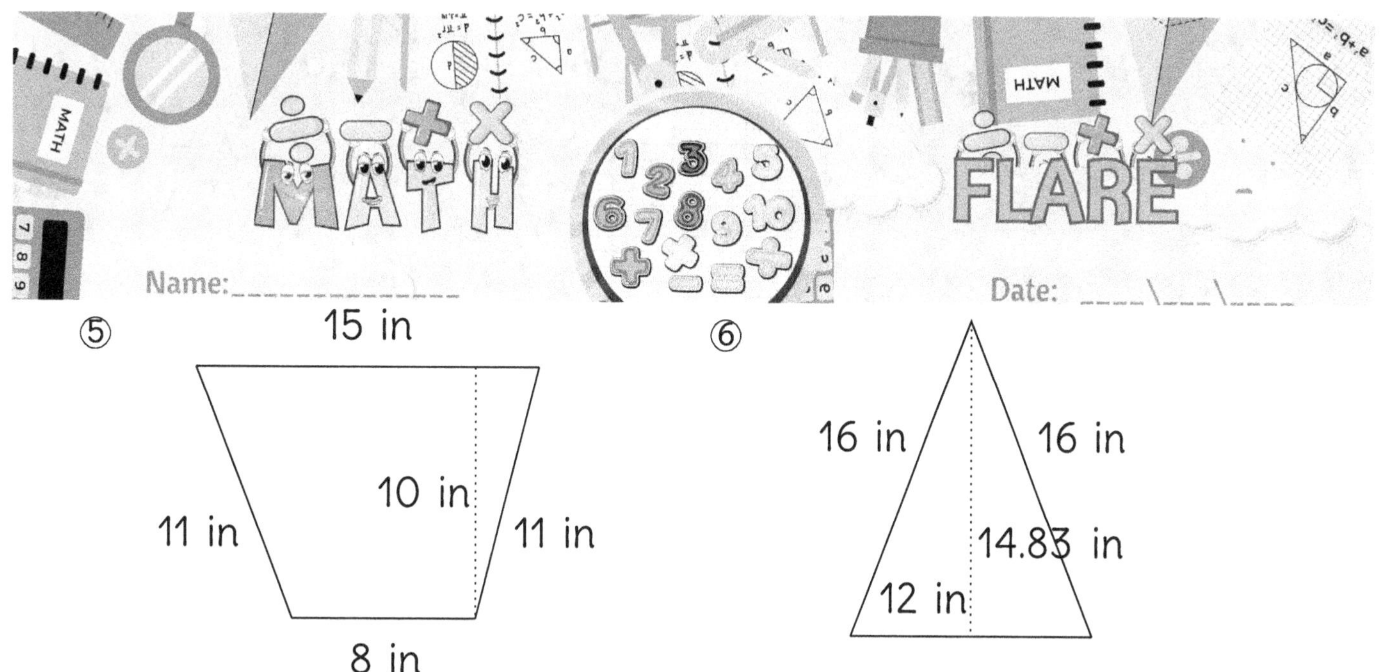

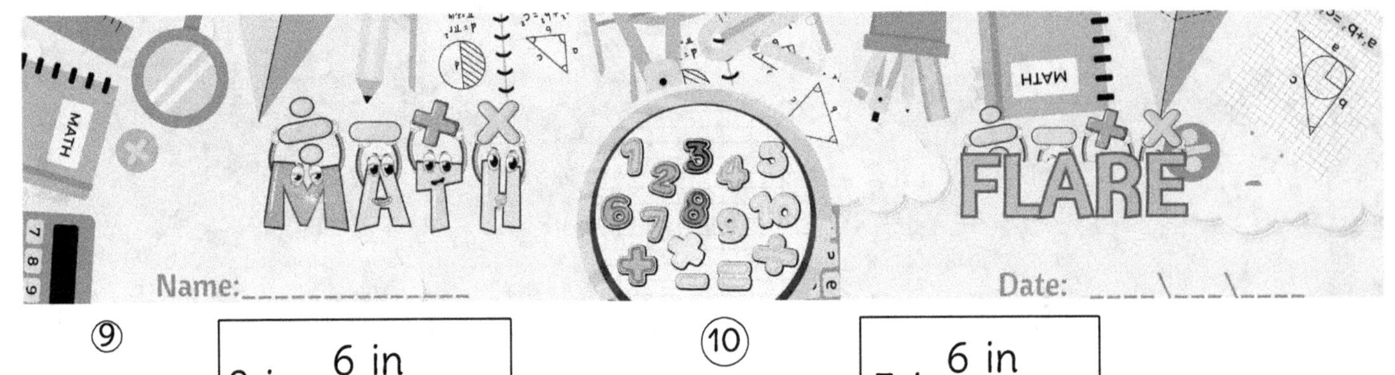

⑨

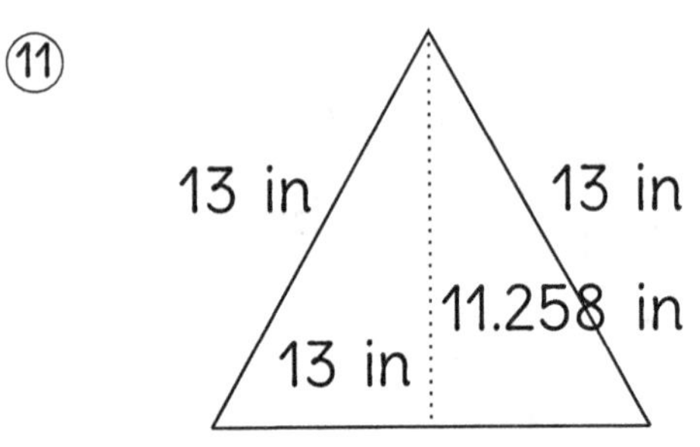

⑩

6 in
3 in
10 in
7 in

⑪

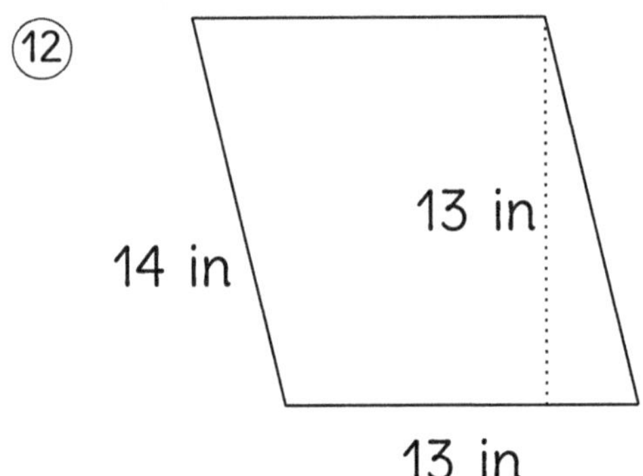

⑫

14 in
13 in
13 in

MATH
FLARE
Name:
Date:

⑬

5 in
9 in
4 in
7 in

⑭

6 in
6 in
5.20 in
6 in

⑮

4 in
8 in
8 in
8 in
8 in
10 in

⑯

13 in
12 in
11.97 in
6 in

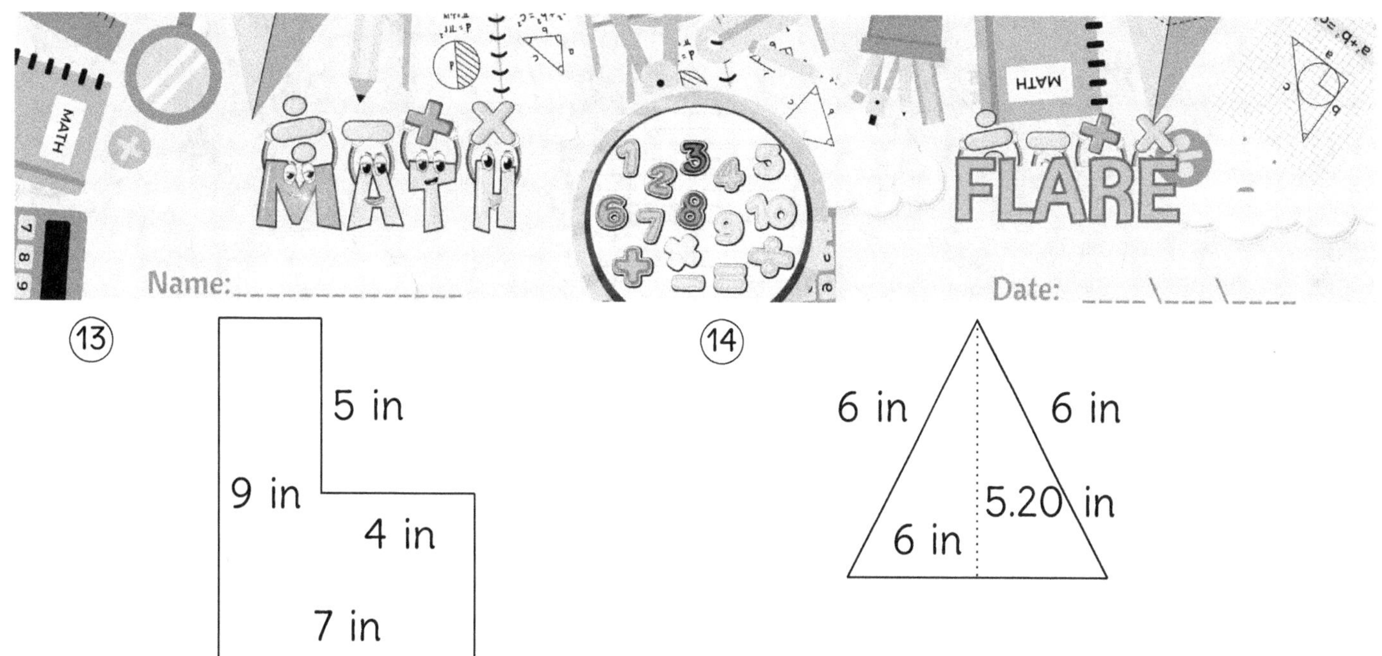

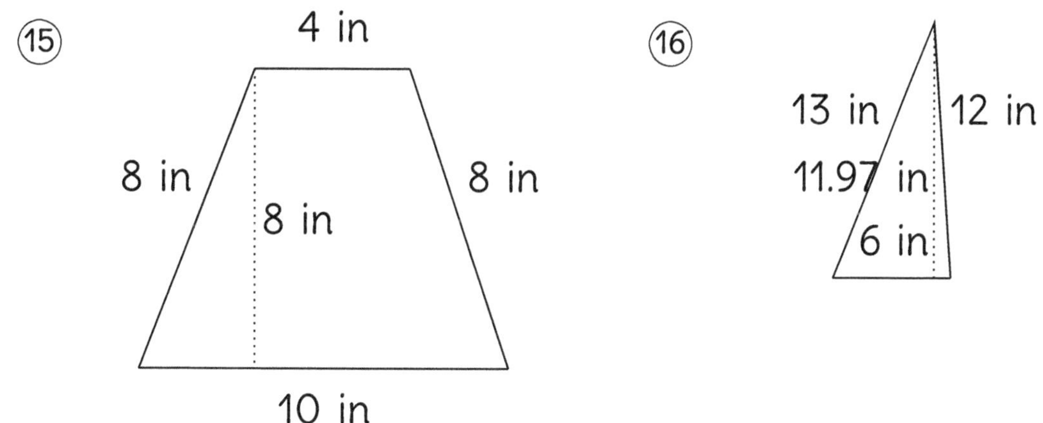

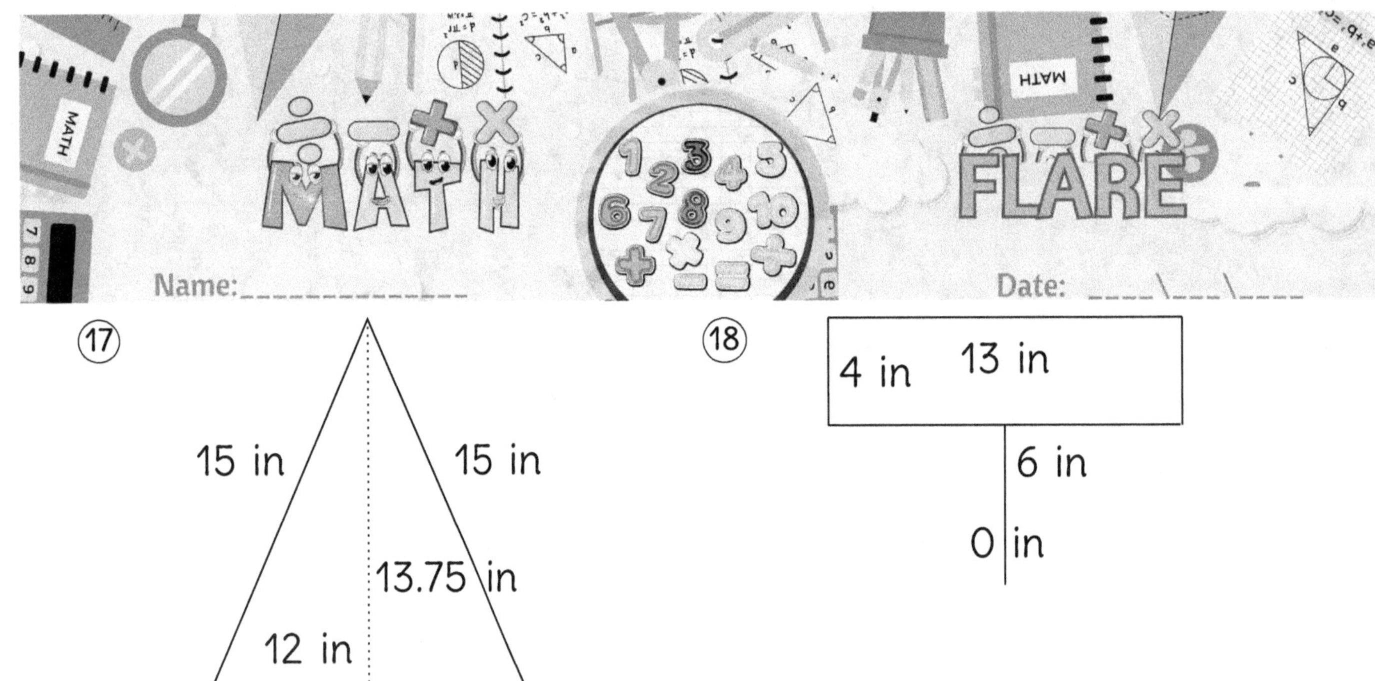
17
15 in
15 in
13.75 in
12 in
18
4 in
13 in
6 in
0 in

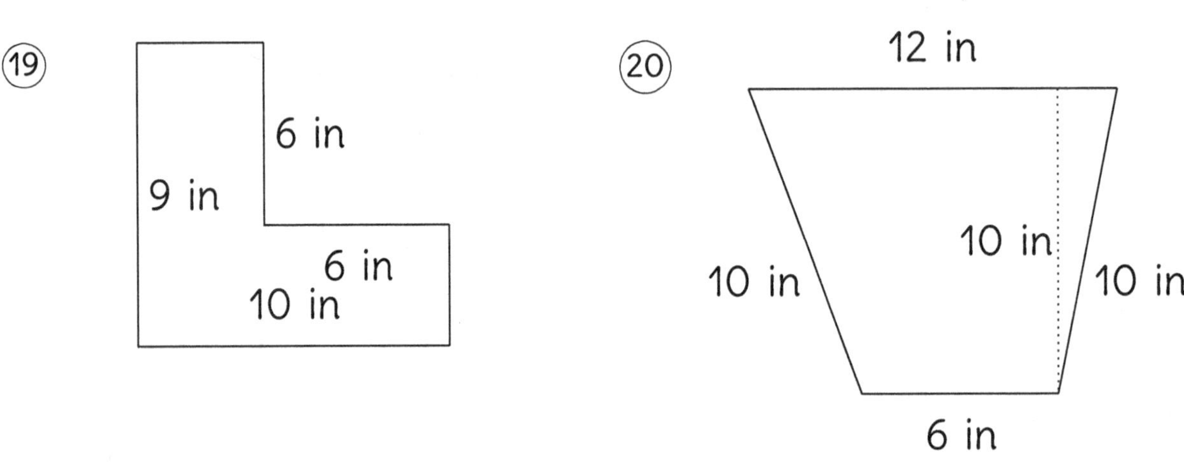
19
6 in
9 in
6 in
10 in
20
12 in
10 in
10 in
10 in
6 in

Name:
Date:
MATH
FLARE

(21)

3 in
9 in
8 in
12 in

(22)

4 in
8 in
4 in
7 in

(23)

3 in
6 in
6 in
6 in
7 in

(24)

9 in
12 in
0 in
12 in

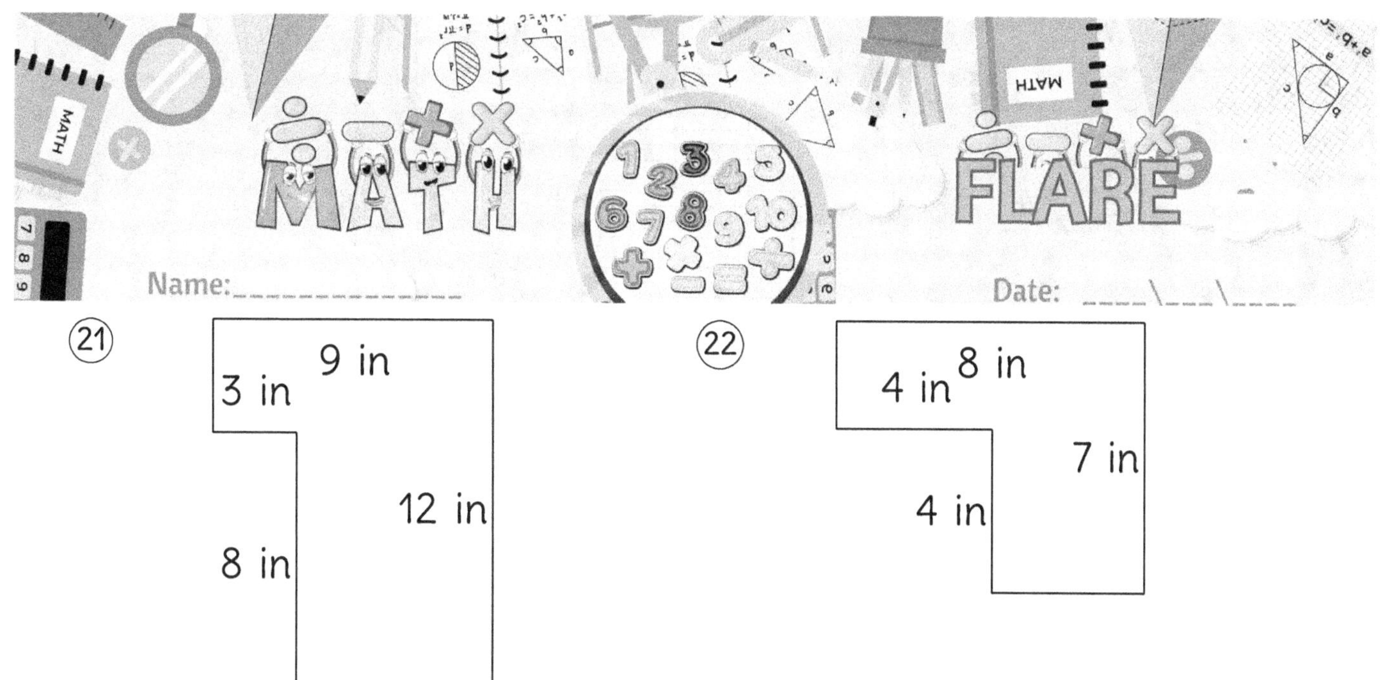

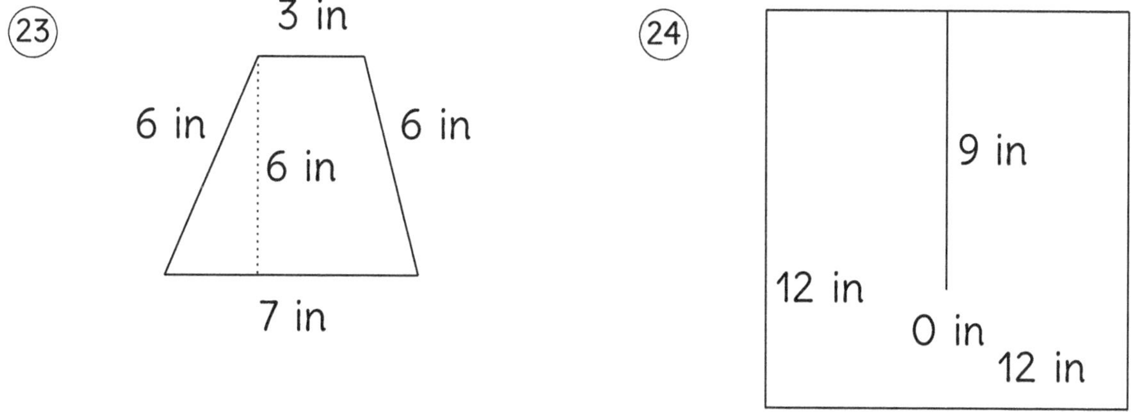

Name:
Date:
MATH
FLARE

(25)

5 in
6 in
0 in 7 in

(26)

6 in   6 in
5.45 in
5 in

(27)

11 in
16 in
0 in 17 in

(28)

14 in
6 in
9 in
0 in

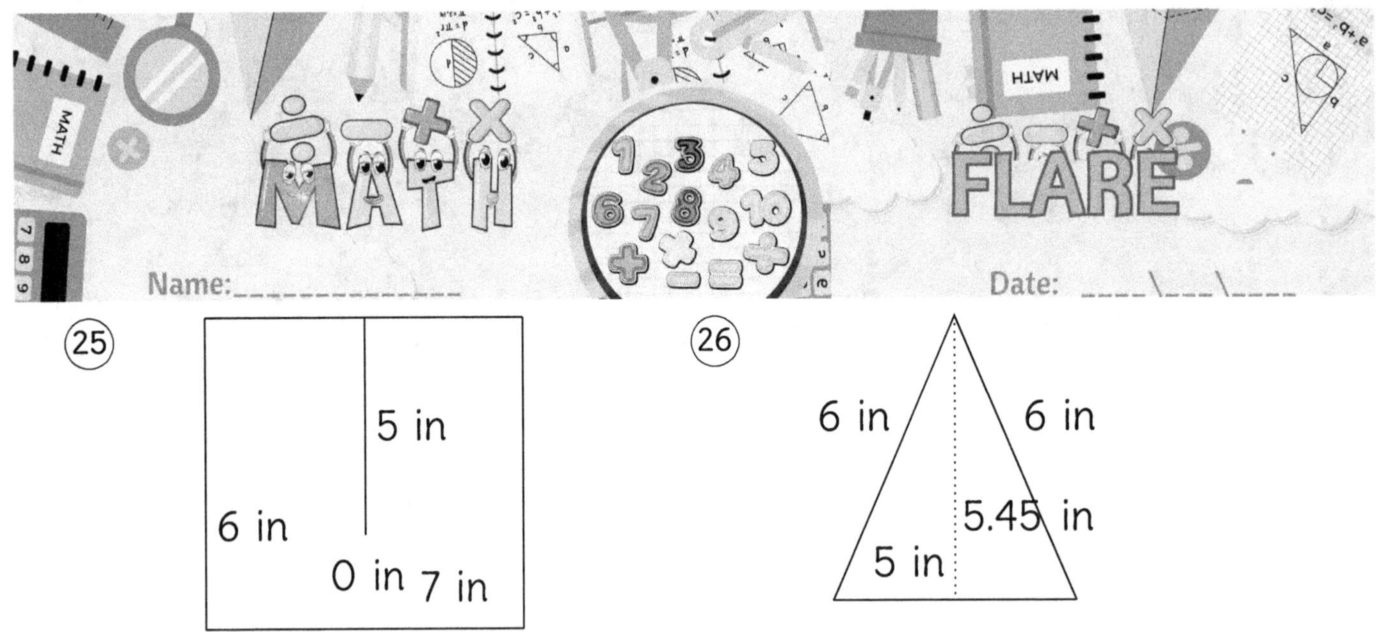

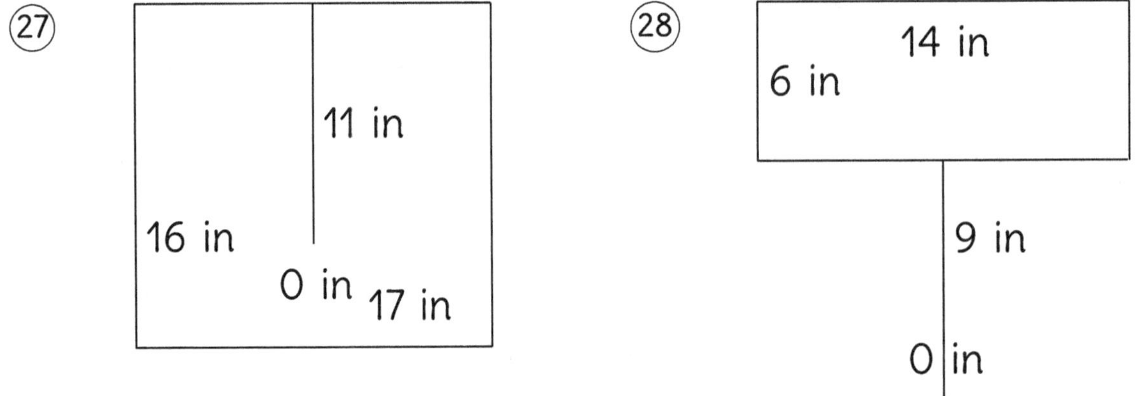

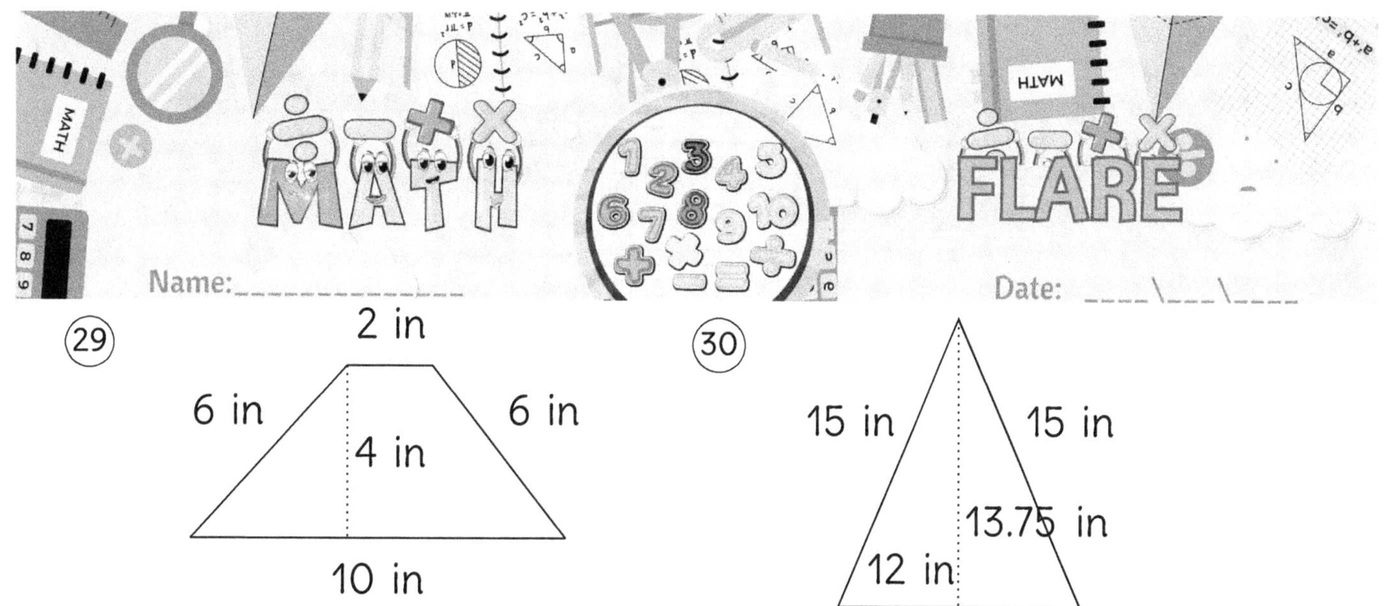

(29)

(30)

(31)

(32)

129

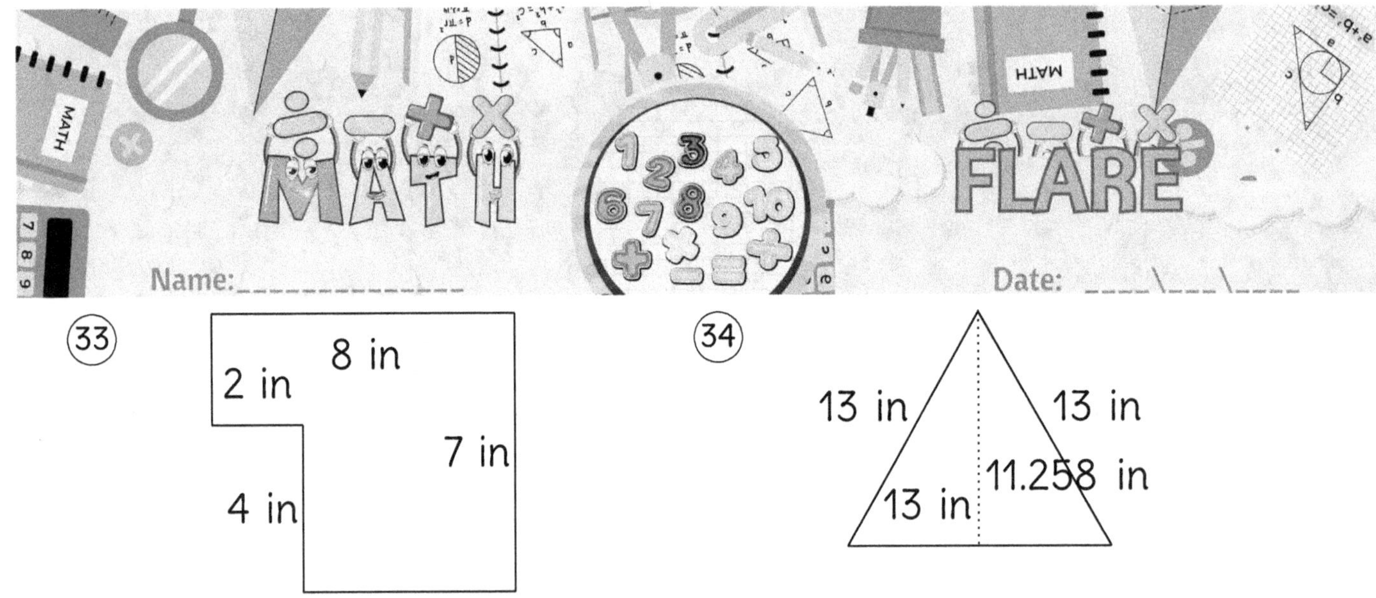

(33)

(34)

(35)

(36)

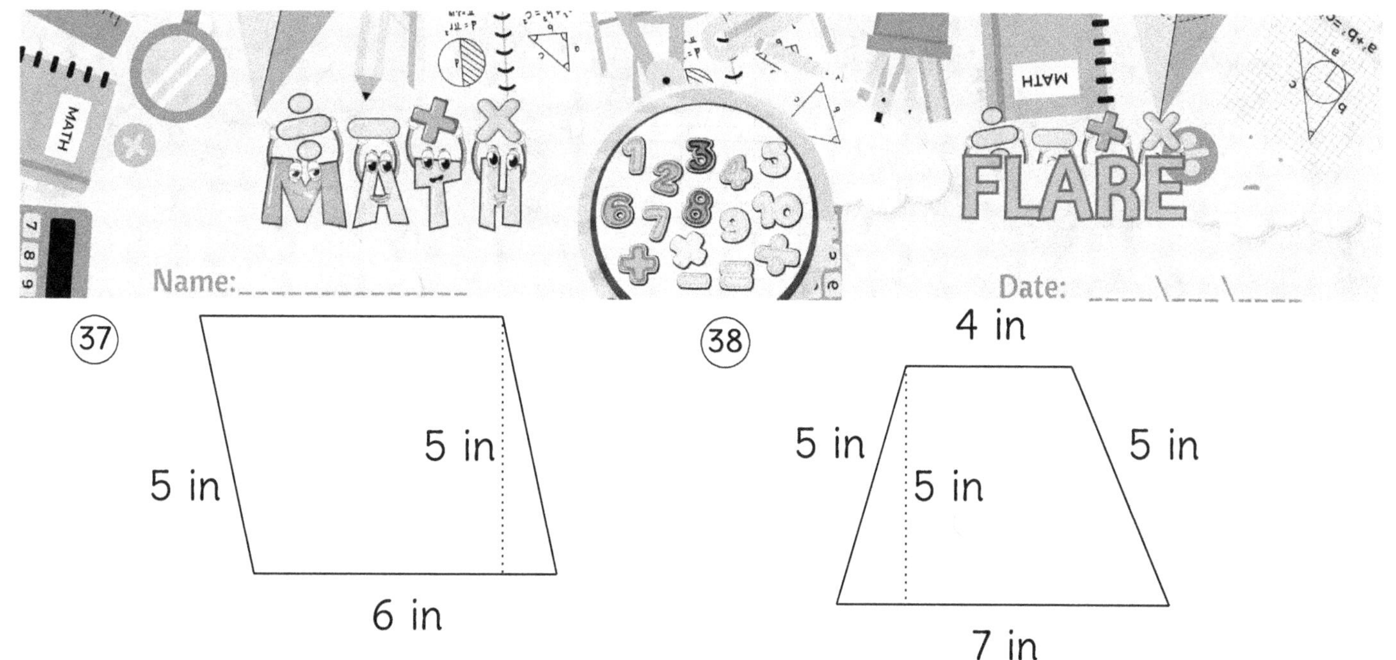

(37)

(38)

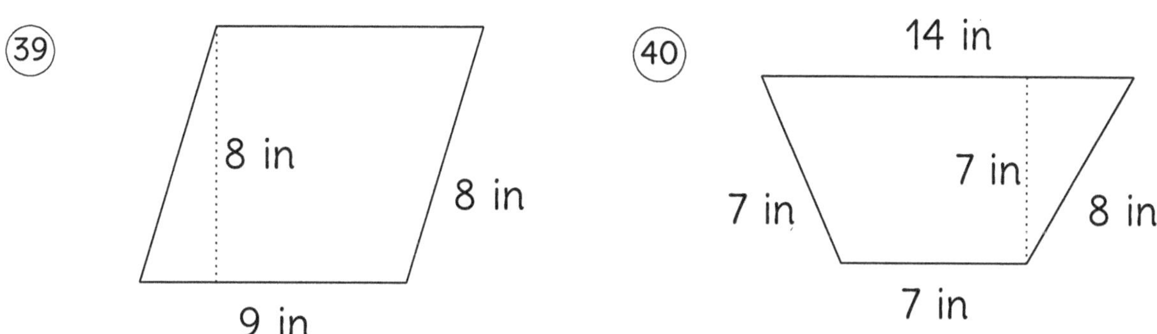

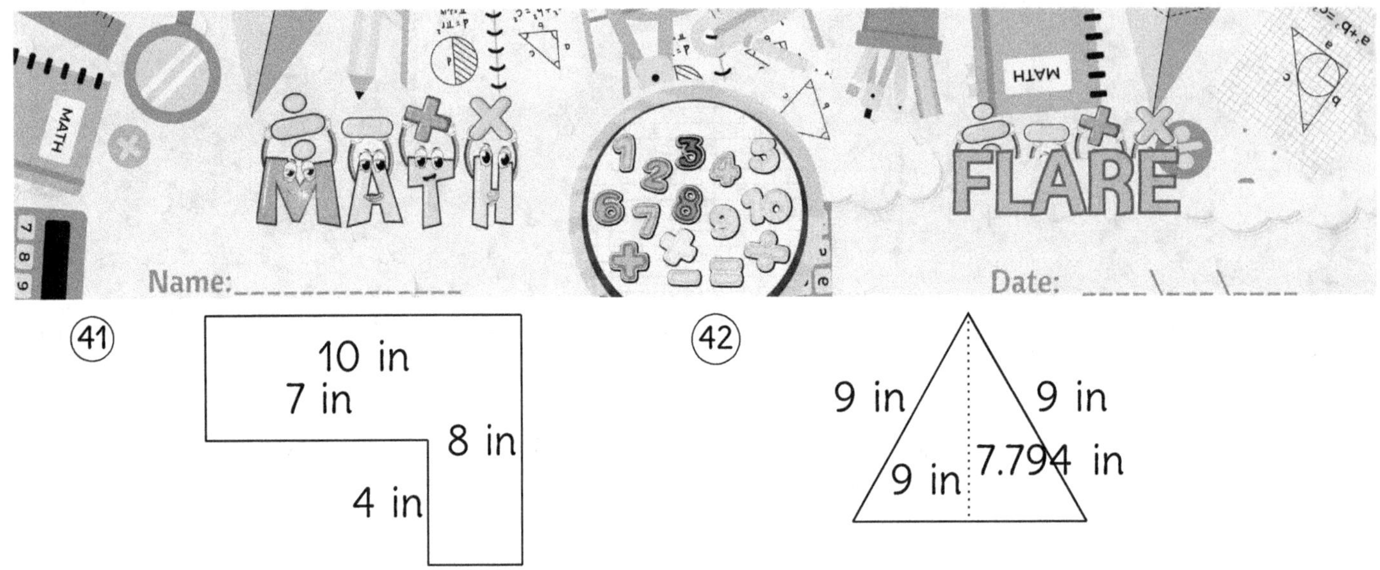

(41)

(42)

(43)

(44)
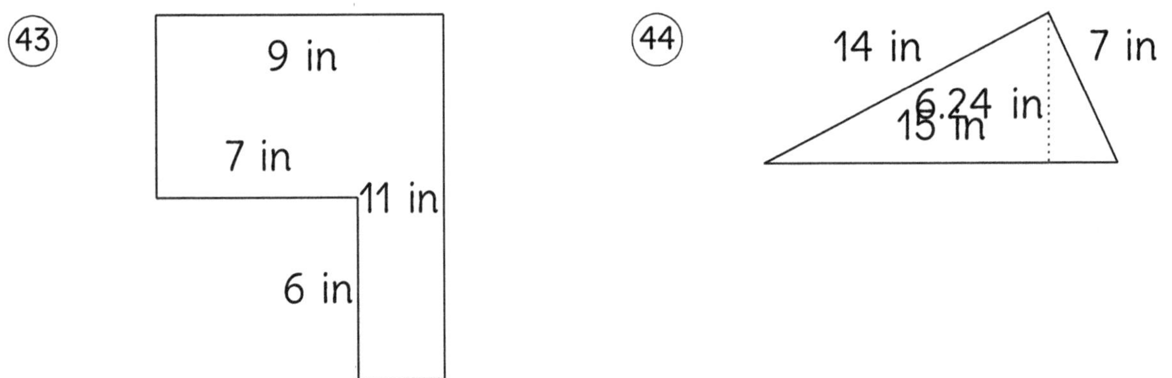

Name:
Date:

45)

15 in
8 in
9 in
10 in
8 in

46)

14 in
13 in
14 in
14 in
6 in

47)

7 in
7 in
6.062 in
7 in

48)

8 in
8 in
6.93 in
8 in

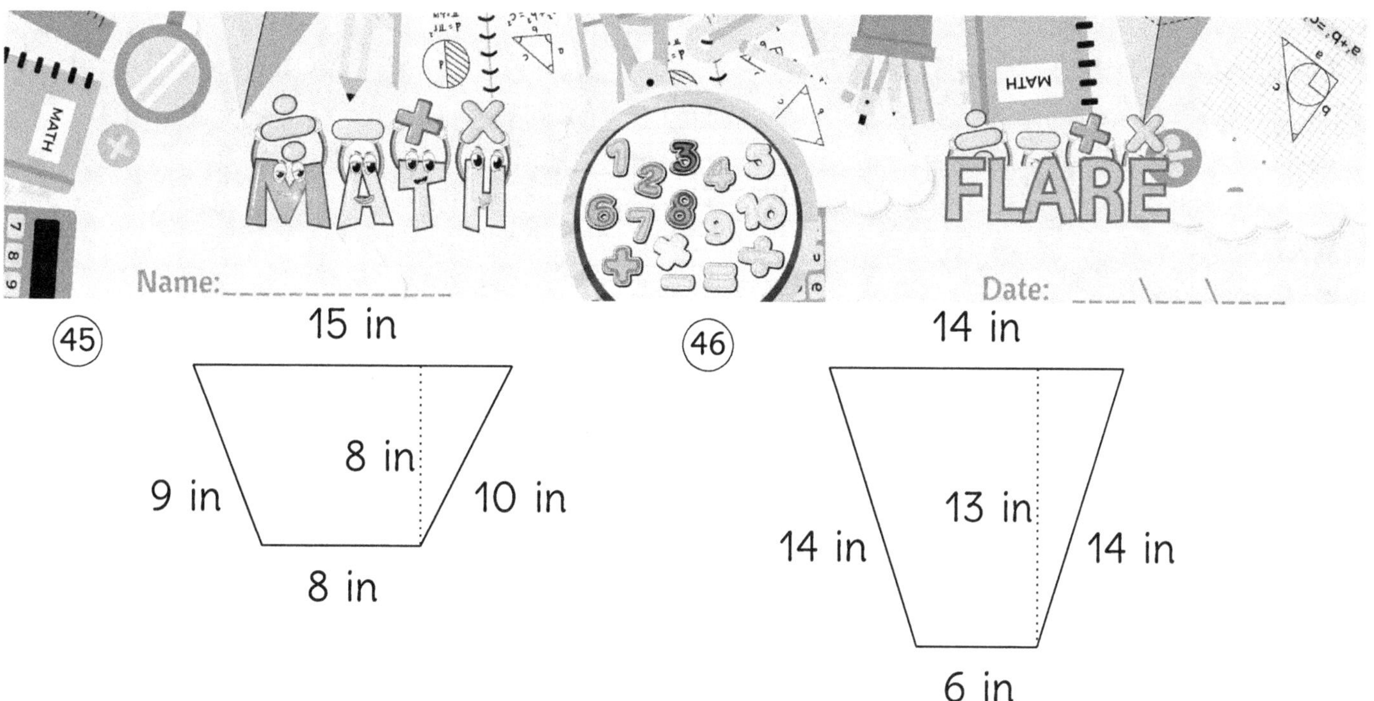

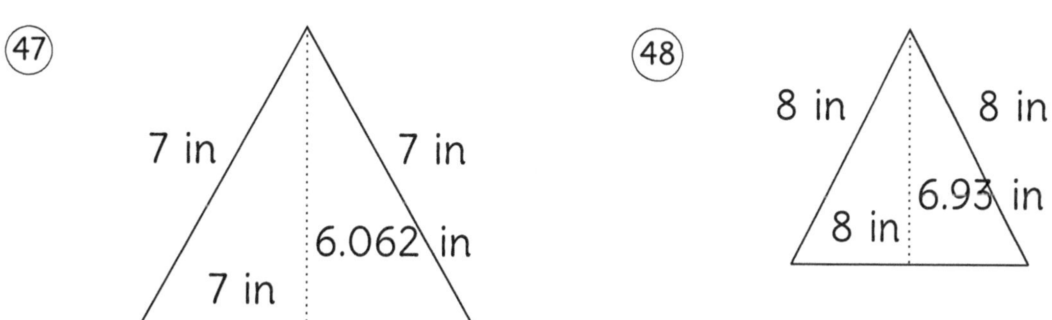

Name:
Date:
MATH
FLARE

49

9 in
6 in
4 in
0 in

50

11 in
11 in
13 in

51

6 in
11 in
0 in
10 in

52

13 in
13 in
12.60 in
6 in

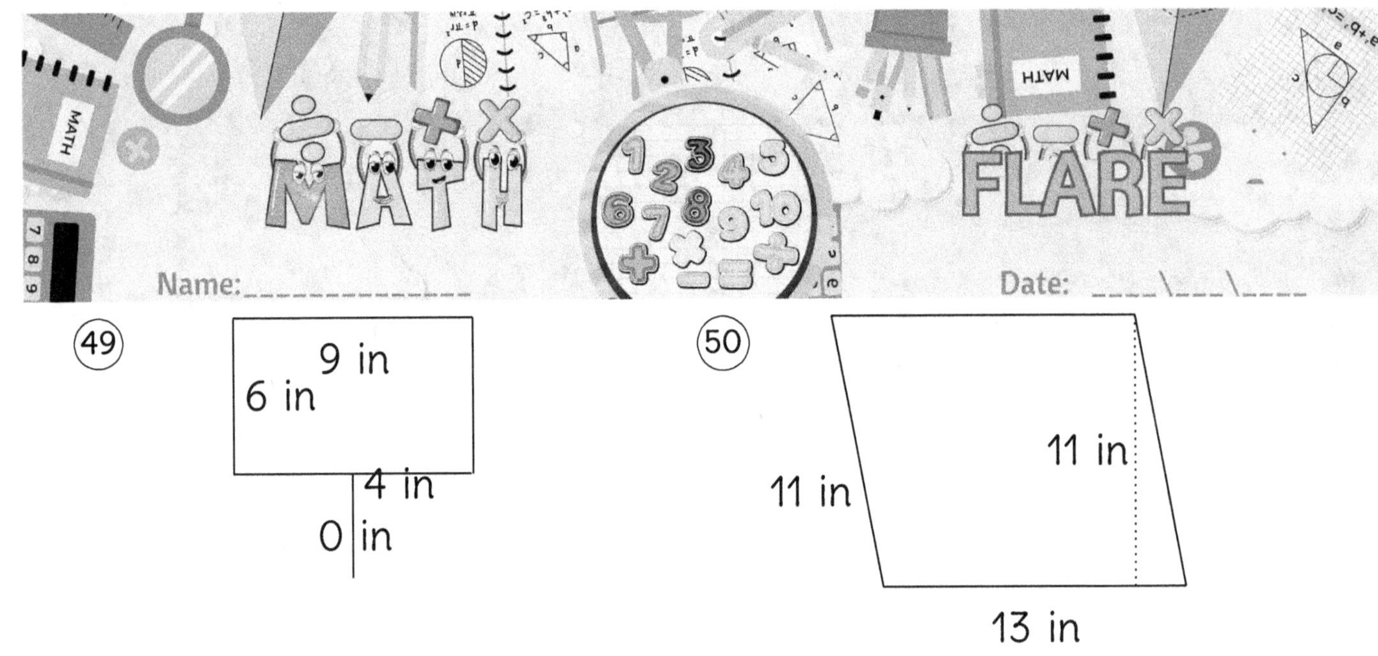

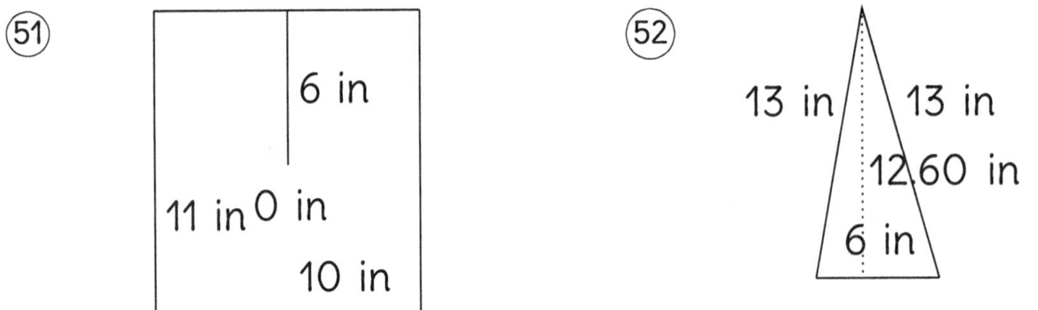

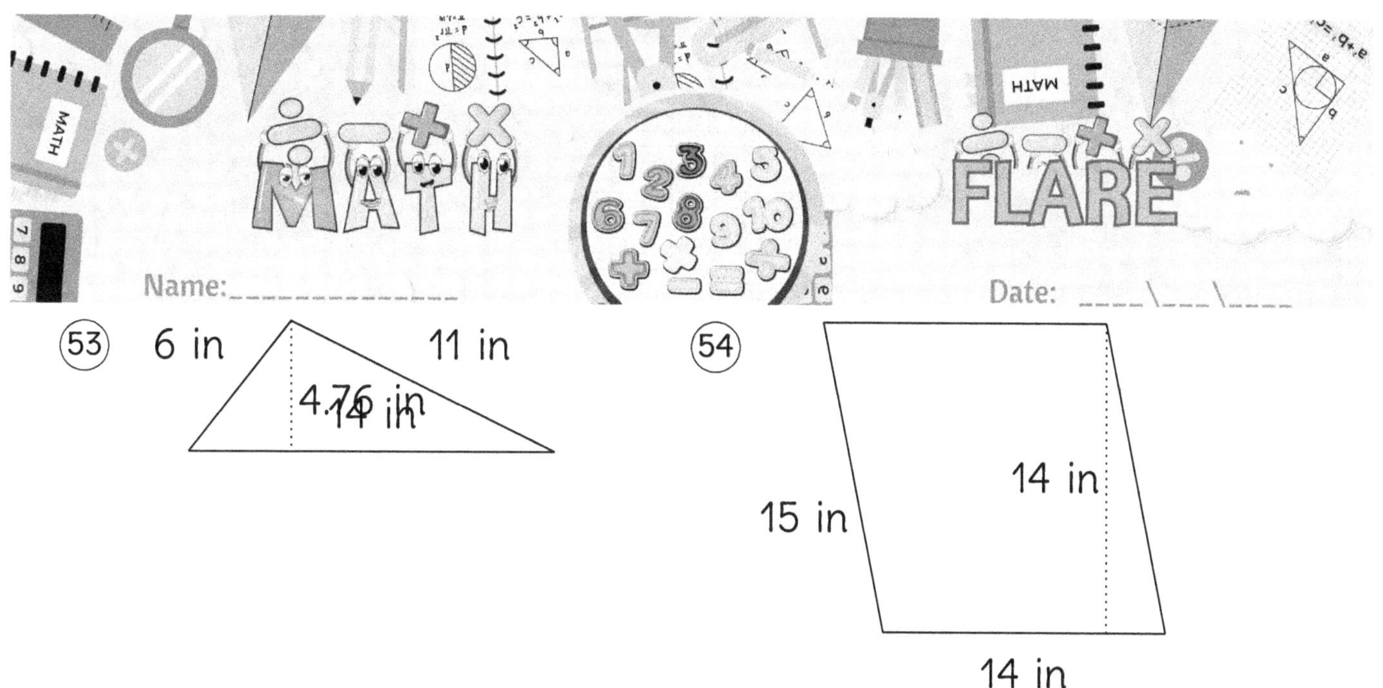

(53) 6 in   11 in
4.76 in
14 in

(54)
14 in
15 in
14 in

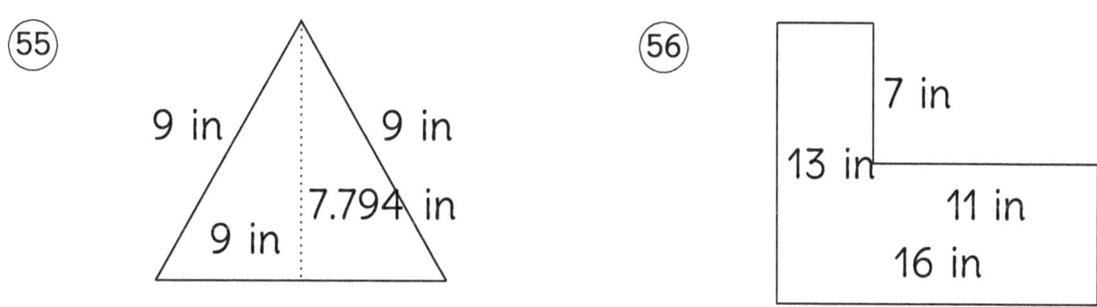

(55)
9 in   9 in
7.794 in
9 in

(56)
7 in
13 in
11 in
16 in

Name:
Date:

(57)

8 in
11 in
8 in

(58)

7 in
7 in
6.062 in
7 in

(59)

9 in
9 in
8.29 in
7 in

(60)

11 in
12 in
8 in

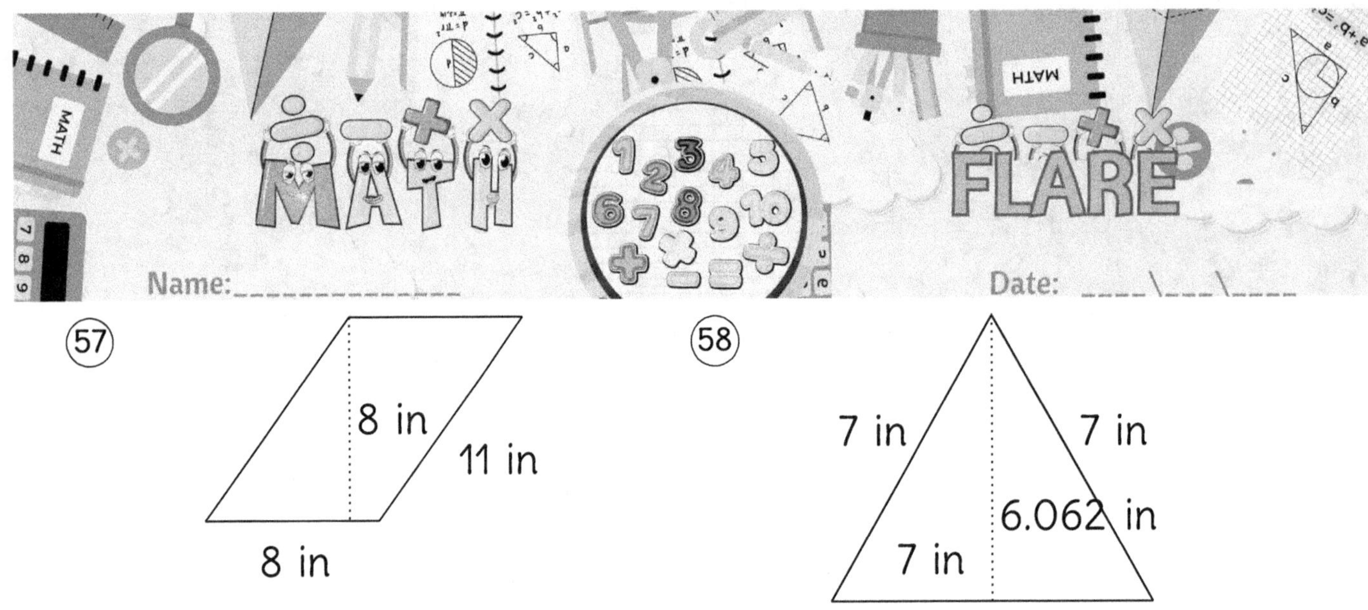

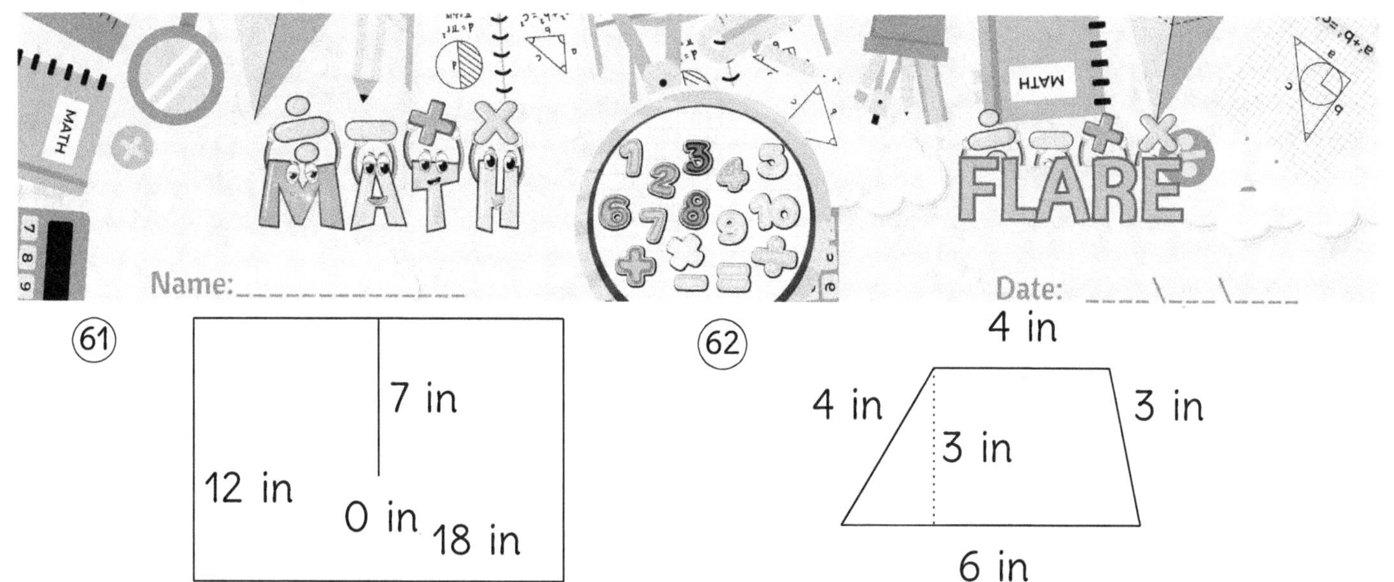

61)

62)

63)

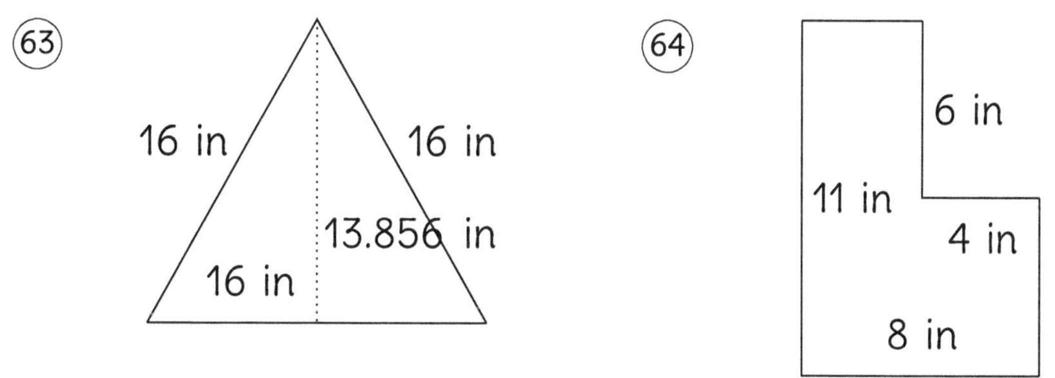

64)

137

Name:
Date:
MATH
FLARE
MATH

(65)

9 in
8 in
8.32 in
3 in

(66)

5 in
11 in
3 in
11 in

(67)

4 in
6 in
5 in
4 in

(68)

13 in
12 in
12.11 in
6 in

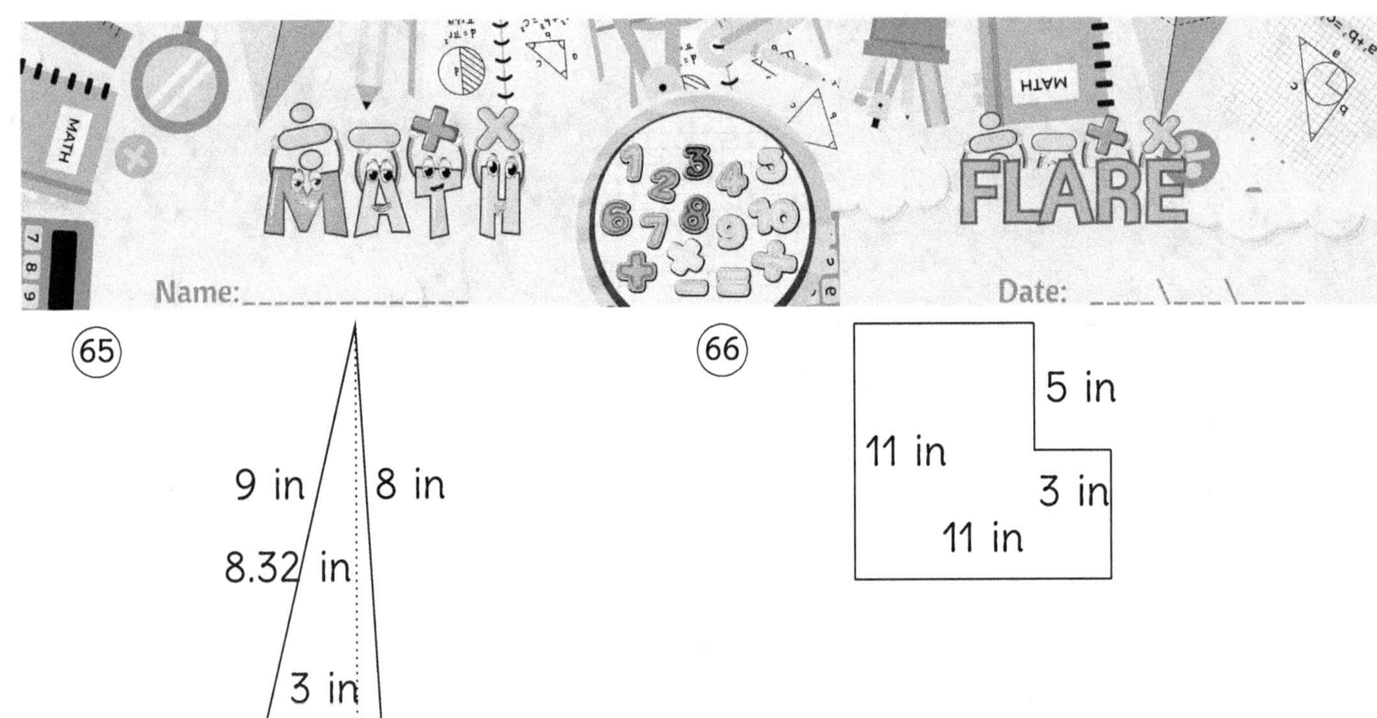

Name:
Date:

(69)

16 in
7 in
11 in
0 in

(70)

9 in
15 in
6 in
14 in

(71)

4 in
7 in
4 in
7 in

(72)

7 in
7 in
6.32 in
6 in

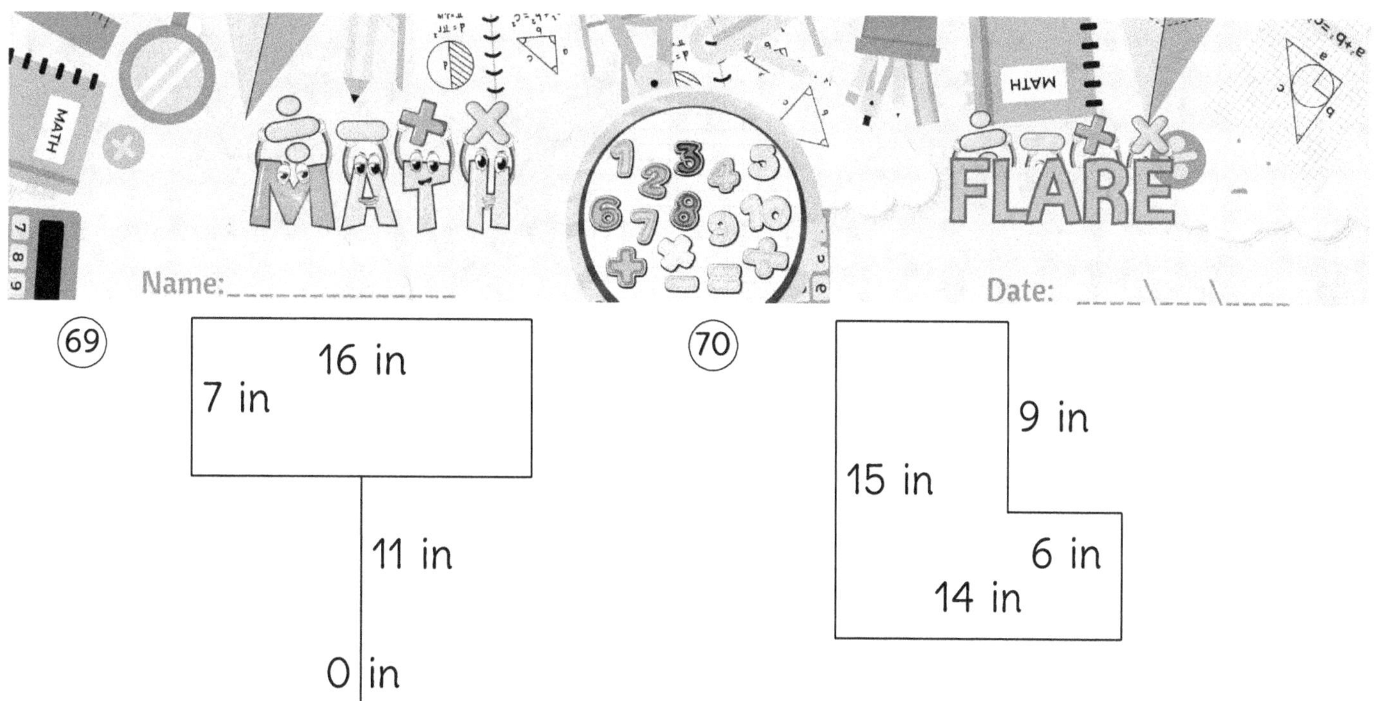

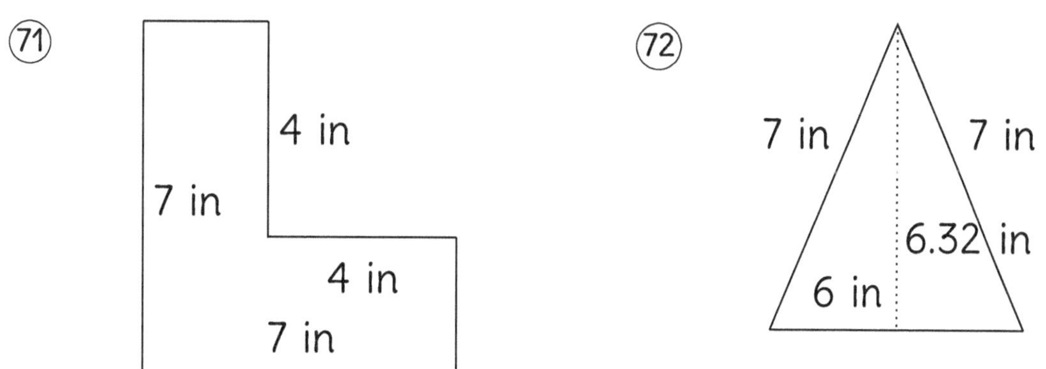

Name:
Date:
MATH
FLARE

73

10 in
11 in
11 in

74

10 in
7 in
11 in
4 in

75

9 in
5 in
8 in
5 in

76

8 in
14 in
6 in
9 in

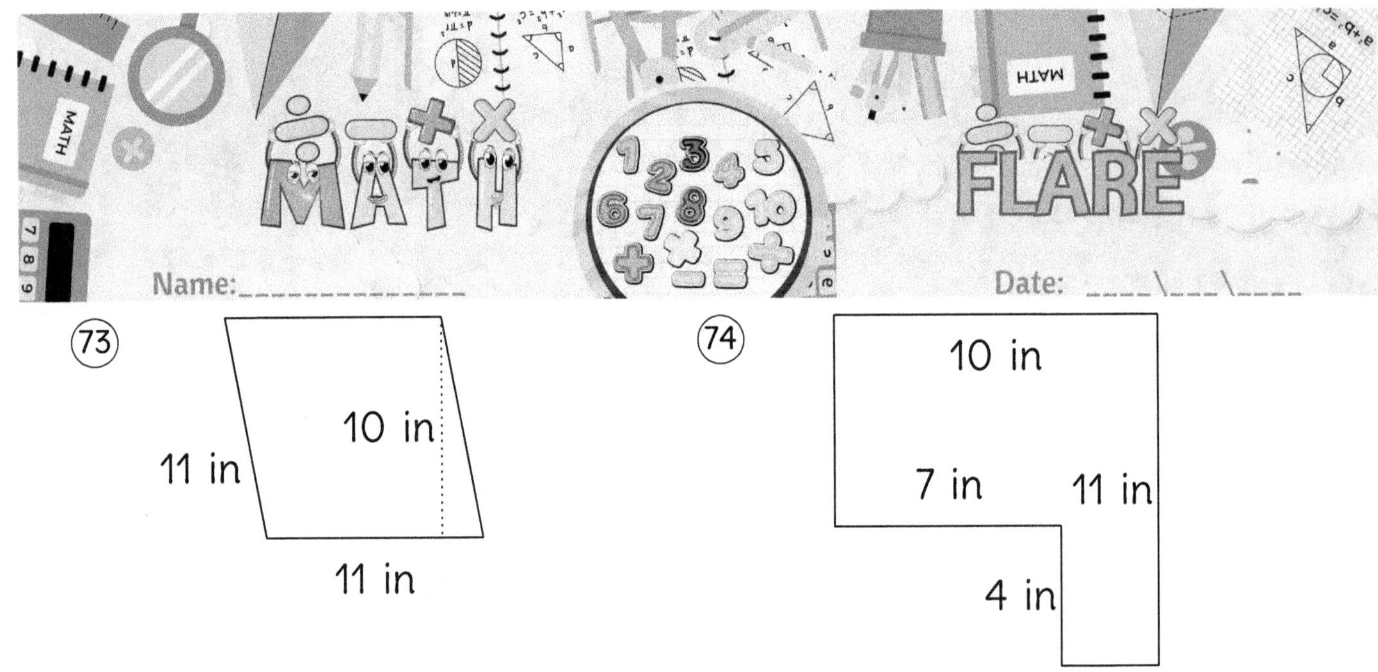

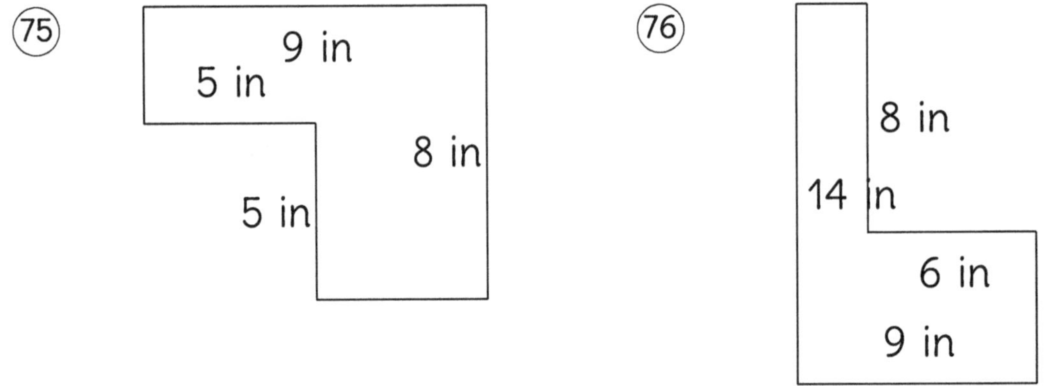

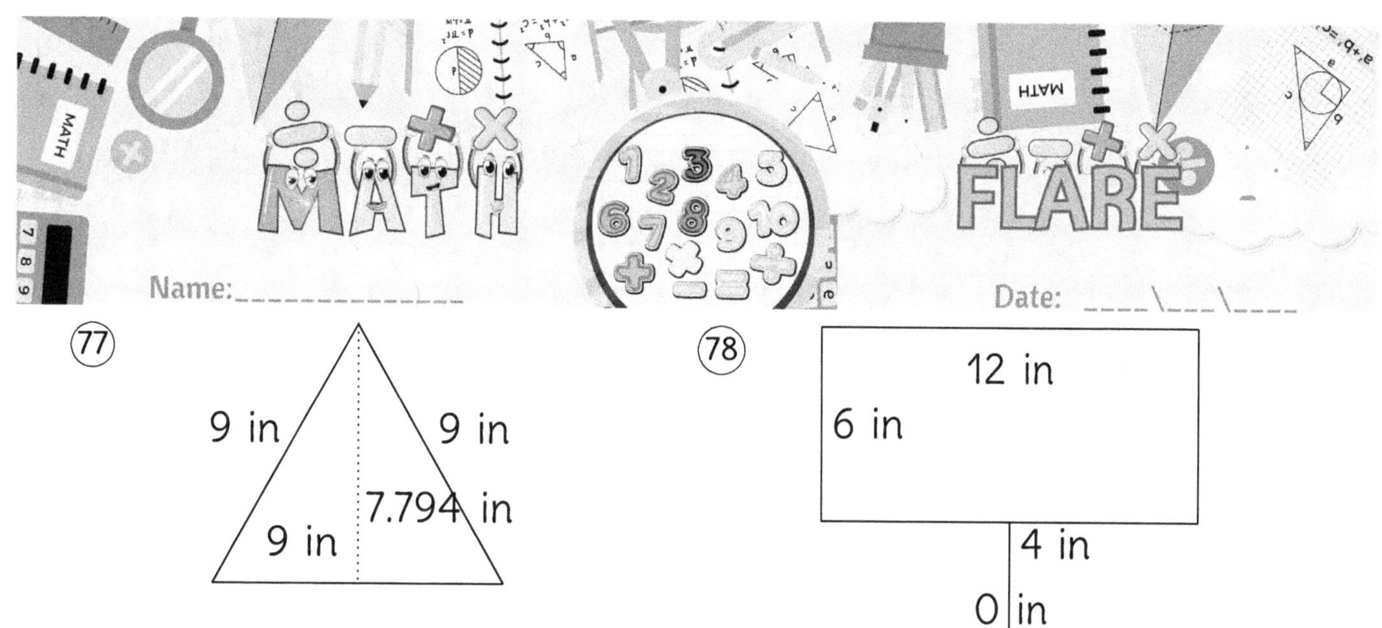

Ⓜ MATH FLARE

⑦⑦

⑦⑧

⑦⑨

⑧⓪

Name: _______________   Date: ____________

Volume and Surface Area

① 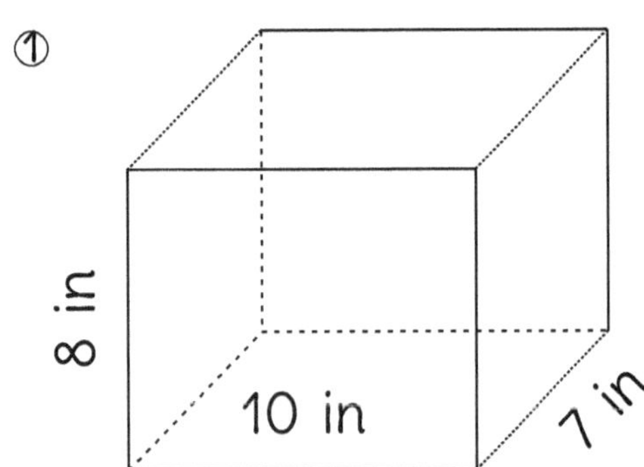

② 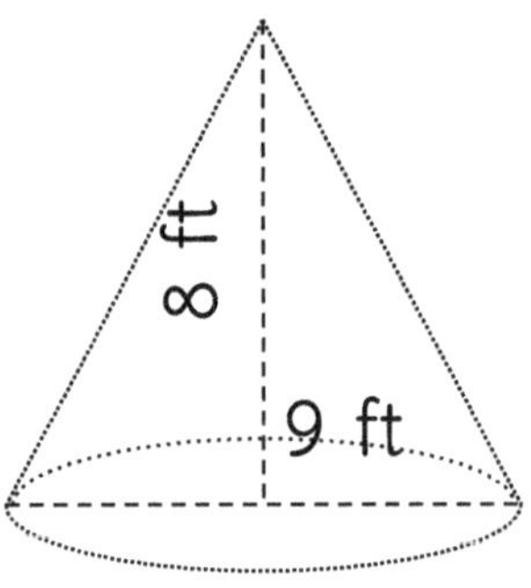

③ 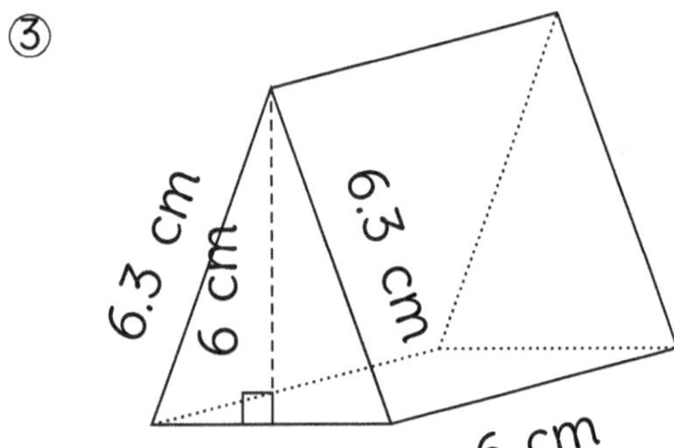

④ 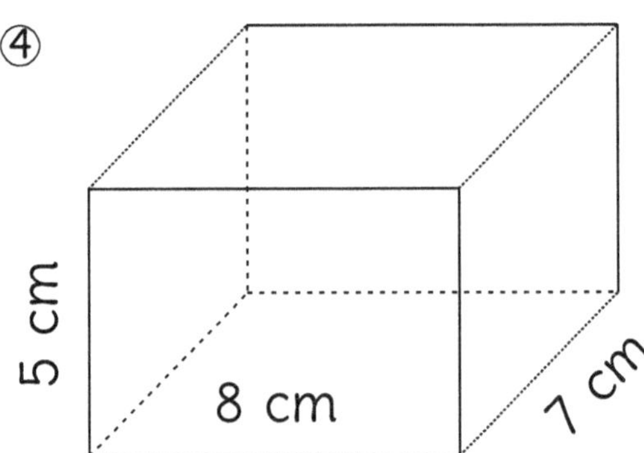

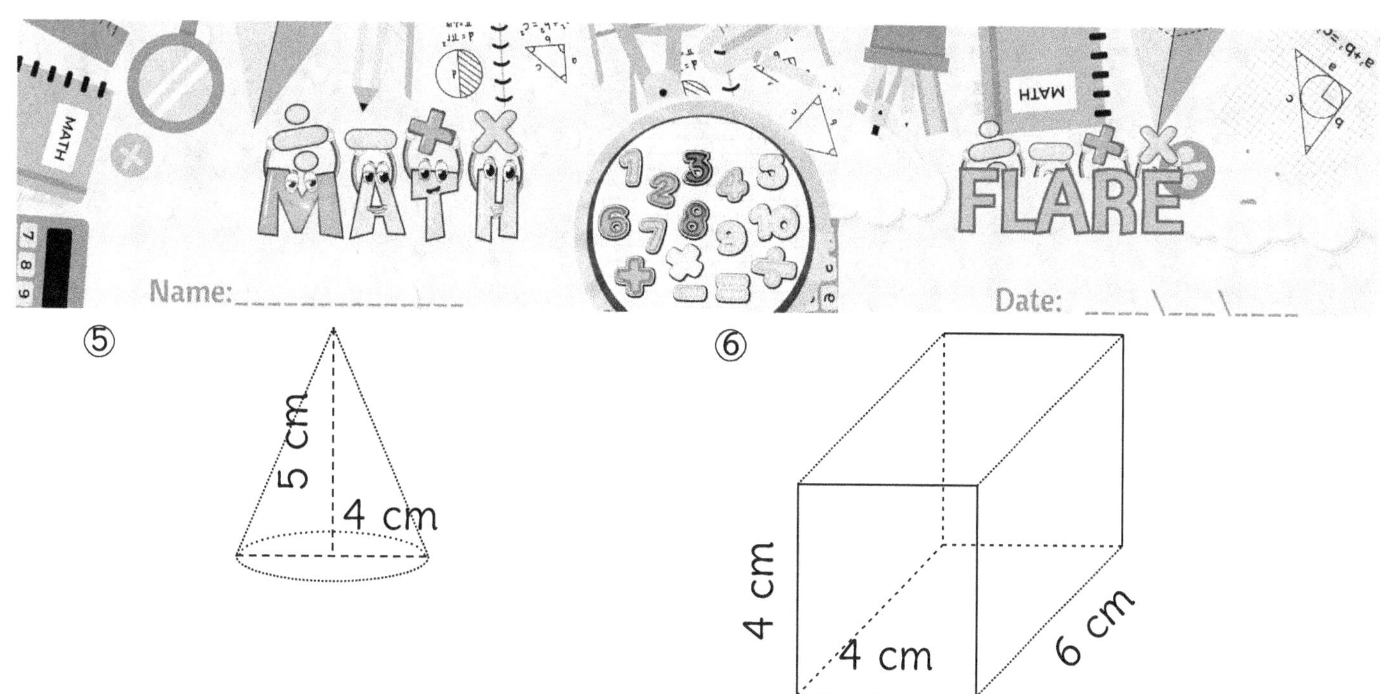

⑤

⑥

⑦ 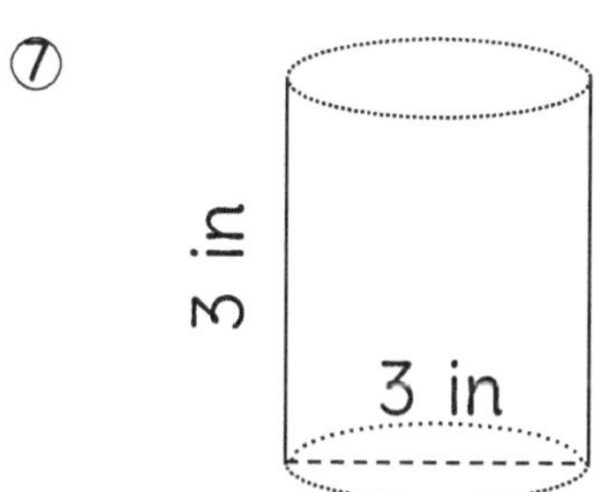

⑧ 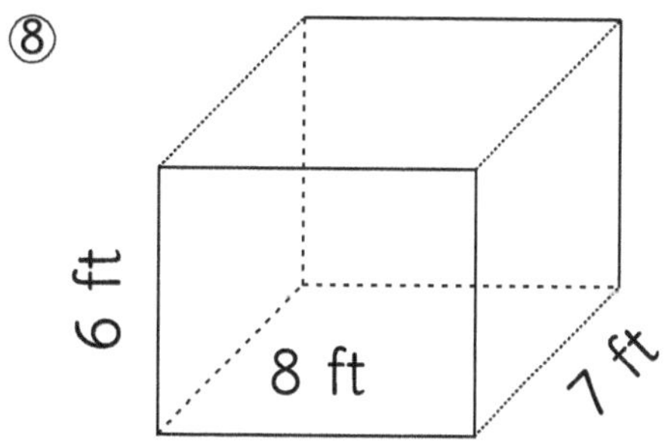

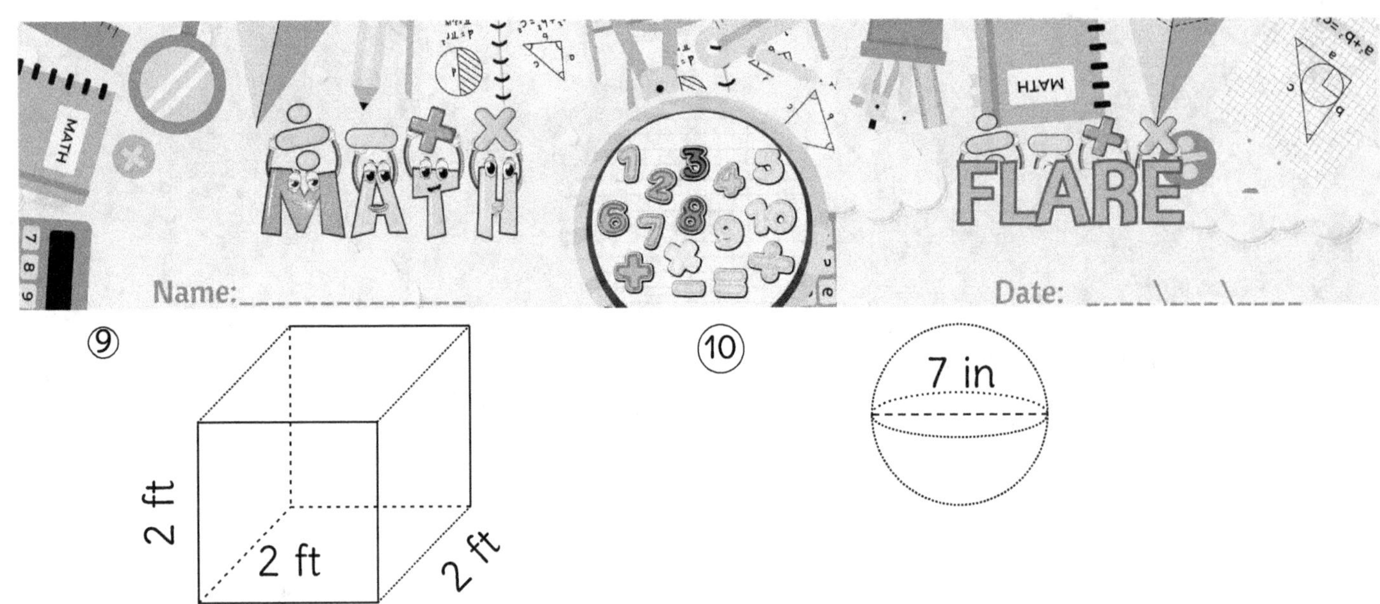

Name:
Date:
⑨
2 ft
2 ft
2 ft
⑩
7 in

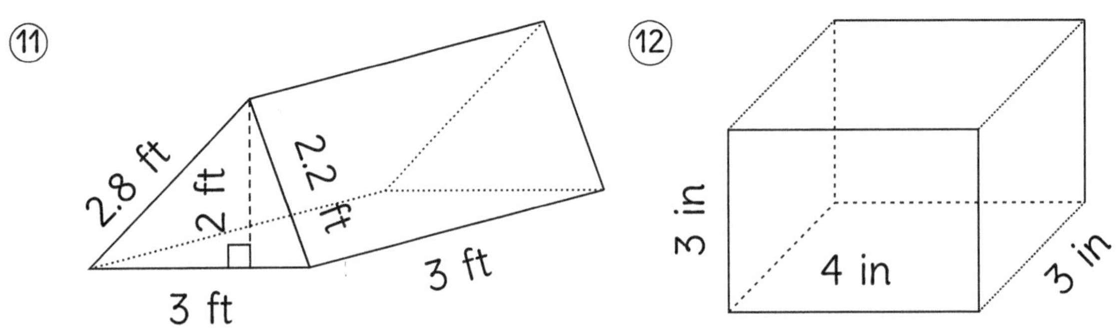

⑪
2.8 ft
2 ft
2.2 ft
3 ft
3 ft
⑫
3 in
4 in
3 in

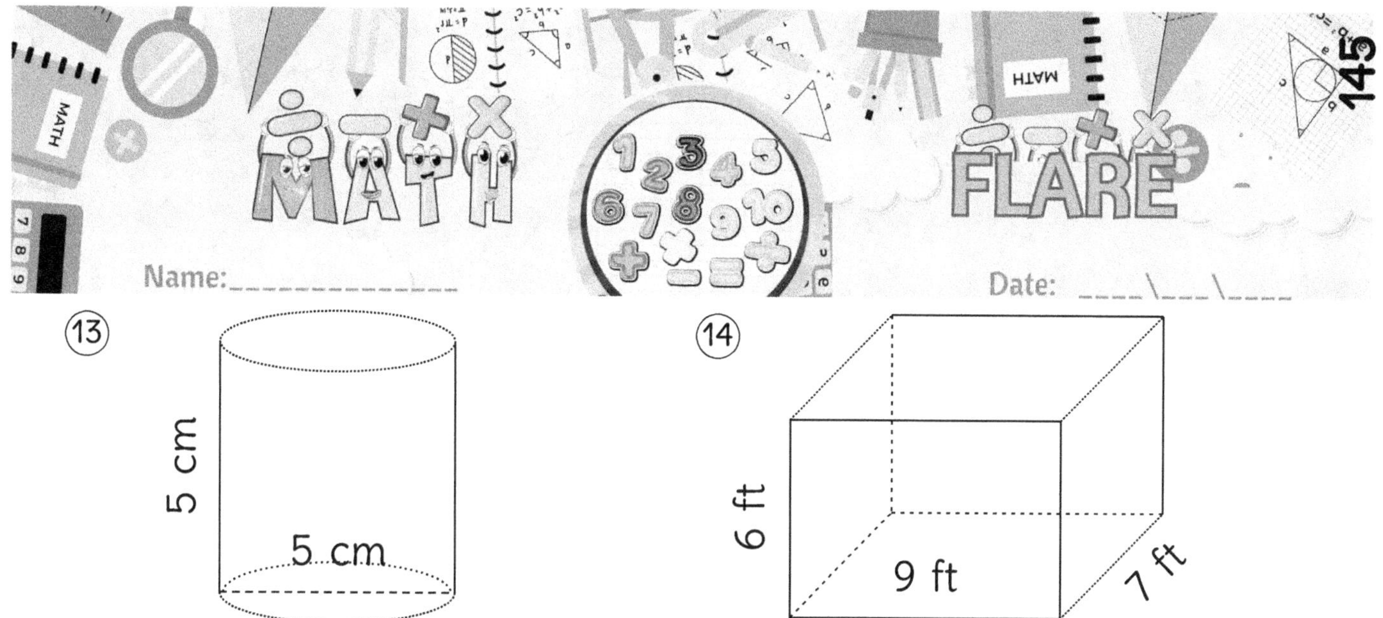

⑬
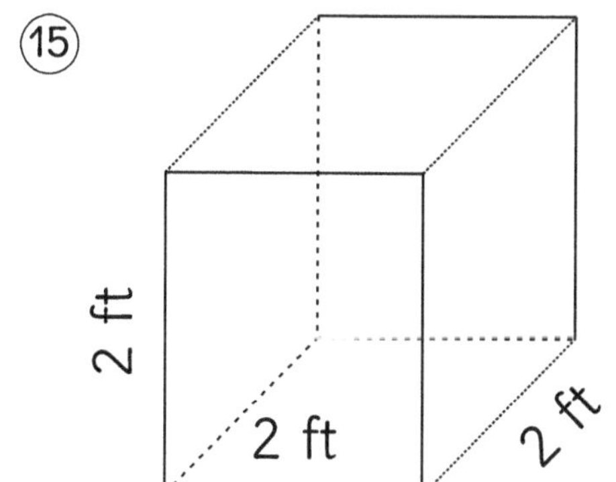

⑭

⑮
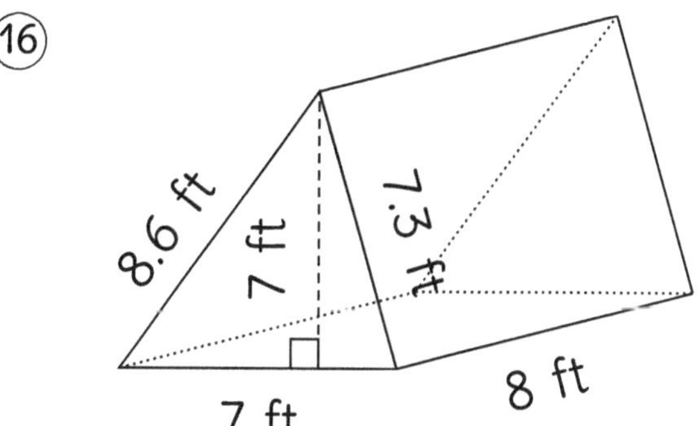

⑯

MathFlare - Math Workbook 8th and 9th Grade

Name: _______________________   Date: _______________

17)

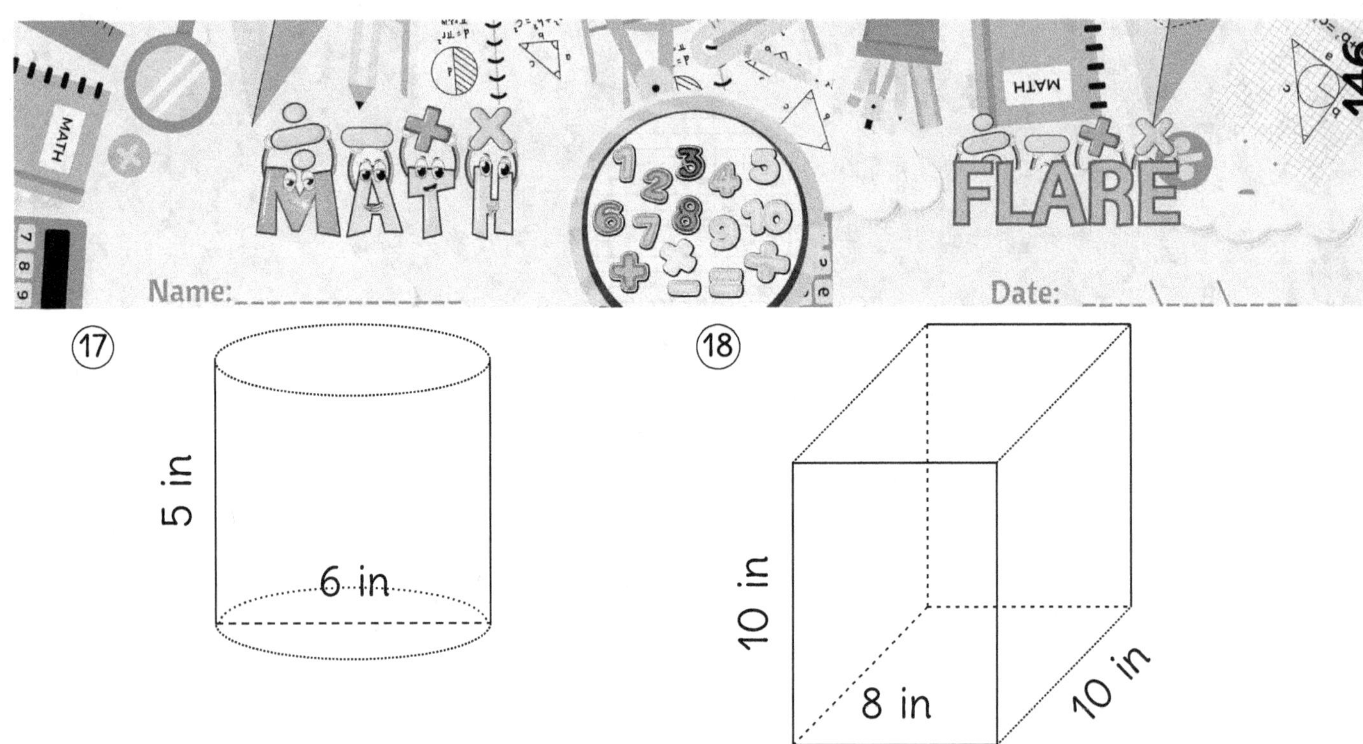

19)

MathFlare - Math Workbook 8th and 9th Grade

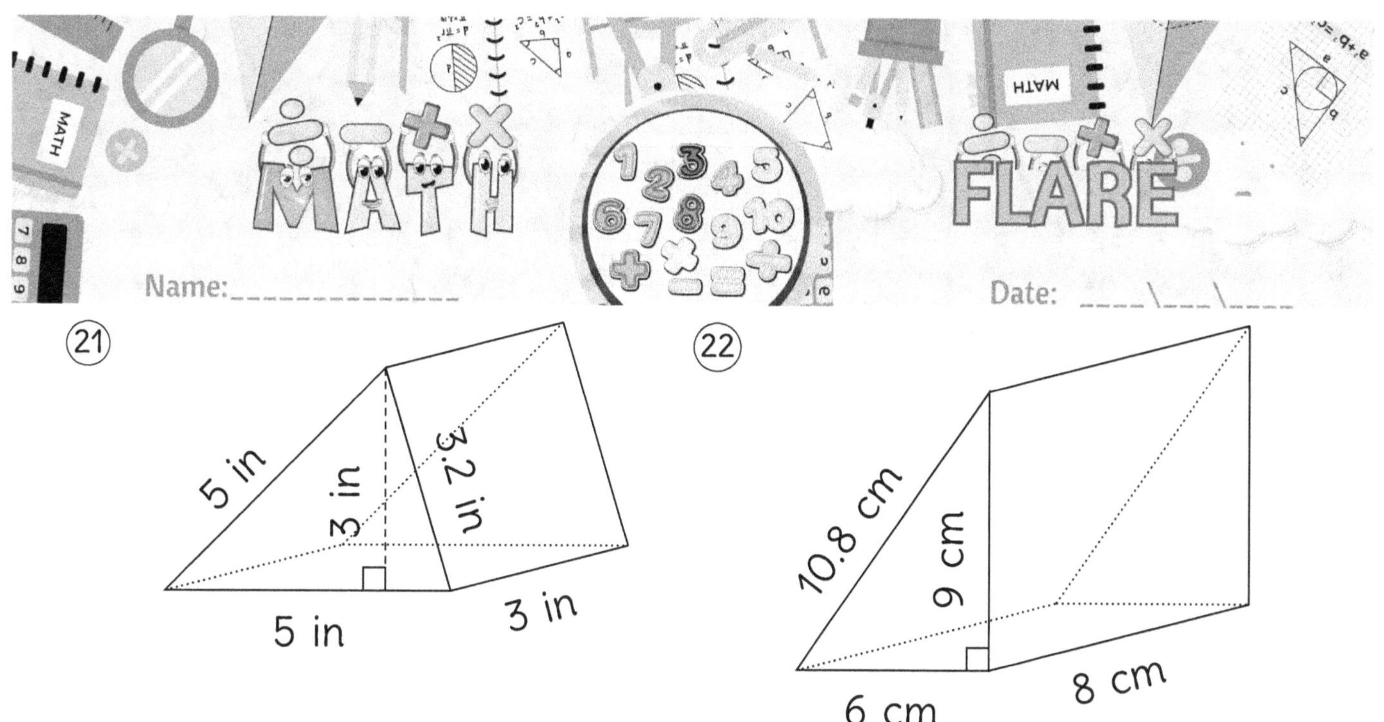
21)
5 in
3 in
3.2 in
5 in
3 in
22)
10.8 cm
9 cm
6 cm
8 cm

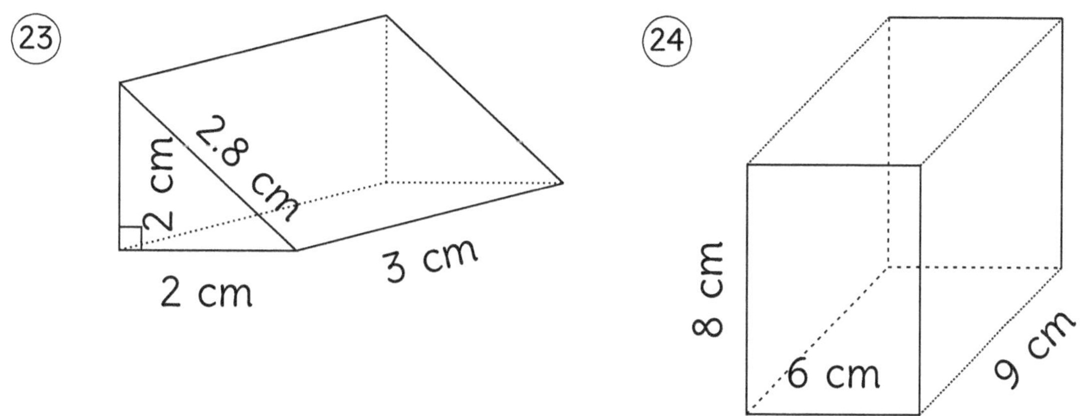
23)
2 cm
2.8 cm
2 cm
3 cm
24)
8 cm
6 cm
9 cm

25) 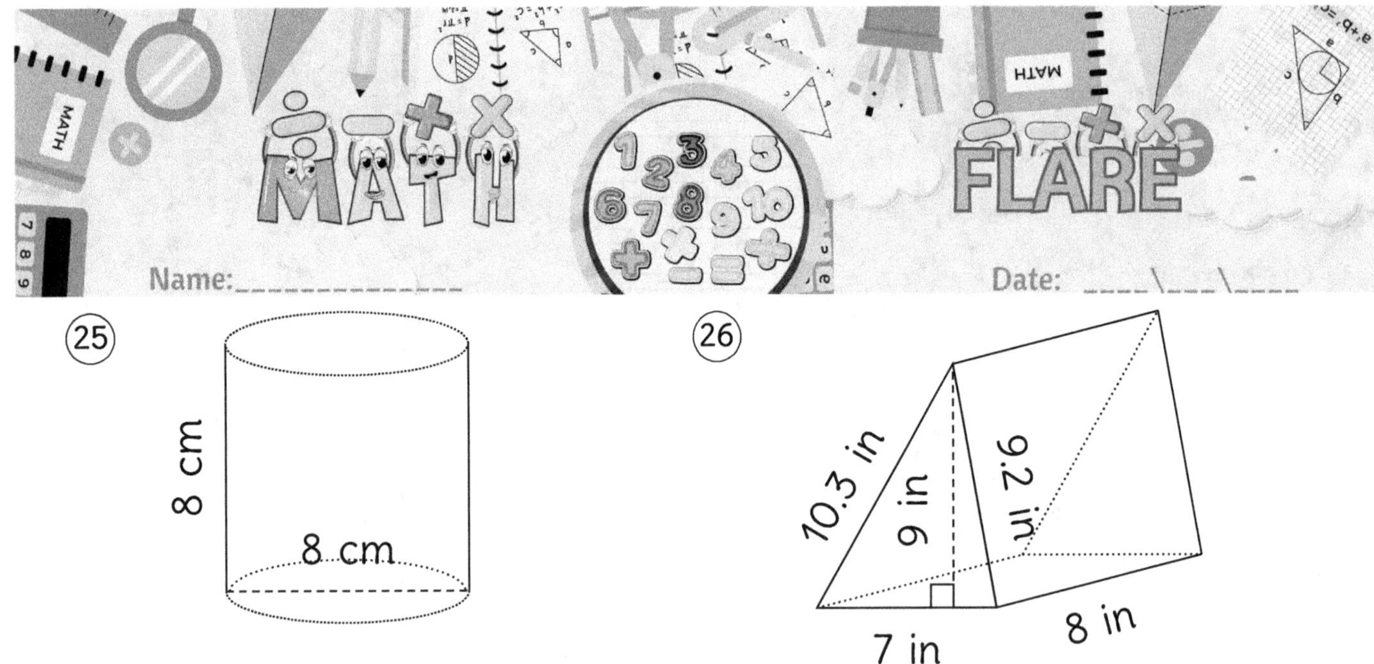

27) 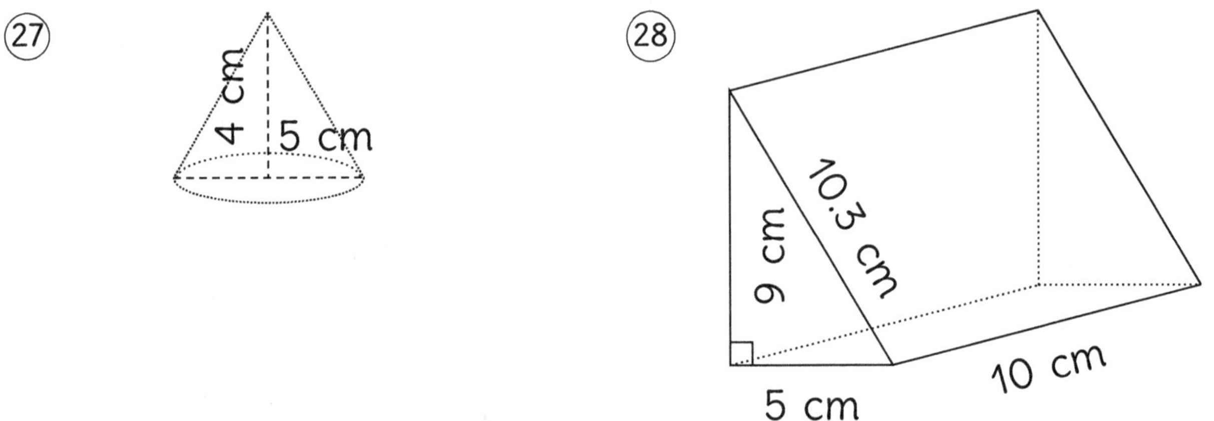

MATH
FLARE
Name:
Date:

(29)

6 in
7 in
8 in

(30)

5 ft
5 ft
6 ft

(31)

4 ft
3 ft

(32)

8 in
8 in
7 in

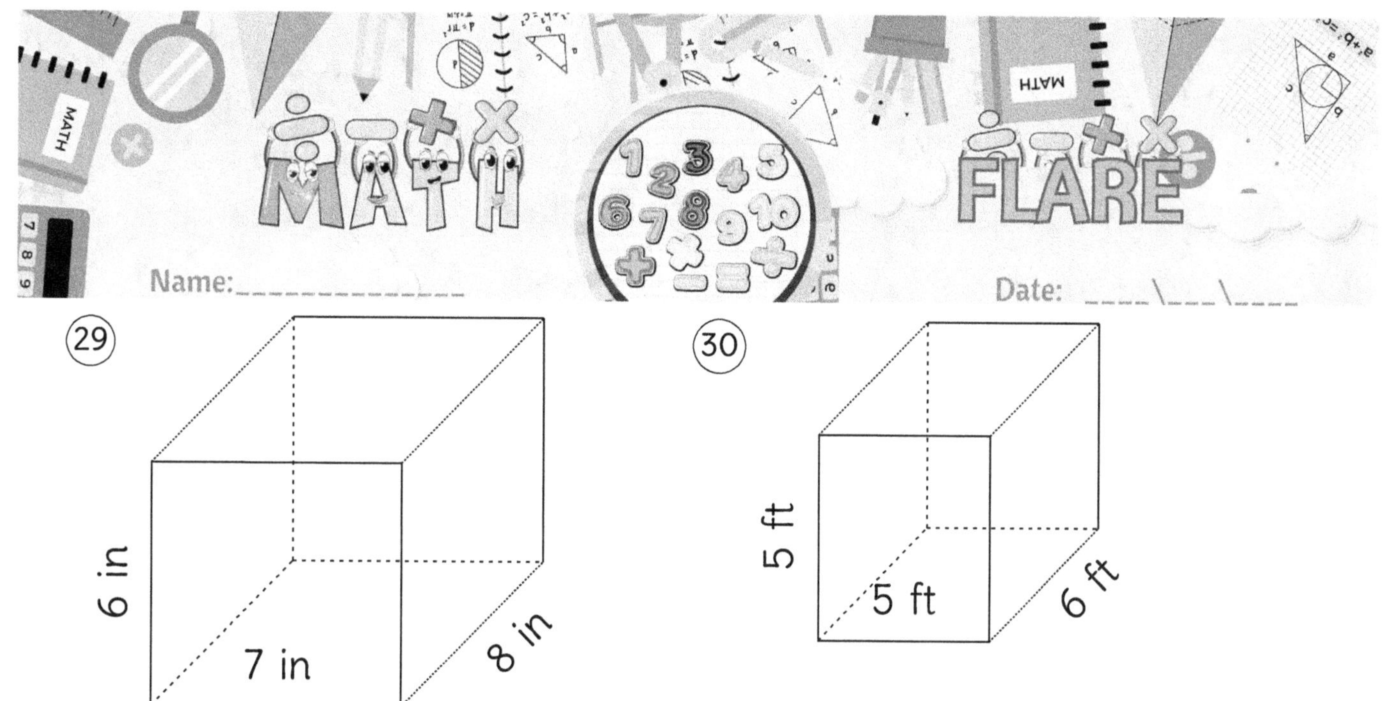

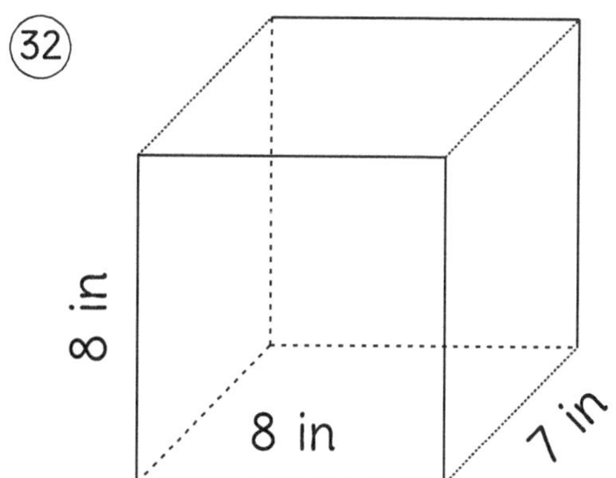

MATH
FLARE
Name:
Date:

(33)

4 cm
8 cm
6 cm

(34)

3 ft
2 ft

(35)

9 ft
7 ft
8 ft

(36)

4 in
5 in
7 in

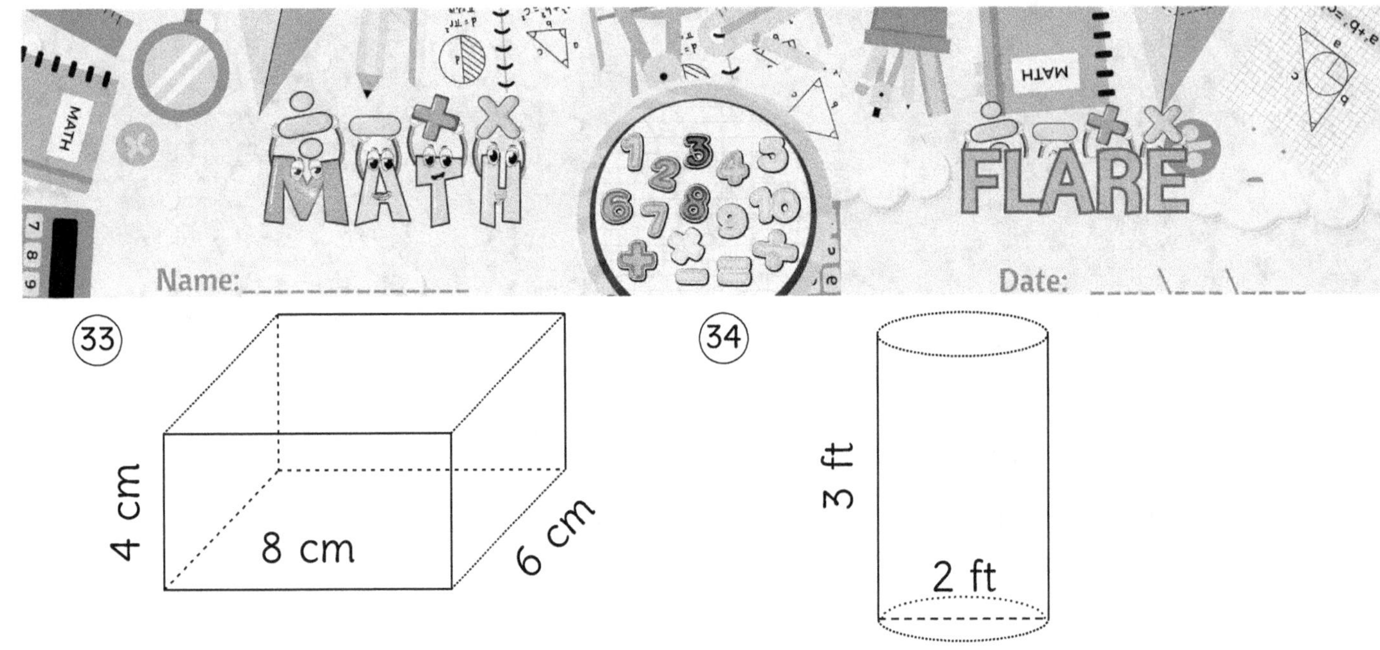

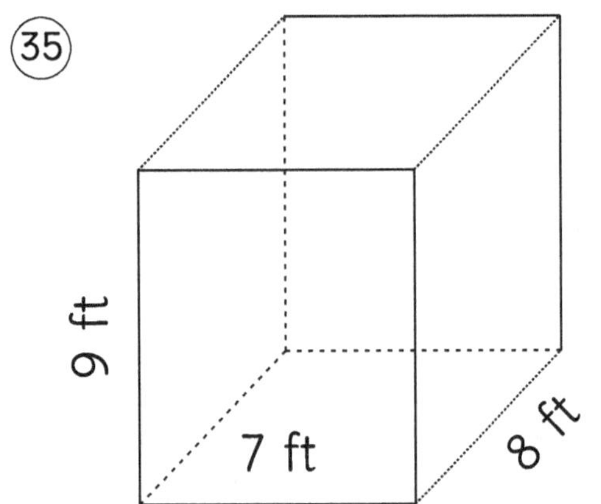

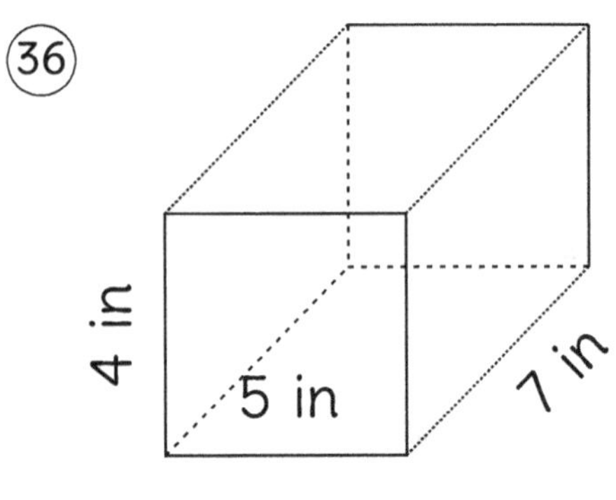

Name:
Date:

(37)

5 ft
9 ft

(38)

3.2 cm
3.2 cm
3 cm
2 cm
4 cm

(39)

7 ft
9.2 ft
6 ft
7 ft

(40)

6 in
11 in
8 in

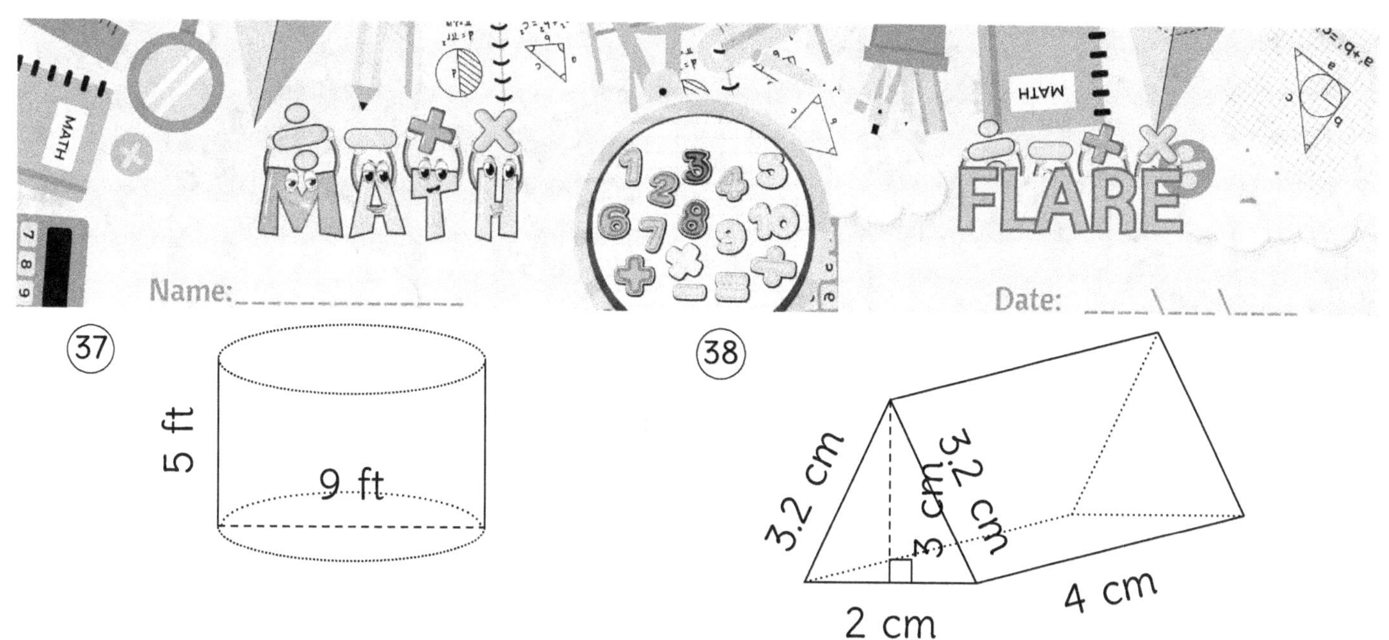

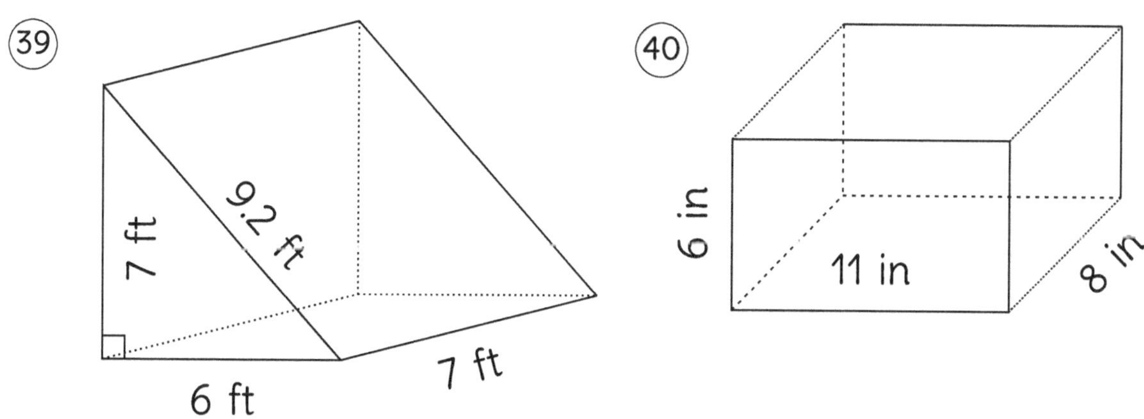

MATH
FLARE
Name:
Date:

41

8 ft
11 ft

42

7 ft
10 ft

43

3 in
3 in
4 in

44

8.5 ft
8 ft
8.5 ft
6 ft
6 ft

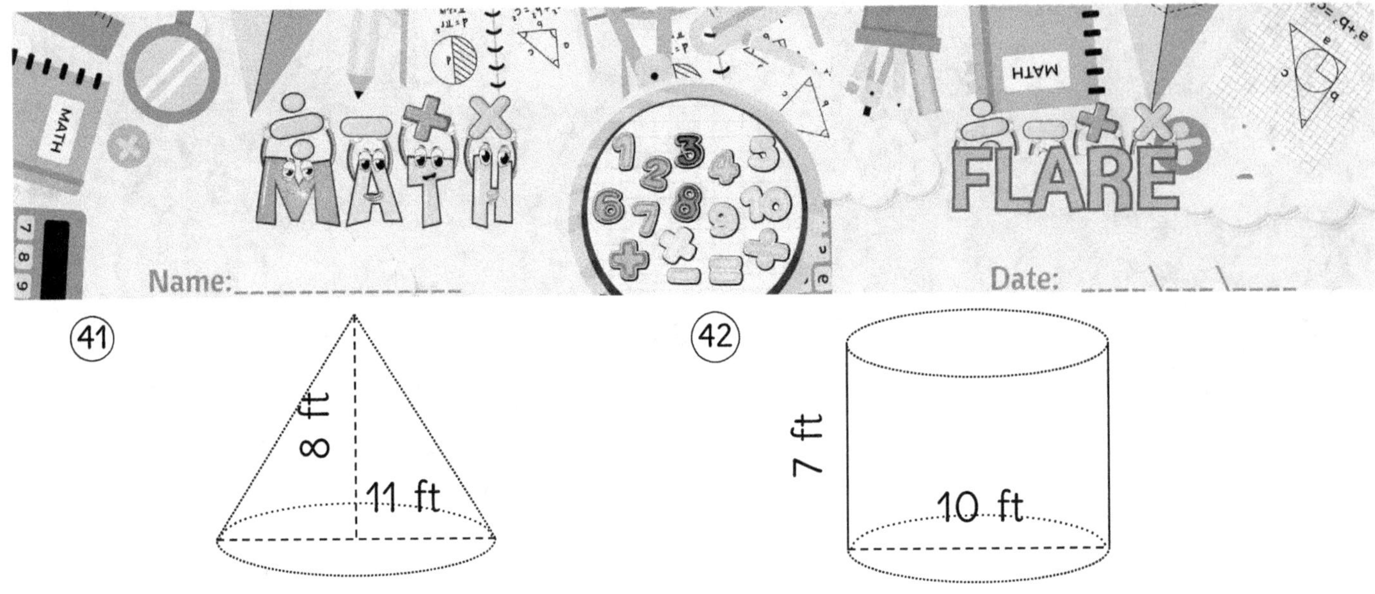

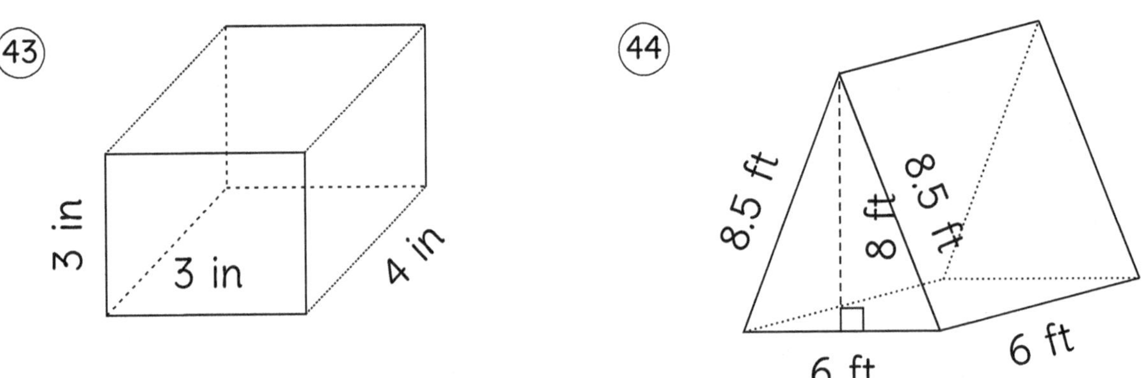

Name:_________________   Date: ____________

45
3.6 cm
3 cm
3.6 cm
4 cm
2 cm
46
4 cm
5 cm
3 cm
4 cm

47
4.5 ft
4 ft
4.5 ft
4 ft
4 ft
48
7 cm
9 cm

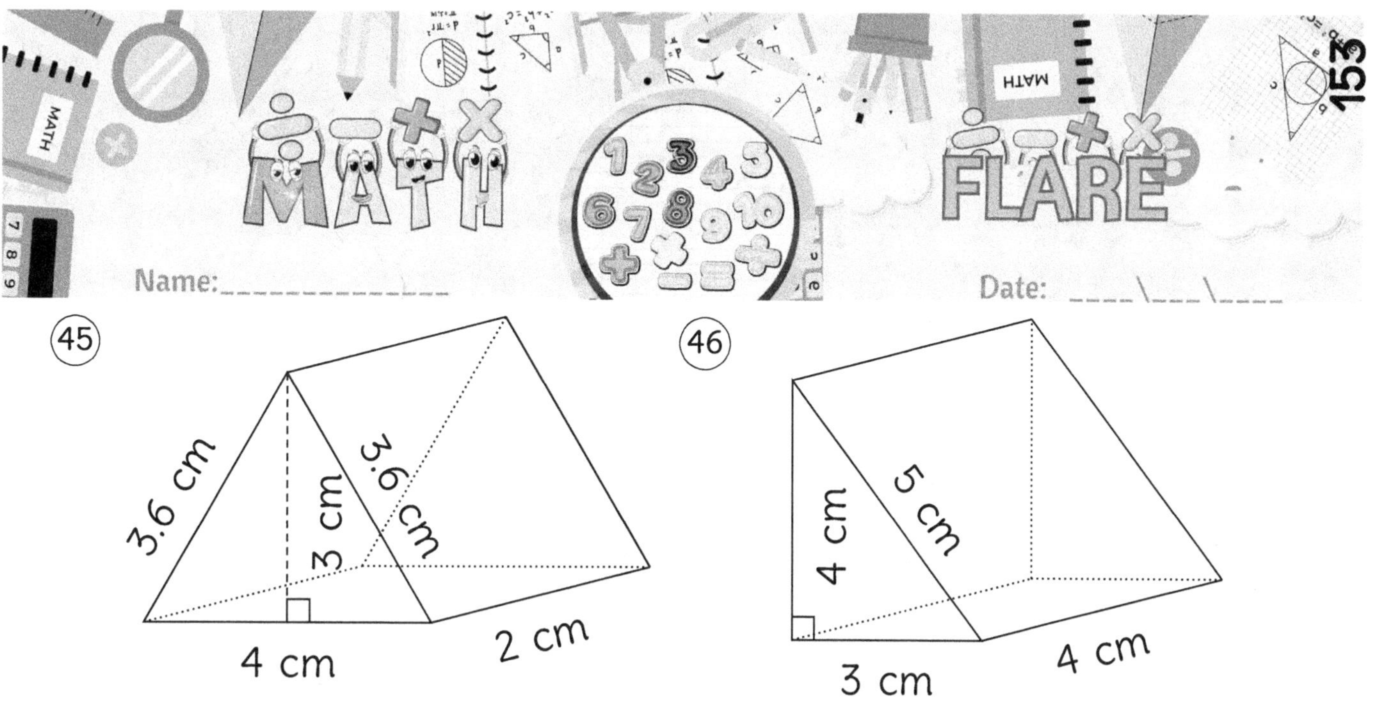

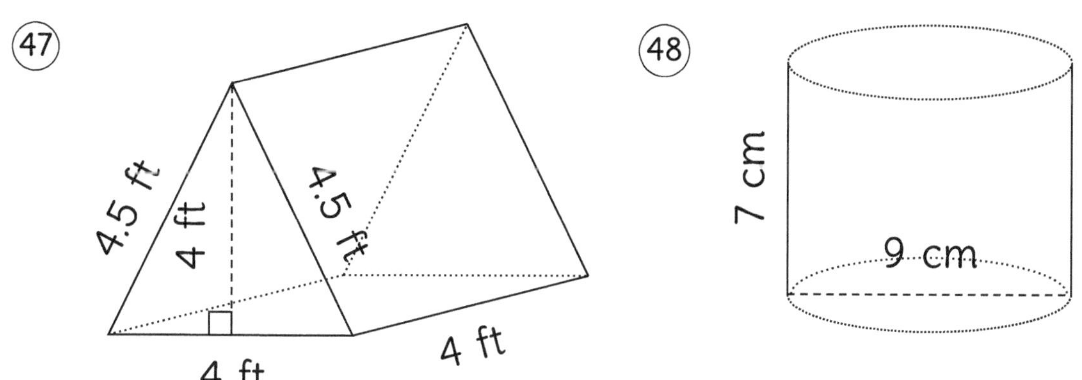

MATH
FLARE
Name:
Date:

(49)

4 in
4 in
4 in

(50)

5 ft
6 ft
4 ft

(51)

6 in
4 in
4 in

(52)

4 ft
3 ft
4 ft

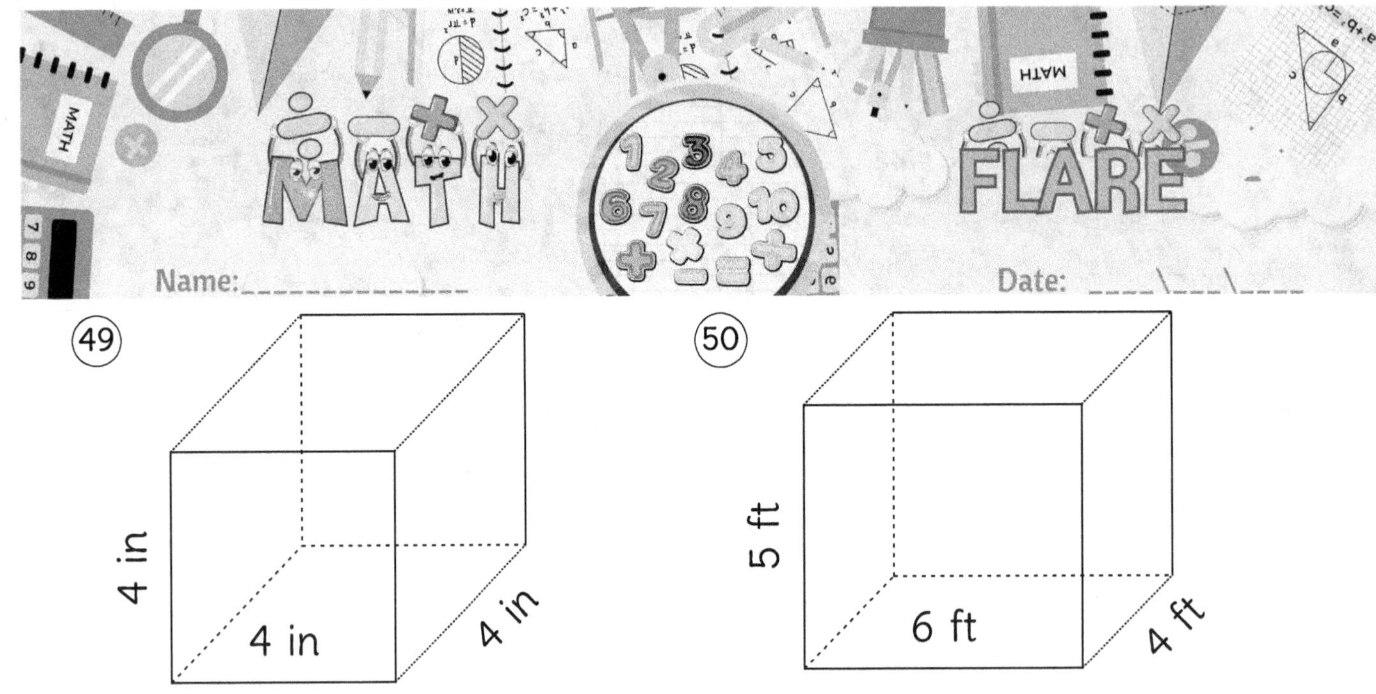

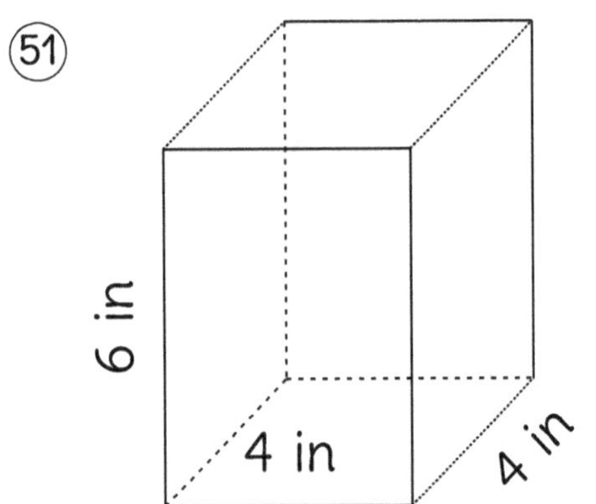

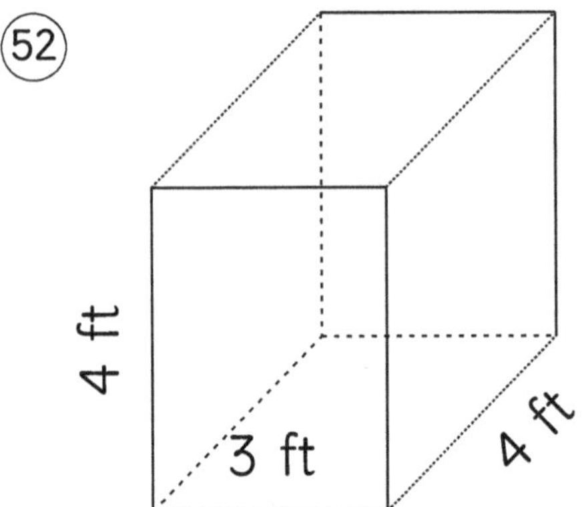

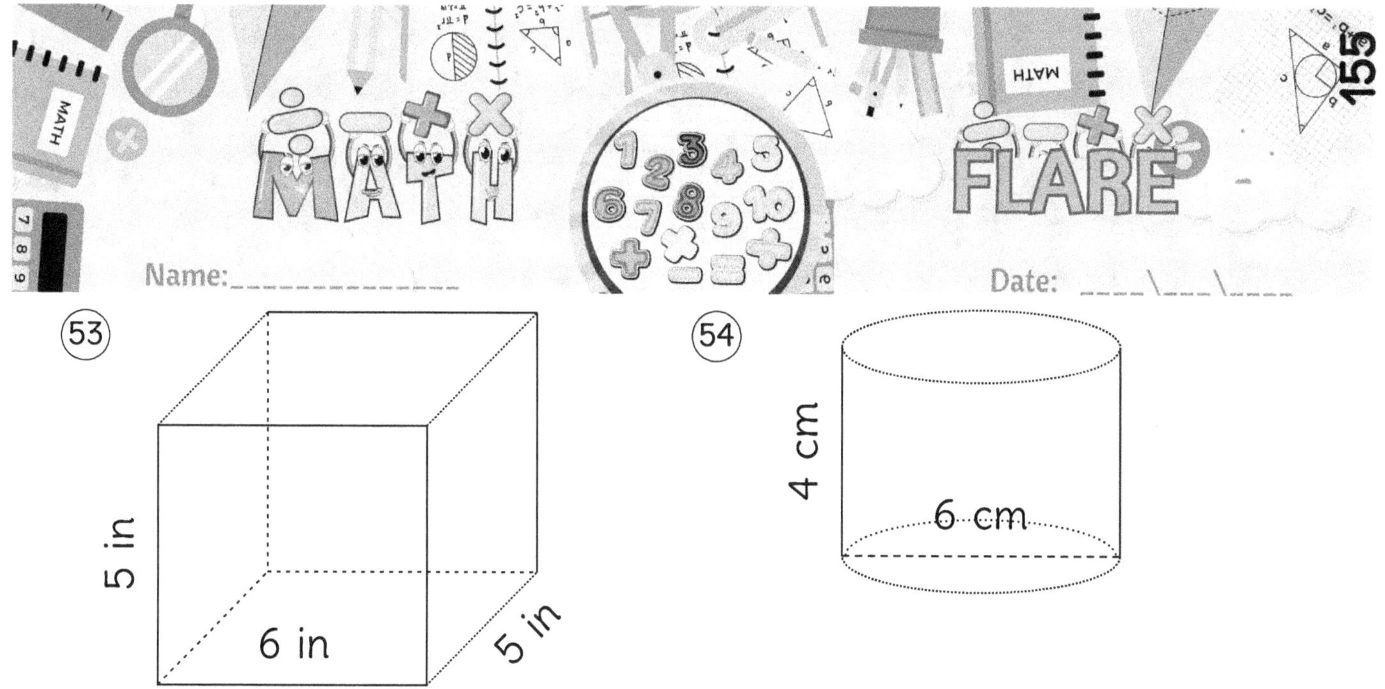

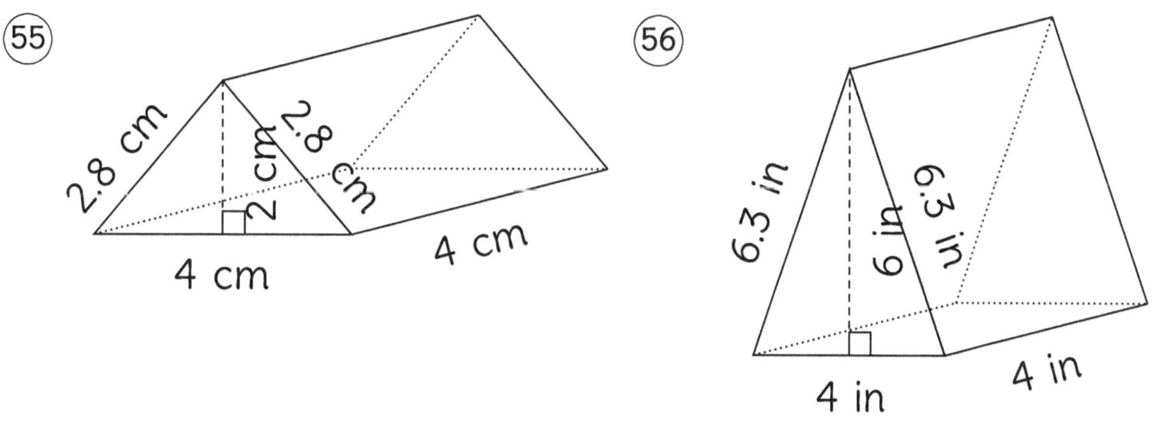

MathFlare - Math Workbook 8th and 9th Grade

Name:________________ Date: ____________

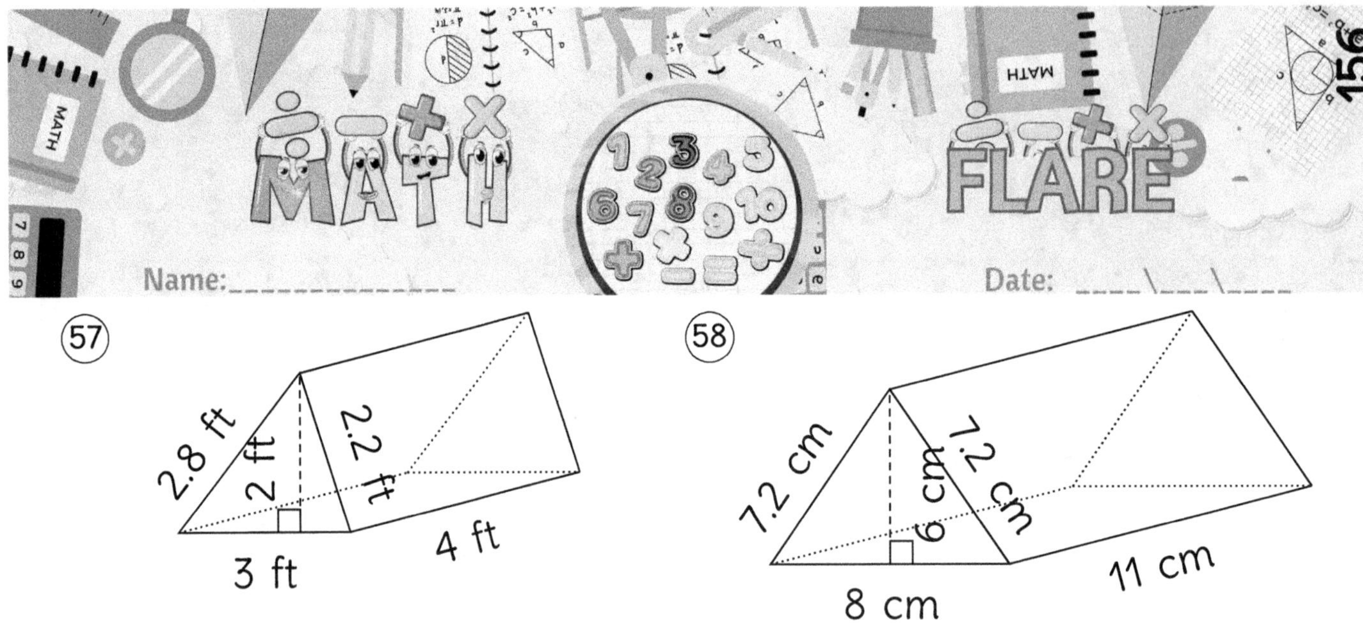

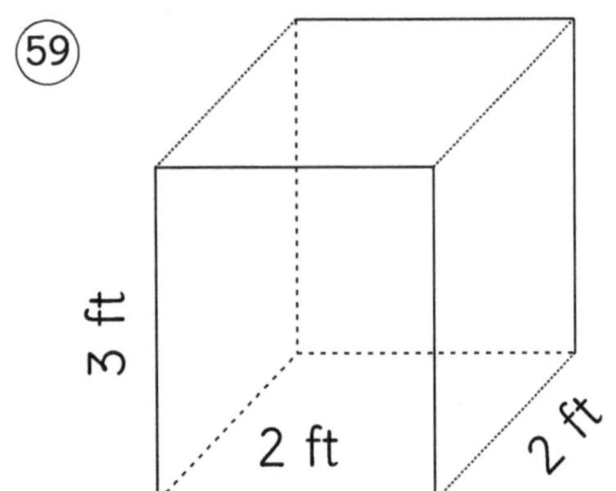

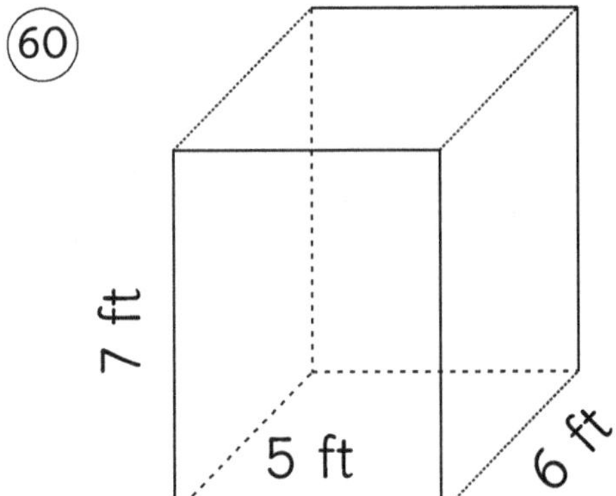

MathFlare - Math Workbook 8th and 9th Grade

Pythagorean Theorem

① 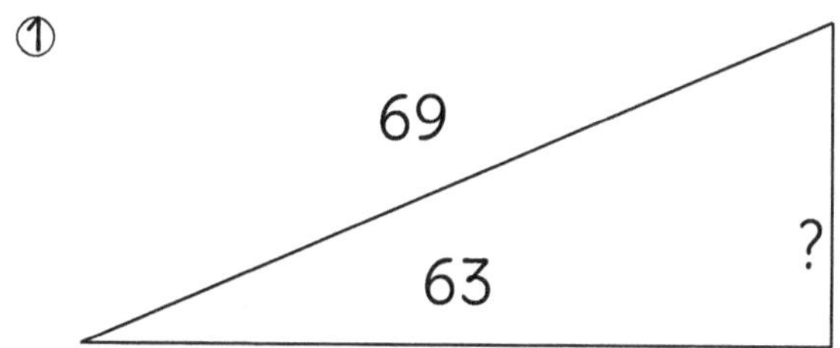

② 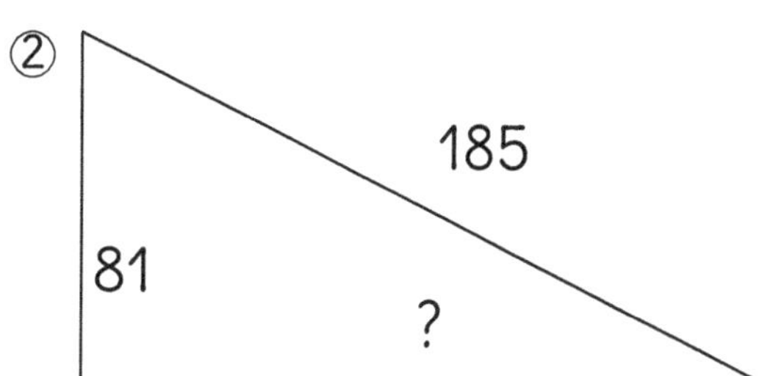

$$c^2 = a^2 + b^2$$
$$69^2 = a^2 + 63^2$$
$$4761 = a^2 + 3969 \quad \text{solve for } a$$
$$4761 - 3969 = a^2 \quad a = \sqrt{792}$$
$$792 = a^2 \quad a \approx 28.14$$

③ 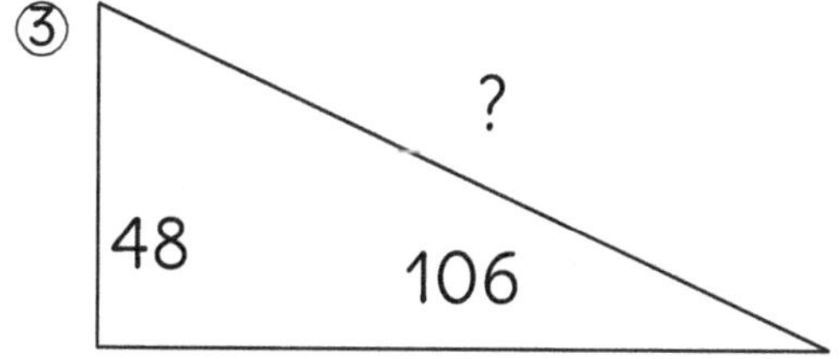

④ 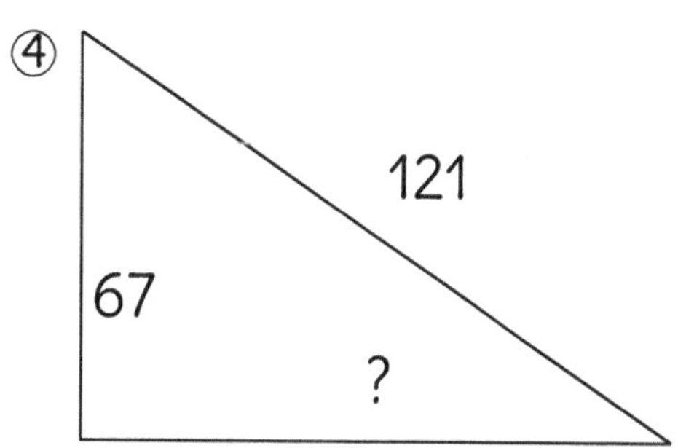

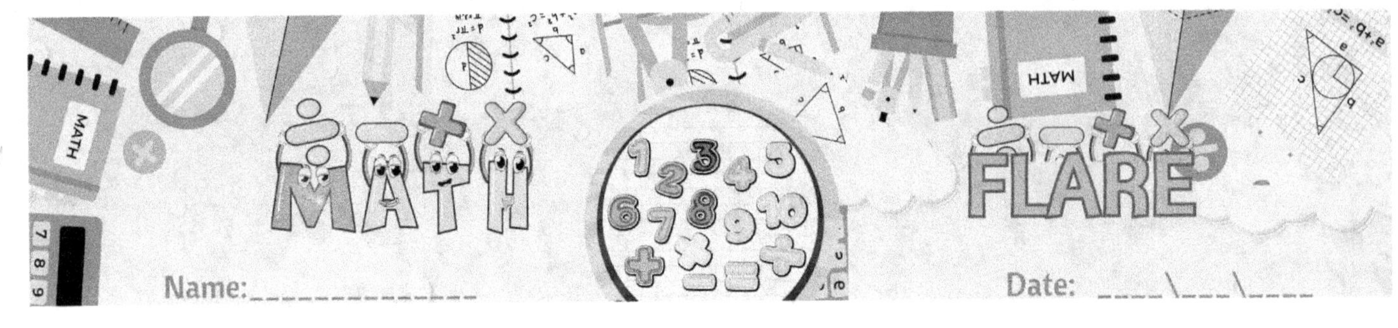

⑤ 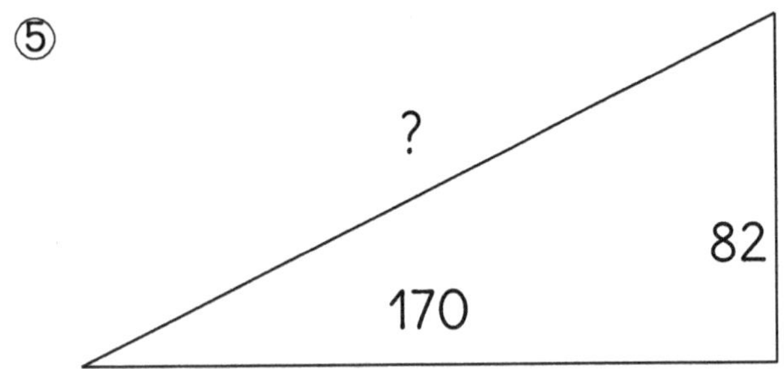

⑥ 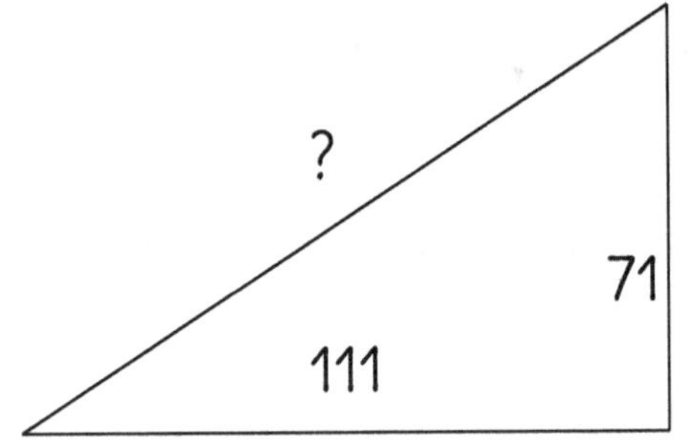

⑦ 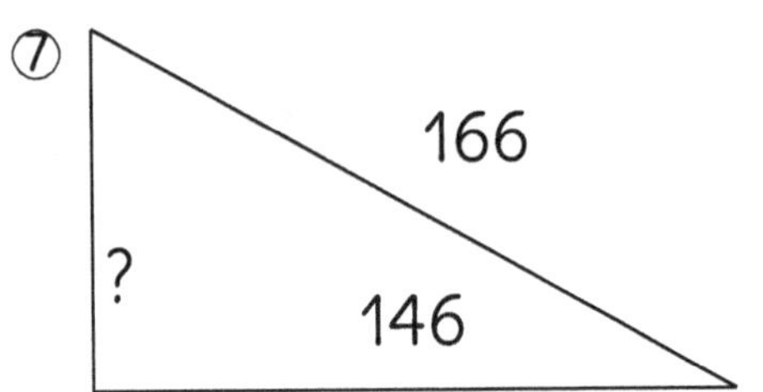

⑧ 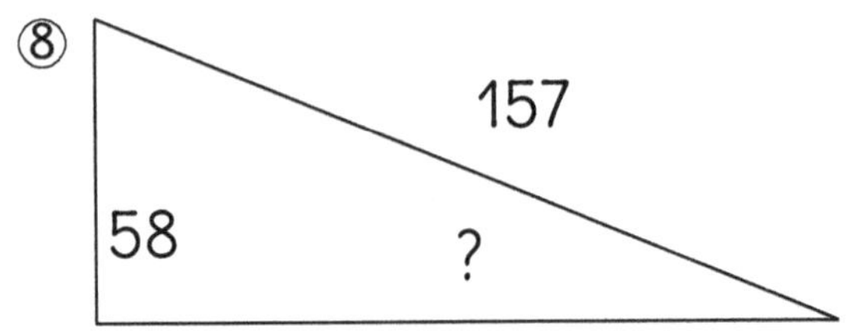

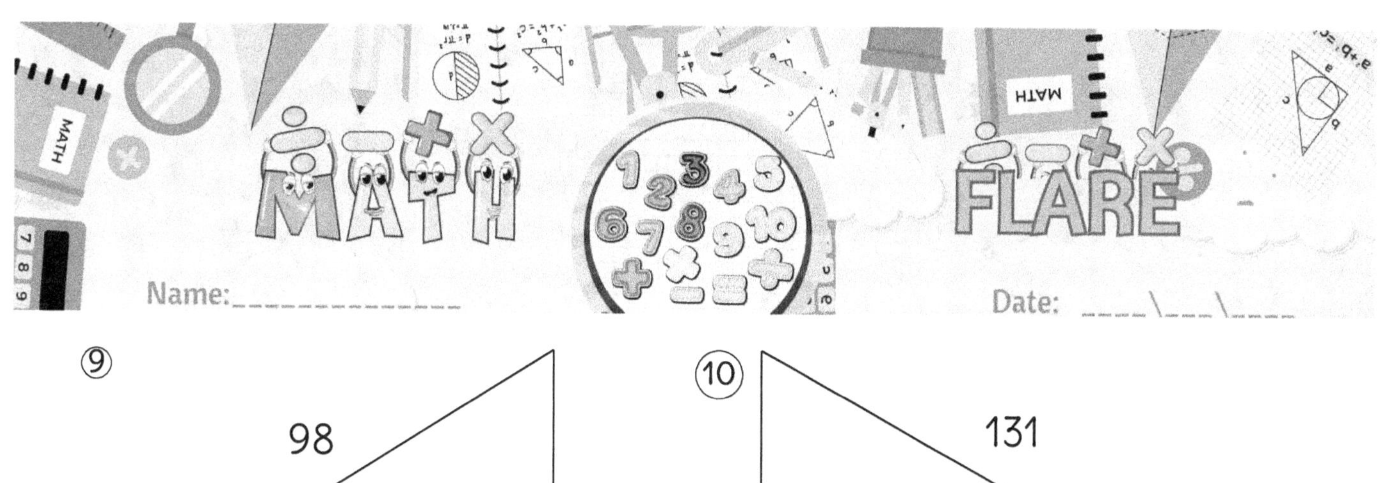

⑨

98

51

?

⑩

131

?

115

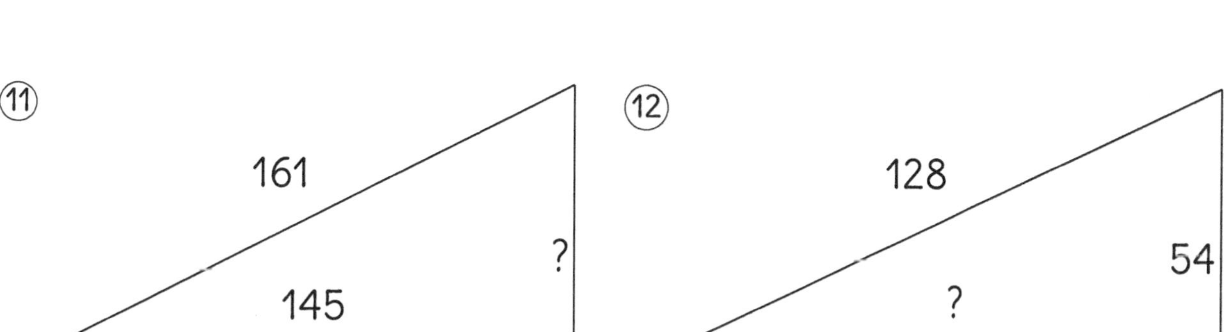

⑪

161

145

?

⑫

128

54

?

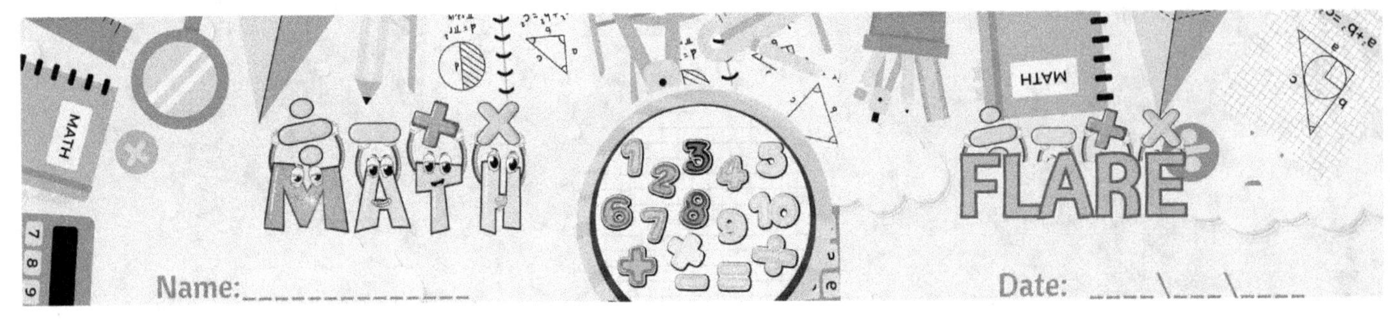
MATH
FLARE
Name:
Date:

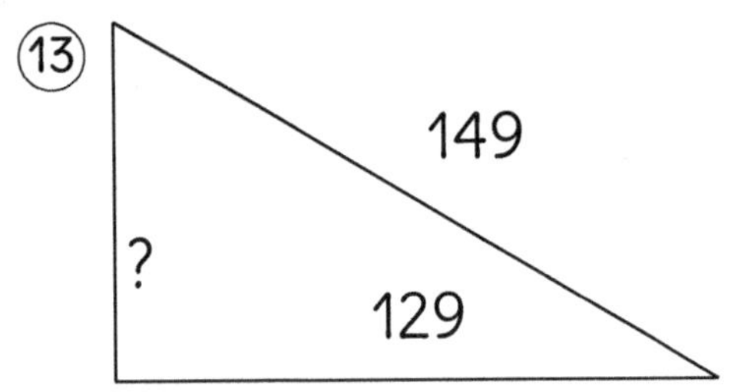
13
149
?
129

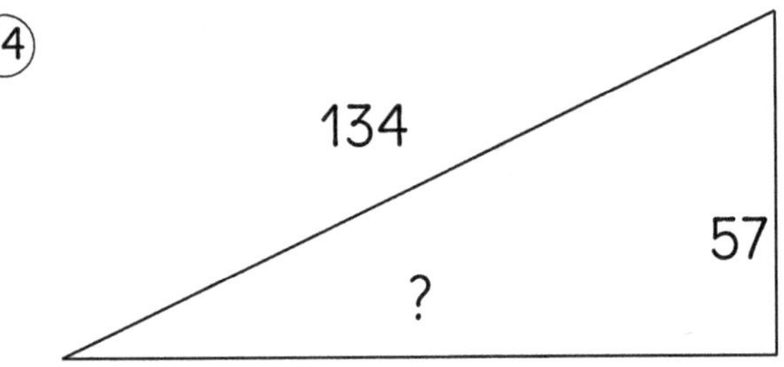
14
134
?
57

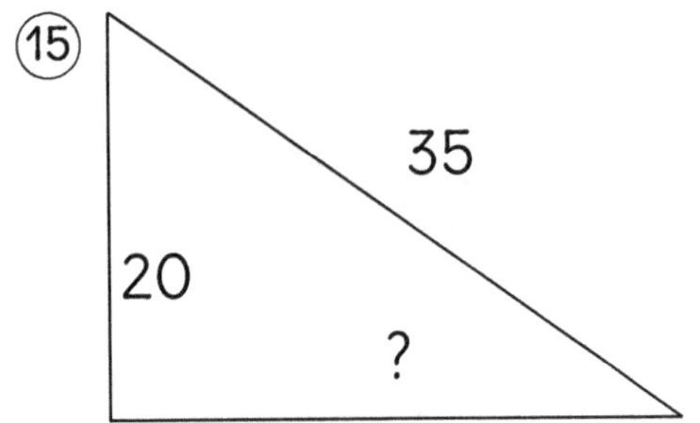
15
35
20
?

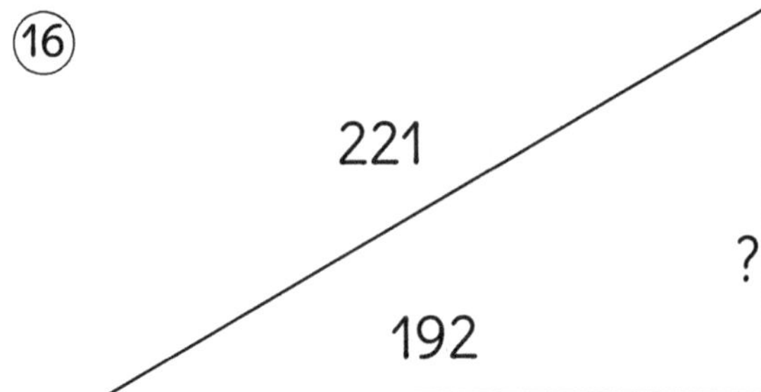
16
221
192
?

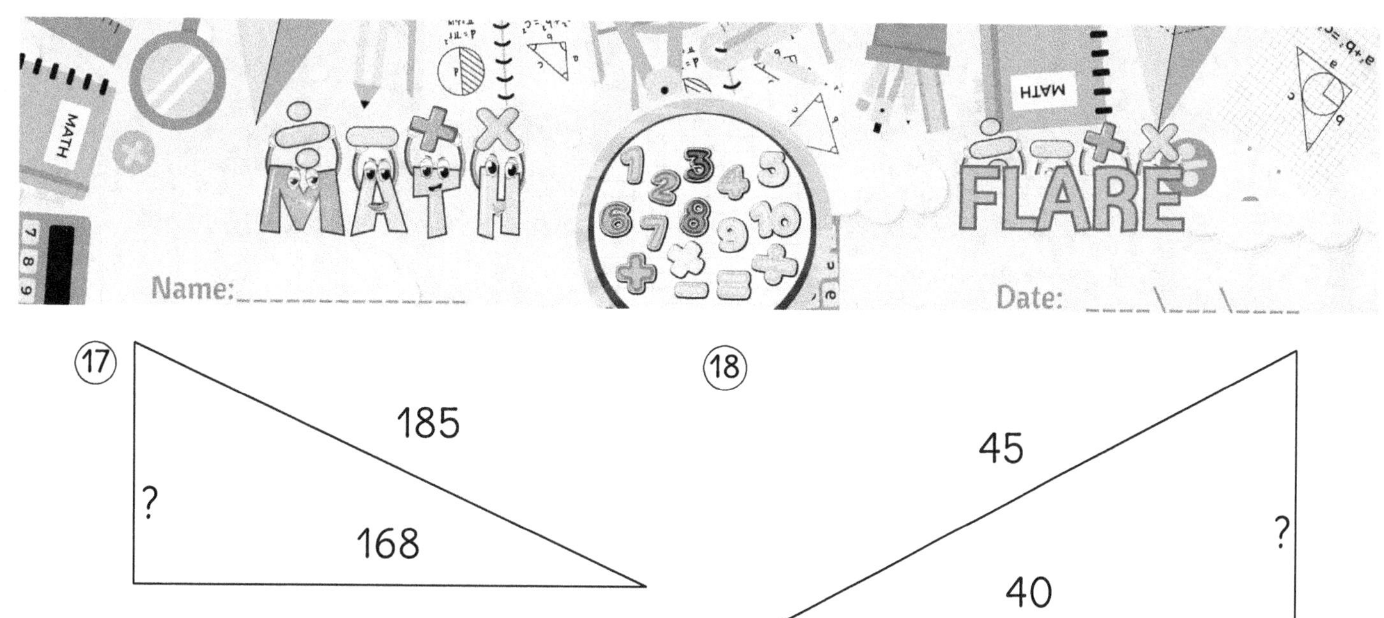

(17)

185

?

168

(18)

45

?

40

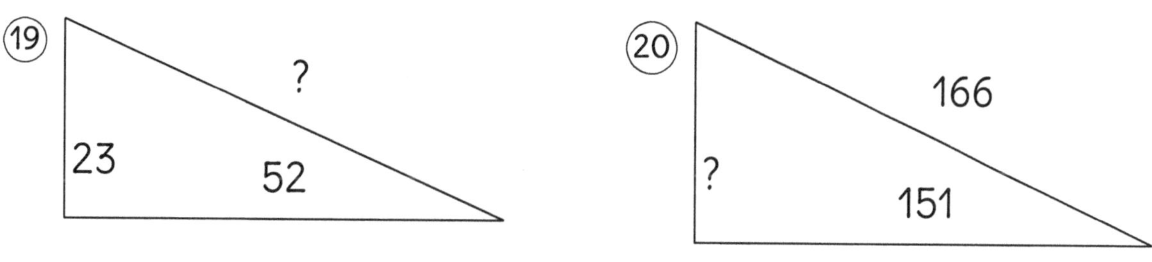

(19)

?

23

52

(20)

166

?

151

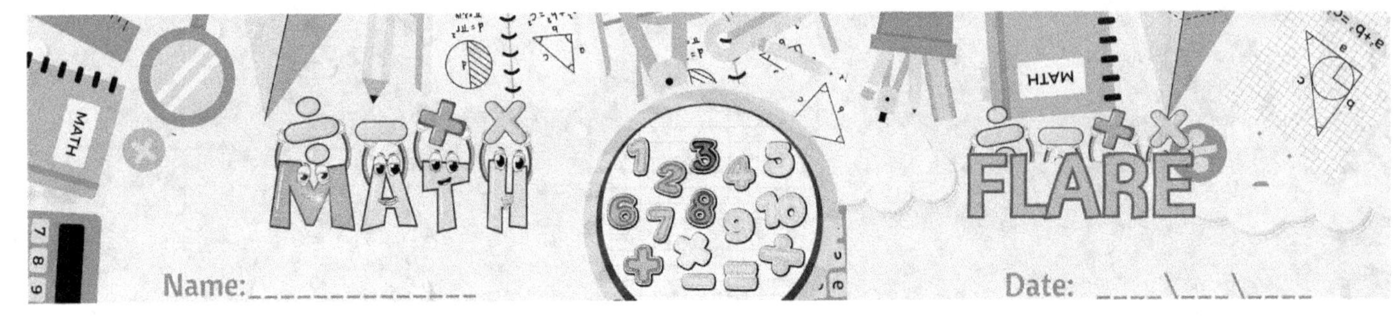

21 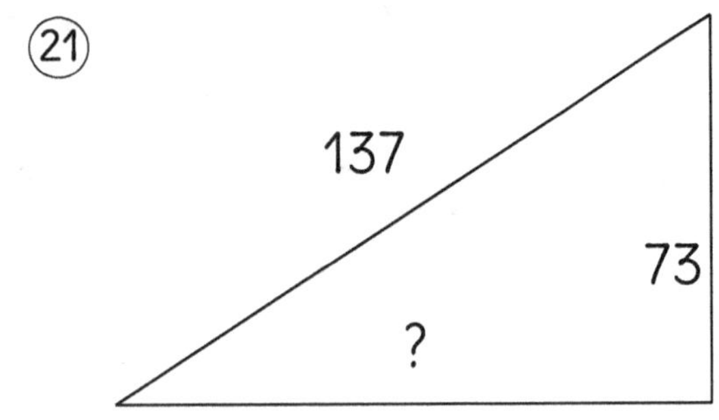

22 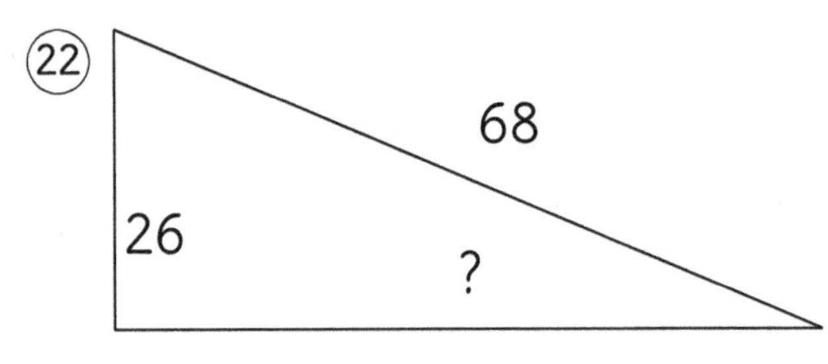

23 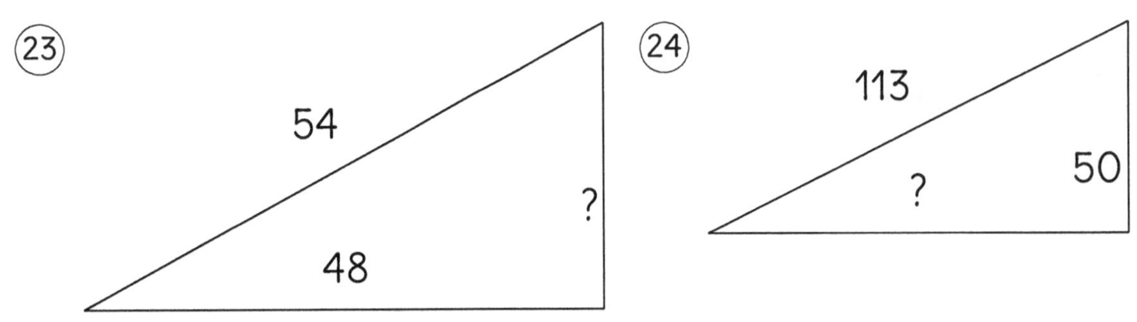

24

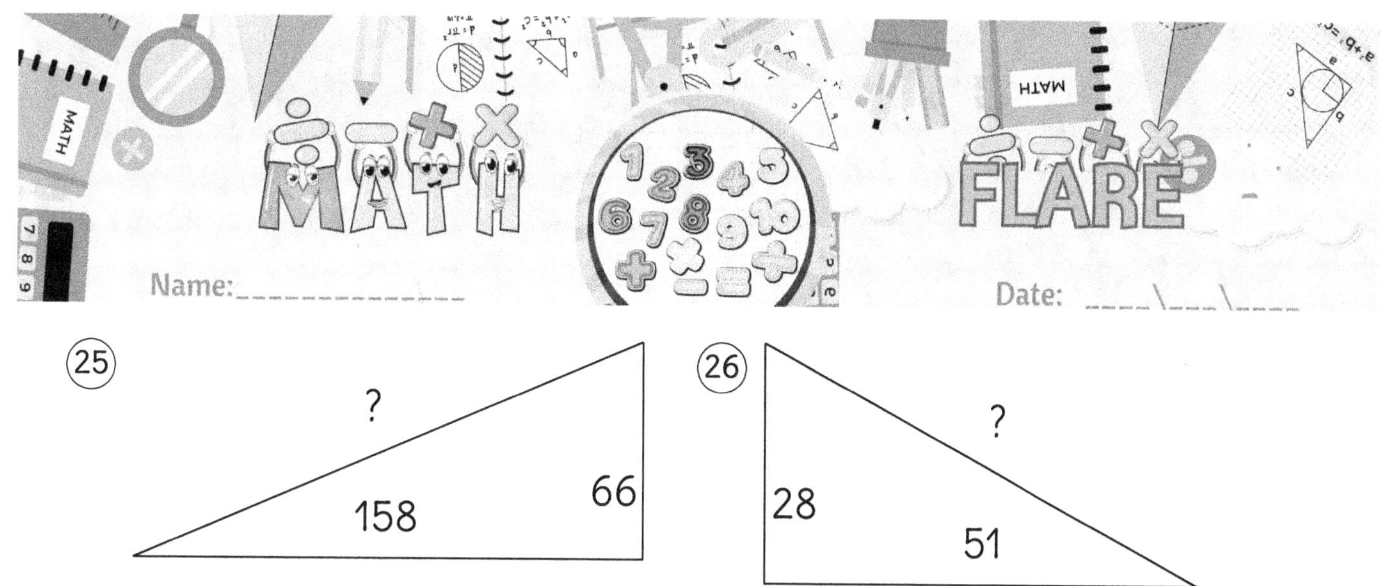

25) 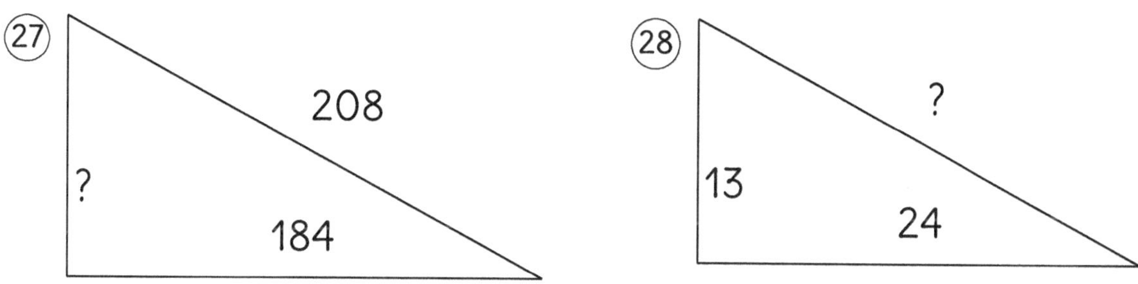

26)

27)

28)

ANSWERS

Page 1: Simplify Expressions

1. -13m - 6	2. 4z	3. 16x - 14	4. -54m + 57
5. 4z + 8	6. 7m	7. 10x + 6	8. 7z - 5
9. m	10. 10x - 2	11. -4m	12. 6k + 7
13. -5z	14. 3z + 6	15. -12m	16. -2x - 7
17. 14x + 6	18. -2z	19. -14x + 11	20. -5y
21. 8x - 10	22. 7k + 8	23. 2m	24. -13y + 2
25. -9z	26. 12k + 10	27. 4y + 5	28. 7m + 10
29. -5z + 14	30. 6k	31. 8x + 1	32. -19z + 21
33. -6m	34. 16x - 6	35. 3x + 1	36. 3k + 3
37. 7	38. -m - 9	39. 72k - 62	40. 3m

Page 9: Order of Operations (PEMDAS)

1. 69	2. 225	3. 4	4. -5	5. 10	6. 210	7. 33
8. 1,027	9. 26	10. -7	11. 48	12. 2	13. 25	14. 4
15. 21	16. 5,187	17. 5	18. 9	19. 2.5	20. -1.8	21. 48
22. 128	23. 60	24. 432	25. 28	26. 16	27. 87	28. 140
29. 19	30. -8	31. 265	32. 12	33. 14	34. 15	35. -3
36. -11	37. 21	38. 5	39. -10	40. 19	41. 10	42. -1
43. 10	44. -13	45. 51	46. 3	47. -0.2	48. 9	

Page 14:   Simplifying Equations
1. -63   2. -15   3. -23   4. 1   5. 27   6. 21   7. -3.7   8. 24

Page 15:   Simplifying Equations
1. -7   2. 1.5   3. 22   4. -0.3   5. -12   6. 4   7. -105   8. -31

Page 16:   Simplifying Equations
1. 5   2. 40   3. 11   4. -59   5. 6   6. 57   7. -75   8. 48

Page 17:   Simplifying Equations
1. -11   2. -31   3. -2   4. 48   5. -7   6. 33   7. 0   8. -8

Page 18:   Simplifying Equations
1. -14   2. 3   3. 5   4. 36   5. -0.6   6. 0.9   7. 16   8. 7

Page 19:   Simplifying Equations
1. -5   2. 0.2   3. 2   4. -17   5. 19   6. -1.2   7. 3   8. -5

Page 20:   Simplifying Equations
1. 28   2. 25   3. 0   4. 69   5. -36   6. -21   7. 30   8. 0.8

Page 21:   Solving Inequalities
1. $k > 8$ 2. $x \leq 5$ 3. $k > -3$ 4. $k > -3$ 5. $y \leq -3$
6. $x \leq -1/3$ 7. $z \leq -4$ 8. $y < 5$ 9. $k > 36$ 10. $z < 5/6$
11. $m < -5$ 12. $m \geq -1$ 13. $z > 3/5$ 14. $m \geq -8$ 15. $m \geq -9$
16. $k \leq -3$ 17. $z \geq 1$ 18. $k > -5/7$ 19. $m \geq 4$ 20. $k > -12$
21. $m \leq 8$ 22. $z > 2/3$ 23. $m < -4$ 24. $m \geq 15$ 25. $m > 12$
26. $k \geq 14$ 27. $k \leq -12$ 28. $z \leq -4/5$ 29. $z \geq 2/3$ 30. $k > 11$
31. $z > 17$ 32. $y < -5$ 33. $m \geq -1$ 34. $z < 2/5$ 35. $y \leq 2$

36. m < 42   37. m ≥ 11   38. z < 40   39. k ≥ 13   40. k ≤ -1

Page 31: Verbal Algebra Expressions

1. 11   2. 3, 12   3. 8, 84   4. 7, 36   5. 6

6. 1, 4   7. 11   8. 7   9. 2, 4   10. 22, 6

11. 0   12. 22, 8   13. 8   14. 10, 1   15. 10

16. 2   17. 9   18. 24   19. 13   20. 7

21. 6   22. 4   23. 9   24. 4, 6   25. 3, 23

26. 18   27. 14   28. 6   29. 12, 9   30. 11

31. 3, 8   32. 1   33. 11   34. 11, 9   35. 7, 14, 35

36. 12   37. 2   38. 21   39. 8   40. 5

41. 2   42. 12   43. 12, 4   44. 8   45. 2

46. 6   47. 10   48. 50   49. 3   50. 6, 15

51. 8, 56   52. 5, 7   53. 3, 18   54. 8   55. 14

56. 15, 6   57. 4, 1   58. 2   59. 3   60. 4, 2

61. 16

Page 45: Equations (Two Sides)

1. $z = 9$ 2. $m = 8$ 3. $x = 2$ 4. $x = 1$ 5. $z = 8$ 6. $x = 1$

7. $x = 3$ 8. $m = 7$ 9. $k = 6$ 10. $x = 3$ 11. $z = 4$ 12. $y = 8$

13. $m = 4$ 14. $z = 6$ 15. $k = 4$ 16. $m = 1$ 17. $y = 5$ 18. $z = 2$

19. $k = 7$ 20. $y = 9$ 21. $y = 4$ 22. $k = 5$ 23. $m = 5$ 24. $m = 8$

25. $y = 4$ 26. $z = 3$ 27. $m = 9$ 28. $x = 6$ 29. $m = 3$ 30. $m = 3$

31. m = 9   32. x = 1   33. x = 8   34. k = 9   35. y = 6   36. m = 6

37. y = 5   38. z = 5   39. y = 3   40. x = 2   41. k = 1   42. k = 7

43. z = 1   44. m = 5   45. z = 4   46. x = 8   47. m = 9   48. x = 9

49. x = 4   50. z = 8   51. m = 7   52. z = 3   53. x = 7   54. m = 3

55. z = 2   56. y = 6   57. z = 2   58. k = 1   59. y = 4   60. k = 5

61. k = 5   62. k = 2   63. k = 7   64. z = 2   65. m = 5   66. x = 6

67. k = 1   68. m = 8   69. k = 7   70. y = 8   71. x = 2   72. z = 1

73. k = 9   74. x = 9   75. y = 2   76. x = 6   77. m = 3   78. z = 7

79. x = 6

Page 61: Percent

1. 2.928   2. 49.0%   3. 2.0%   4. 1.944   5. 0.2%

6. 55.97   7. 6   8. 0.6%   9. 4   10. 8.9%

11. 2   12. 28.6%   13. 0.8%   14. 1.377   15. 2.214

16. 0.008   17. 0.544   18. 0.024   19. 0.5%   20. 5.2%

21. 1.112   22. 8.6%   23. 0.8%   24. 85.05   25. 333

26. 49.434   27. 7   28. 8.6%   29. 0.388   30. 6.8%

31. 47   32. 0.072   33. 0.3%   34. 564   35. 30.87

36. 38   37. 2   38. 691   39. 186.438   40. 7.9%

41. 94   42. 1.7%   43. 6   44. 28.9   45. 763

46. 0.624

Page 66: Convert: Ratio, Fraction, Percent, and Decimals

1.

	Ratio	Fraction	Percent	Decimal
a.	12:15	12/15	80%	0.8
b.	1:2	1/2	50%	0.5
c.	4:15	4/15	26.7%	0.267
d.	2:6	2/6	33.3%	0.333
e.	5:7	5/7	71.4%	0.714
f.	7:18	7/18	38.9%	0.389
g.	3:6	3/6	50%	0.5
h.	2:4	2/4	50%	0.5
i.	4:7	4/7	57.1%	0.571
j.	7:12	7/12	58.3%	0.583
k.	1:1	1/1	100%	1
l.	3:19	3/19	15.8%	0.158
m.	3:7	3/7	42.9%	0.429
n.	13:15	13/15	86.7%	0.867
o.	7:16	7/16	43.8%	0.438

2.

	Ratio	Fraction	Percent	Decimal
a.	5:6	5/6	83.3%	0.833
b.	18:20	18/20	90%	0.9
c.	12:19	12/19	63.2%	0.632
d.	3:7	3/7	42.9%	0.429
e.	13:13	13/13	100%	1
f.	1:2	1/2	50%	0.5
g.	2:16	2/16	12.5%	0.125
h.	2:5	2/5	40%	0.4
i.	1:19	1/19	5.3%	0.053
j.	1:15	1/15	6.7%	0.067
k.	1:4	1/4	25%	0.25
l.	14:16	14/16	87.5%	0.875
m.	8:18	8/18	44.4%	0.444
n.	7:13	7/13	53.8%	0.538
o.	8:17	8/17	47.1%	0.471

3.

	Ratio	Fraction	Percent	Decimal
a.	2:2	2/2	100%	1
b.	4:10	4/10	40%	0.4
c.	8:10	8/10	80%	0.8
d.	1:4	1/4	25%	0.25
e.	3:19	3/19	15.8%	0.158
f.	13:17	13/17	76.5%	0.765
g.	2:8	2/8	25%	0.25
h.	14:20	14/20	70%	0.7
i.	2:6	2/6	33.3%	0.333
j.	4:20	4/20	20%	0.2
k.	15:16	15/16	93.8%	0.938
l.	3:8	3/8	37.5%	0.375
m.	5:7	5/7	71.4%	0.714
n.	11:16	11/16	68.8%	0.688
o.	1:18	1/18	5.6%	0.056

4.

	Ratio	Fraction	Percent	Decimal
a.	3:4	3/4	75%	0.75
b.	1:1	1/1	100%	1
c.	9:13	9/13	69.2%	0.692
d.	1:7	1/7	14.3%	0.143
e.	4:11	4/11	36.4%	0.364
f.	4:6	4/6	66.7%	0.667
g.	6:19	6/19	31.6%	0.316
h.	11:16	11/16	68.8%	0.688
i.	4:16	4/16	25%	0.25
j.	2:4	2/4	50%	0.5
k.	1:2	1/2	50%	0.5
l.	5:18	5/18	27.8%	0.278
m.	6:20	6/20	30%	0.3
n.	2:8	2/8	25%	0.25
o.	4:12	4/12	33.3%	0.333

5.

	Ratio	Fraction	Percent	Decimal
a.	7:18	7/18	38.9%	0.389
b.	2:6	2/6	33.3%	0.333
c.	1:3	1/3	33.3%	0.333
d.	2:4	2/4	50%	0.5
e.	1:8	1/8	12.5%	0.125
f.	1:1	1/1	100%	1
g.	3:5	3/5	60%	0.6
h.	15:18	15/18	83.3%	0.833
i.	10:16	10/16	62.5%	0.625
j.	1:18	1/18	5.6%	0.056
k.	3:18	3/18	16.7%	0.167
l.	5:19	5/19	26.3%	0.263
m.	2:3	2/3	66.7%	0.667
n.	8:15	8/15	53.3%	0.533
o.	7:16	7/16	43.8%	0.438

Page 71: Word Problems: Percent

1. $101.00   2. 12   3. 68   4. 81   5. $114.00

6. 8   7. $21.00   8. $14.00   9. 4   10. 2

11. 36   12. 2   13. 1   14. 32   15. $1.00

16. $27.00   17. $108.00   18. 1   19. 2   20. $1.00

21. 21   22. 24   23. $52.00   24. 72   25. 9

26. 54   27. $12.00   28. $27.00   29. 11   30. $11.00

Page 78: Linear Equations

1. -3   2. -7   3. -10   4. -7   5. 3   6. 1   7. 4   8. 3   9. -10

10. 9   11. -4   12. -6   13. -3   14. 2   15. 8   16. -4   17. 1   18. -3

19. 8   20. -9   21. -2   22. -8

Page 81: Slope from Two Points

1. 5   2. -10   3. -10   4. -2   5. 3   6. -3   7. 5   8. -3   9. 8

10. 4   11. -2   12. 3   13. 3   14. -6   15. -1   16. 2   17. 5   18. 6

19. 10   20. 6

Page 84: Plotting Lines

1.
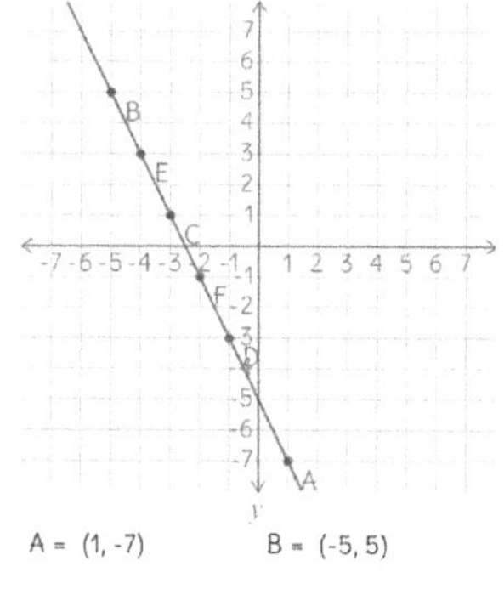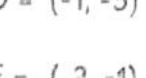

A = (1, -7)   B = (-5, 5)

C = (-3, 1)   D = (-1, -3)

F = (-4, 3)   F = (2, -1)

2.
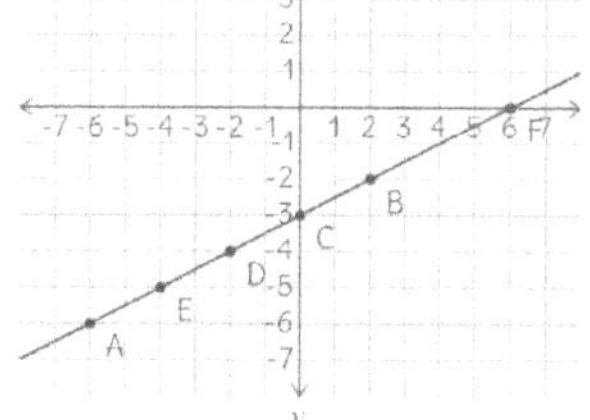

A = (-6, -6)   B = (2, -2)

C = (0, -3)   D = (-2, -4)

E = (-4, -5)   F = (6, 0)

3.
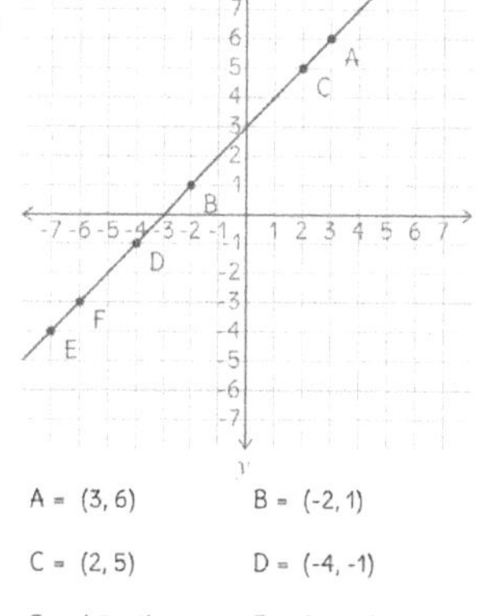

A = (3, 6)   B = (-2, 1)

C = (2, 5)   D = (-4, -1)

E = (-7, -4)   F = (-6, -3)

4.
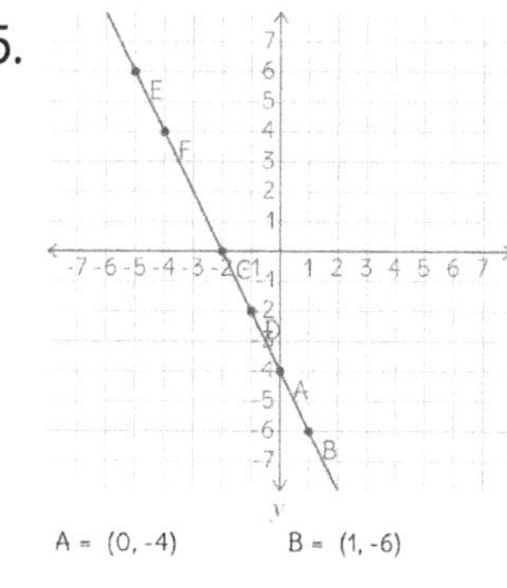

A = (-3, 1)   B = (5, -7)

C = (-7, 5)   D = (-5, 3)

E = (3, -5)   F = (2, -4)

5.

A = (0, -4)   B = (1, -6)

C = (-2, 0)   D = (-1, -2)

E = (-5, 6)   F = (-4, 4)

6.
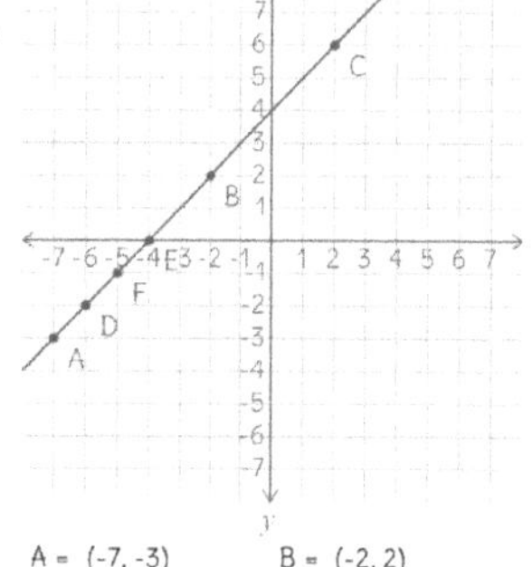

A = (-7, -3)   B = (-2, 2)

C = (2, 6)   D = (-6, -2)

E = (-4, 0)   F = (-5, -1)

7. 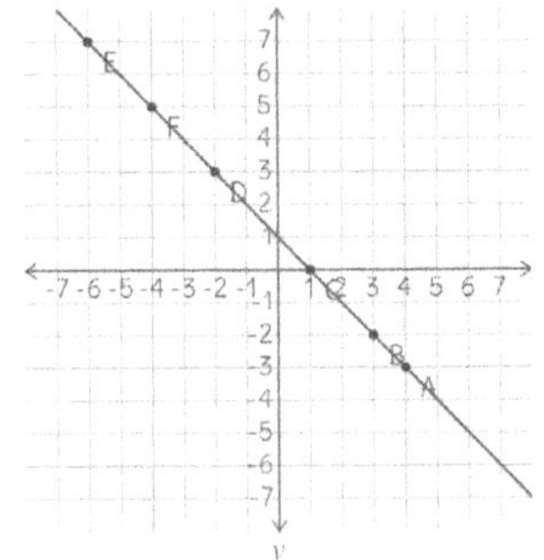

A = (4, -3)   B = (3, -2)

C = (1, 0)   D = (-2, 3)

E = (-6, 7)   F = (-4, 5)

8. 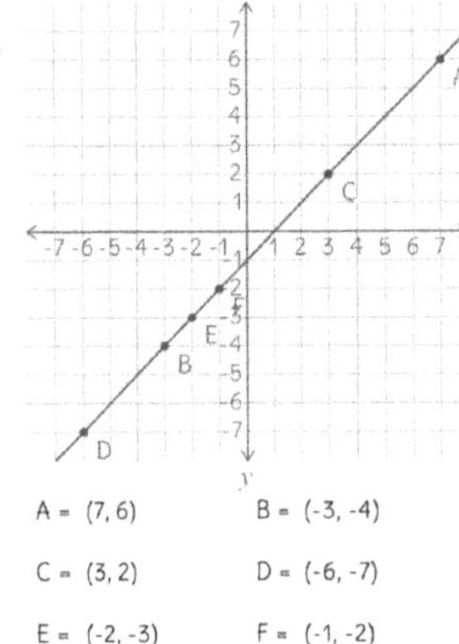

A = (7, 6)   B = (-3, -4)

C = (3, 2)   D = (-6, -7)

E = (-2, -3)   F = (-1, -2)

9. 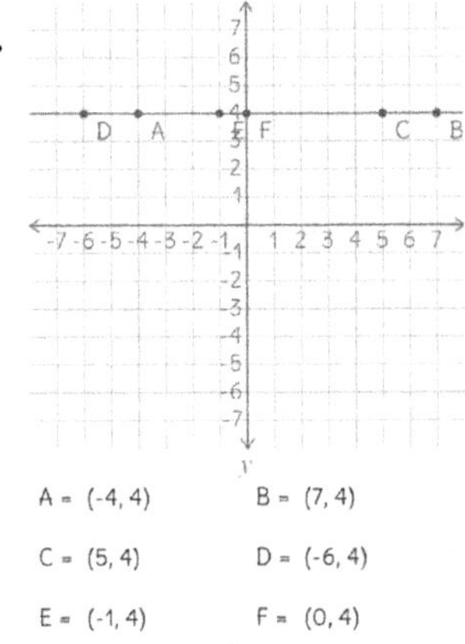

A = (-4, 4)   B = (7, 4)

C = (5, 4)   D = (-6, 4)

E = (-1, 4)   F = (0, 4)

10. 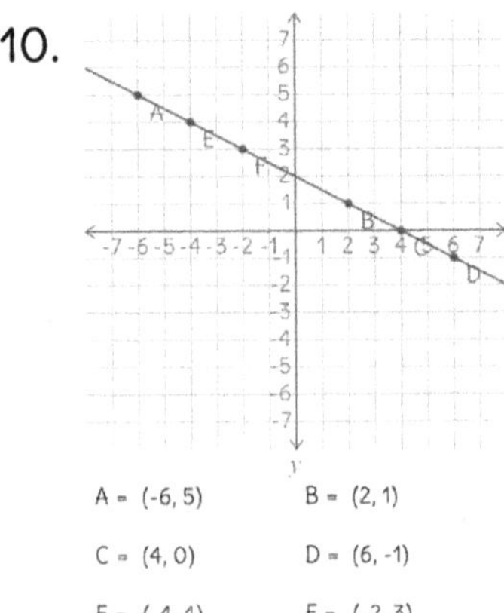

A = (-6, 5)   B = (2, 1)

C = (4, 0)   D = (6, -1)

E = (-4, 4)   F = (-2, 3)

Page 94: Graphing Linear Equations

1. $y = \frac{11}{4}x + 4$

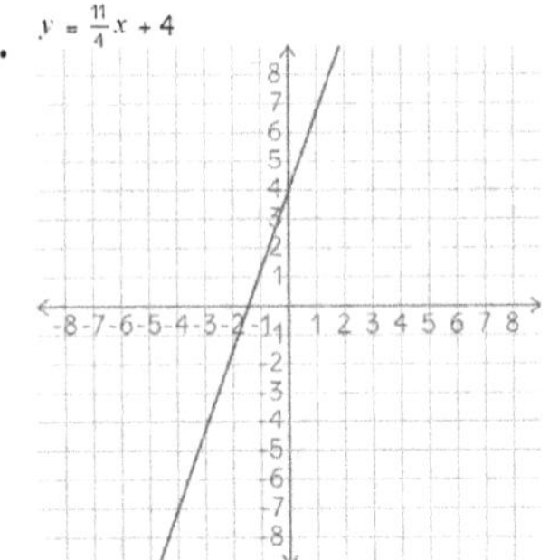

2. $y = \frac{5}{4}x + 5$

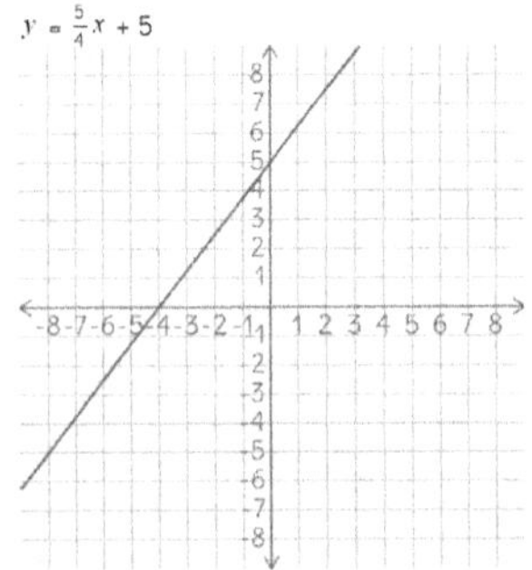

3. $x = 4$

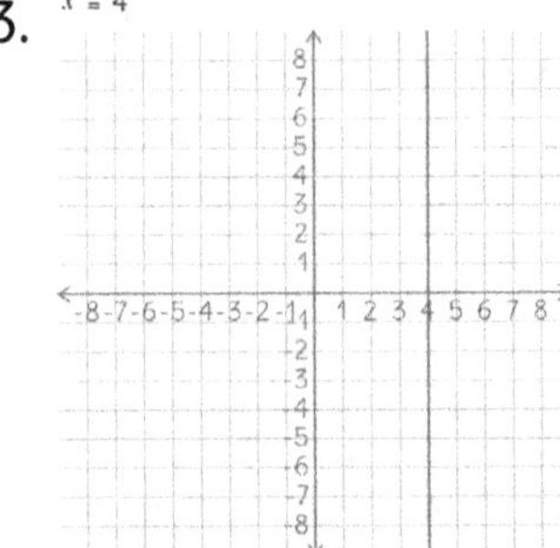

4. $x = -5$

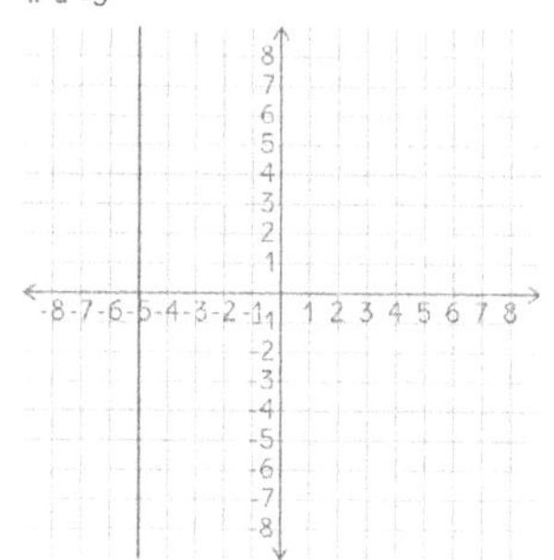

5. $y = -\frac{3}{4}x + 6$

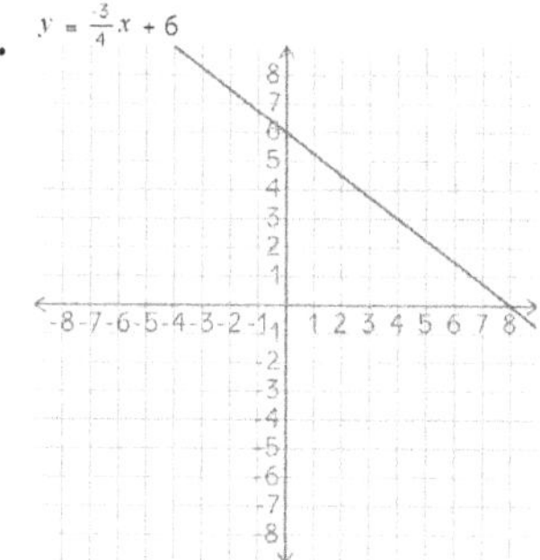

6. $y = -3x + 4$

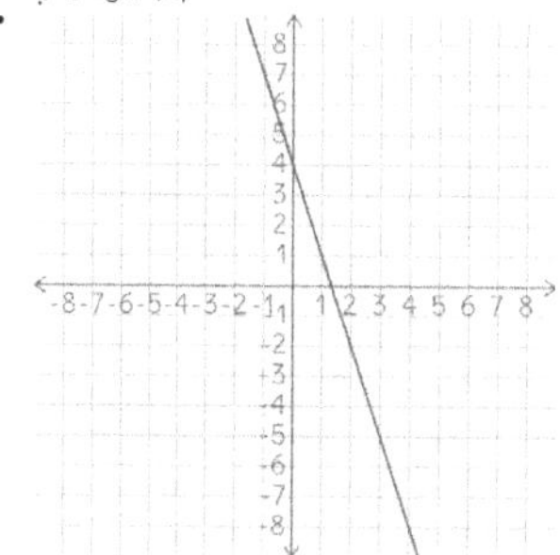

7. $y = 3x + 7$

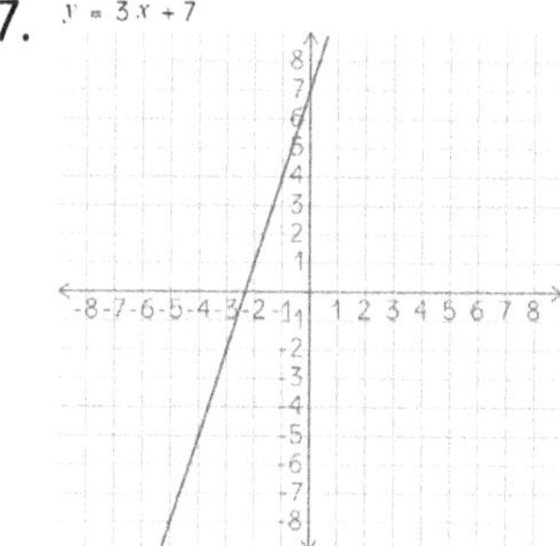

8. $y = -x + 4$

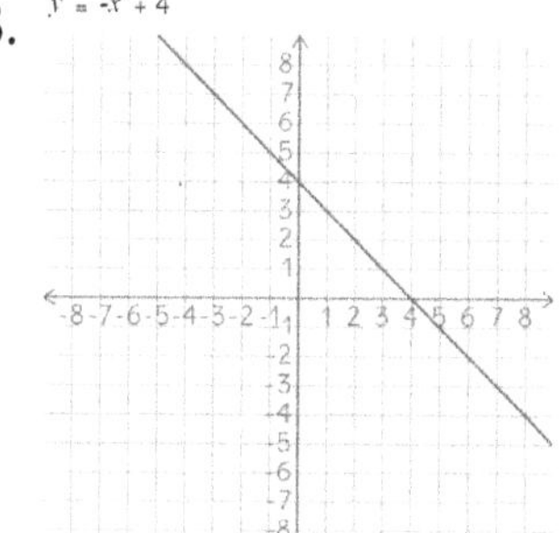

9. $y = -2x + 4$

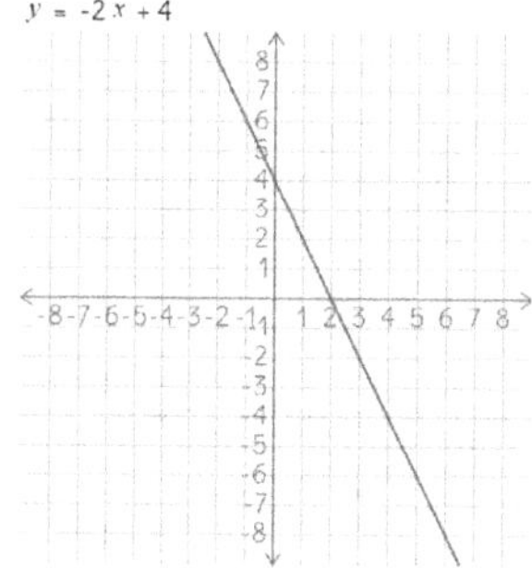

10. $y = \frac{7}{4}x - 6$

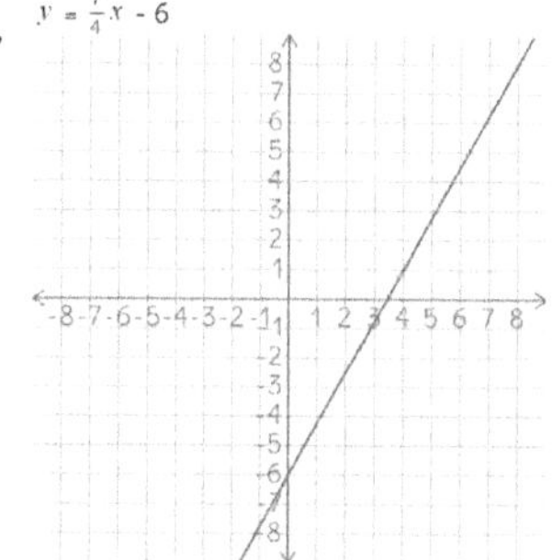

Page 104: System of Equations

1. x = 0.15, y = 1.08

2. x = -0.61, y = 0.58

3. x = 0.47, y = 0.6

4. x = 0.53, y = 0.79

5. x = -0.5, y = 0.93

6. x = 2.0, y = -2.0

7. x = 0.33, y = 0.67

8. x = -0.91, y = 1.31

9. x = 3.62, y = -0.12

10. x = 0.52, y = 0.61

11. x = -0.88, y = 1.23

12. x = -4.4, y = 9.4

13. x = -0.0, y = 0.88

14. x = 1.62, y = 0.12

15. x = 0.4, y = 0.2

16. . x = -2.64, y = 2.55   17. x = -0.23, y = 0.87   18. x = 3.18, y = -0.36

19. x = 0.17, y = 0.67   20. x = 0.03, y = 1.4   21. x = -1.15, y = 2.69

22. x = -0.06, y = 0.24   23. x = -0.5, y = 1.0   24. x = -0.43, y = 0.86

Page 112:   Cartesian Coordinates

1. 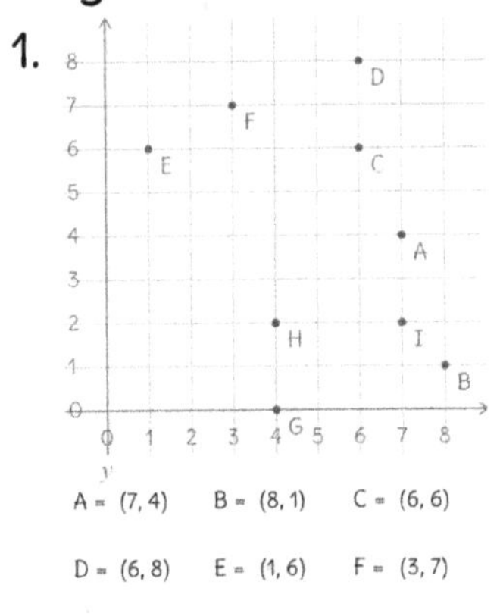

A = (7, 4)   B = (8, 1)   C = (6, 6)

D = (6, 8)   E = (1, 6)   F = (3, 7)

G = (4, 0)   H = (4, 2)   I = (7, 2)

2. 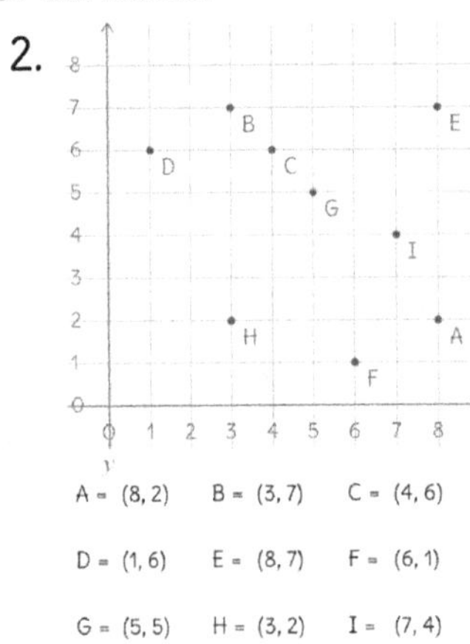

A = (8, 2)   B = (3, 7)   C = (4, 6)

D = (1, 6)   E = (8, 7)   F = (6, 1)

G = (5, 5)   H = (3, 2)   I = (7, 4)

3. 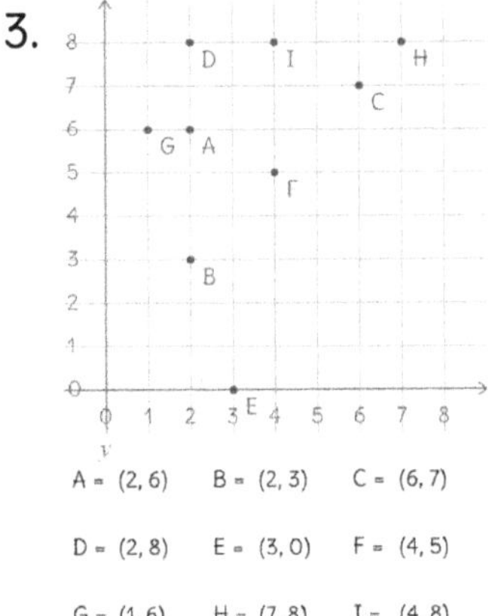

A = (2, 6)   B = (2, 3)   C = (6, 7)

D = (2, 8)   E = (3, 0)   F = (4, 5)

G = (1, 6)   H = (7, 8)   I = (4, 8)

4. 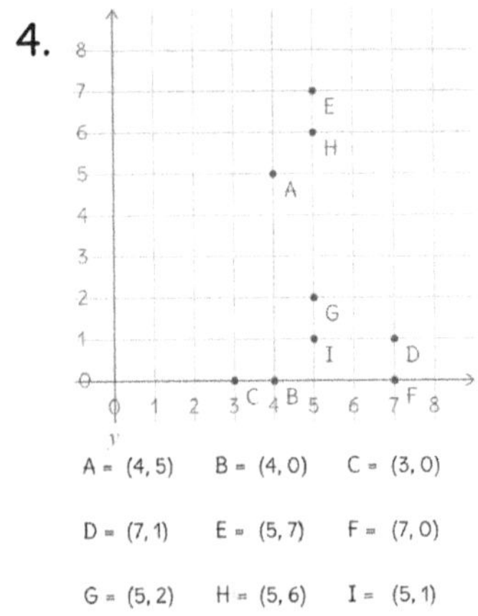

A = (4, 5)   B = (4, 0)   C = (3, 0)

D = (7, 1)   E = (5, 7)   F = (7, 0)

G = (5, 2)   H = (5, 6)   I = (5, 1)

5. 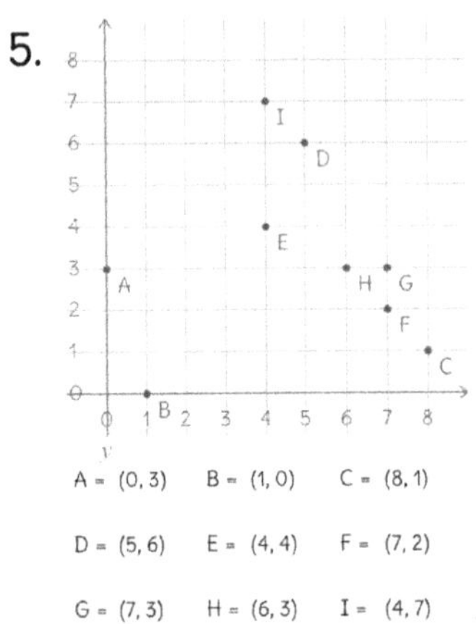

A = (0, 3)   B = (1, 0)   C = (8, 1)

D = (5, 6)   E = (4, 4)   F = (7, 2)

G = (7, 3)   H = (6, 3)   I = (4, 7)

Page 117:   Cartesian Coordinates

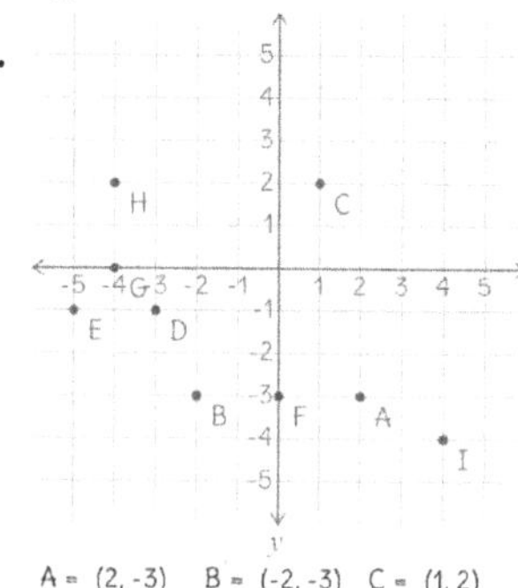

1.

A = (2, -3)   B = (-2, -3)   C = (1, 2)

D = (-3, -1)   E = (-5, -1)   F = (0, -3)

G = (-4, 0)   H = (-4, 2)   I = (4, -4)

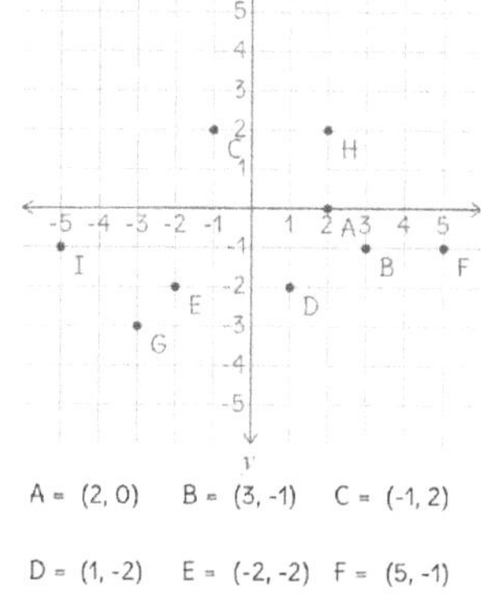

2.

A = (2, 0)   B = (3, -1)   C = (-1, 2)

D = (1, -2)   E = (-2, -2)   F = (5, -1)

G = (-3, -3)   H = (2, 2)   I = (-5, -1)

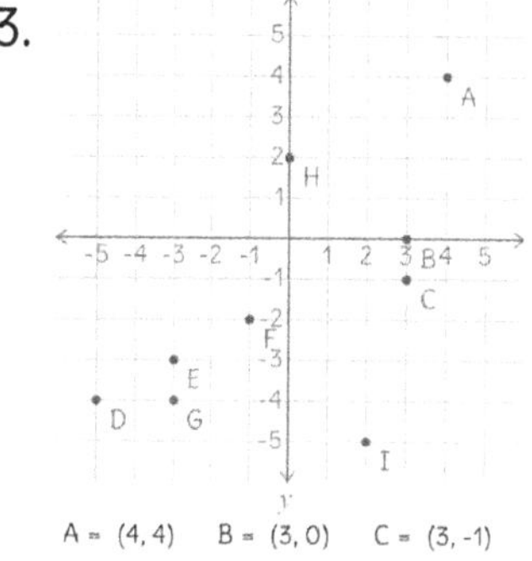

3.

A = (4, 4)   B = (3, 0)   C = (3, -1)

D = (-5, -4)   E = (-3, -3)   F = (-1, -2)

G = (-3, -4)   H = (0, 2)   I = (2, -5)

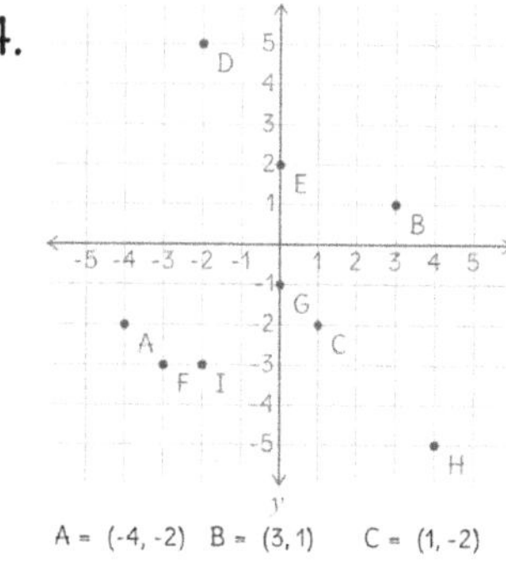

4.

A = (-4, -2)   B = (3, 1)   C = (1, -2)

D = (-2, 5)   E = (0, 2)   F = (-3, -3)

G = (0, -1)   H = (4, -5)   I = (-2, -3)

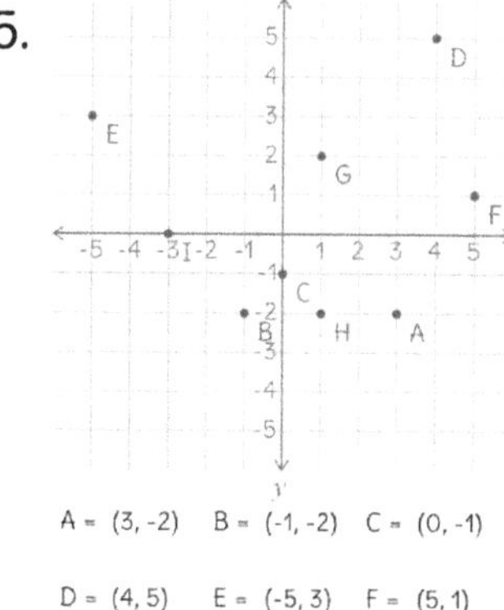

5.

A = (3, -2)   B = (-1, -2)   C = (0, -1)

D = (4, 5)   E = (-5, 3)   F = (5, 1)

G = (1, 2)   H = (1, -2)   I = (-3, 0)

Page 122:   Area and Perimeter

1. P=21 A=27
2. P=28 A=36
3. P=38 A=45

4. P=46 A=66
5. P=45 A=115
6. P=44 A=88.98

7. P=44 A=60
8. P=21 A=21.22
9. P=28 A=38

10. P=32 A=39
11. P=39 A=73.18
12. P=54 A=169

13. P=32 A=43
14. P=18 A=15.6
15. P=30 A=56

16. P=31 A=35.91
17. P=42 A=82.5
18. P=46 A=52

19. P=38 A=54

20. P=38 A=90

21. P=42 A=84

22. P=30 A=40

23. P=22 A=30

24. P=66 A=144

25. P=36 A=42

26. P=17 A=13.62

27. P=88 A=272

28. P=58 A=84

29. P=24 A=24

30. P=42 A=82.5

31. P=35 A=48.16

32. P=38 A=49

33. P=30 A=48

34. P=39 A=73.18

35. P=28 A=37

36. P=72 A=225

37. P=22 A=30

38. P=21 A=28

39. P=34 A=72

40. P=36 A=74

41. P=36 A=52

42. P=27 A=35.07

43. P=40 A=57

44. P=36 A=46.8

45. P=42 A=92

46. P=48 A=130

47. P=21 A=21.22

48. P=24 A=27.72

49. P=38 A=54

50. P=48 A=143

51. P=54 A=110

52. P=32 A=37.8

53. P=31 A=33.32

54. P=58 A=196

55. P=27 A=35.07

56. P=58 A=131

57. P=38 A=64

58. P=21 A=21.22

59. P=25 A=29.02

60. P=40 A=88

61. P=74 A=216

62. P=17 A=15

63. P=48 A=110.85

64. P=38 A=64

65. P=20 A=12.48

66. P=44 A=106

67. P=22 A=14

68. P=31 A=36.33

69. P=68 A=112

70. P=58 A=156

71. P=28 A=33

72. P=20 A=18.96

73. P=44 A=110

74. P=42 A=82

75. P=34 A=47

76. P=46 A=78

77. P=27 A=35.07

78. P=44 A=72

79. P=46 A=65

80. P=68 A=169

Page 142: Volume and Surface Area

1. V=560 in³ in³ SA=412 in² in²

2. V=170 ft³ ft³ SA=193 ft² ft²

3. V=72 cm³ cm³ SA=123.6 cm² cm²

4. V=280 cm³ cm³ SA=262 cm² cm²

5. V=21 cm³ cm³ SA=46 cm² cm²

6. V=96 cm³ cm³ SA=128 cm² cm²

7. V=21.21 in³ in³ SA=42 in² in²

8. V=336 ft³ ft³ SA=292 ft² ft²

9. V=8 ft³ ft³ SA=24 ft² ft²

10. V=180 in³ in³ SA=154 in² in²

11. V=9 ft³ ft³ SA=30.0 ft² ft²

12. V=36 in³ in³ SA=66 in² in²

13. V=98.17 cm³ cm³ SA=118 cm² cm²

14. V=378 ft³ ft³ SA=318 ft² ft²

15. V=8 ft³ ft³ SA=24 ft² ft²

16. V=196 ft³ ft³ SA=232.2 ft² ft²

17. V=141.37 in³ in³ SA=151 in² in²

18. V=800 in³ in³ SA=520 in² in²

19. V=57 in³ in³ SA=91 in² in²

20. V=60 ft³ ft³ SA=94 ft² ft²

21. V=22 in³ in³ SA=54.6 in² in²

22. V=216 cm³ cm³ SA=260.4 cm² cm²

23. V=6 cm³ cm³ SA=24.4 cm² cm²

24. V=432 cm³ cm³ SA=348 cm² cm²

25. V=402.12 cm³ cm³ SA=302 cm² cm²

26. V=252 in³ in³ SA=275.0 in² in²

27. V=26 cm³ cm³ SA=57 cm² cm²

28. V=225 cm³ cm³ SA=288.0 cm² cm²

29. V=336 in³ in³ SA=292 in² in²

30. V=150 ft³ ft³ SA=170 ft² ft²

31. V=9 ft³ ft³ SA=27 ft² ft²

32. V=448 in³ in³ SA=352 in² in²

33. V=192 cm³ cm³ SA=208 cm² cm²

34. V=9.42 ft³ ft³ SA=25 ft² ft²

35. V=504 ft³ ft³ SA=382 ft² ft²

36. V=140 in³ in³ SA=166 in² in²

37. V=318.09 ft³ ft³ SA=269 ft² ft²

38. V=12 cm³ cm³ SA=39.6 cm² cm²

39. V=147 ft³ ft³ SA=197.4 ft² ft²

40. V=528 in³ in³ SA=404 in² in²

41. V=253 ft³ ft³ SA=263 ft² ft²

42. V=549.78 ft³ ft³ SA=377 ft² ft²

43. V=36 in³ in³ SA=66 in² in²

44. V=144 ft³ ft³ SA=186.0 ft² ft²

45. V=12 cm³ cm³ SA=34.4 cm² cm²

46. V=24 cm³ cm³ SA=60 cm² cm²

47. V=32 ft³ ft³ SA=68.0 ft² ft²

48. V=445.32 cm³ cm³ SA=325 cm² cm²

49. V=64 in³ in³ SA=96 in² in²

50. V=120 ft³ ft³ SA=148 ft² ft²

51. V=96 in³ in³ SA=128 in² in²

52. V=48 ft³ ft³ SA=80 ft² ft²

53. V=150 in³ in³ SA=170 in² in²

54. V=113.10 cm³ cm³ SA=132 cm² cm²

55. V=16 cm³ cm³ SA=46.4 cm² cm²

56. V=48 in³ in³ SA=90.4 in² in²

57. V=12 ft³ ft³ SA=38.0 ft² ft²

58. V=264 cm³ cm³ SA=294.4 cm² cm²

59. V=12 ft³ ft³ SA=32 ft² ft²

60. V=210 ft³ ft³ SA=214 ft² ft²

Page 157: Pythagorean Theorem

1. S=28.142   2. S=166.325   3. S=116.362   4. S=100.757

5. S=188.743   6. S=131.765   7. S=78.994   8. S=145.894

9. S=83.684   10. S=62.738   11. S=69.971   12. S=116.052

13. S=74.565   14. S=121.272   15. S=28.723   16. S=109.439

17. S=77.466   18. S=20.616   19. S=56.859   20. S=68.957

21. S=115.931   22. S=62.833   23. S=24.739   24. S=101.336

25. S=171.231   26. S=58.181   27. S=96.995   28. S=27.295